BOETHIUS AND

DIALOGUE

SETH LERER

BOETHIUS AND DIALOGUE

LITERARY METHOD IN
The Consolation of Philosophy

PRINCETON UNIVERSITY PRESS

PRINCETON, NEW JERSEY

Copyright © 1985 by Princeton University Press
Published by Princeton University Press, 41 William Street
Princeton, New Jersey 08540
In the United Kingdom
Princeton University Press, Guildford, Surrey

All Rights Reserved

Library of Congress Cataloging in Publication Data will be
found on the last printed page of this book

ISBN 0-691-06653-1

Publication of this book has been aided by
the Whitney Darrow Publication Fund of Princeton University Press

This book has been composed in Linotron Bembo

Clothbound editions of Princeton University Press books
are printed on acid-free paper, and binding materials
are chosen for strength and durability

Printed in the United States of America
by Princeton University Press
Princeton, New Jersey

For Nancy

CONTENTS

A NOTE ON TEXTS

All quotations from foreign language sources are presented in English translation in the text, with original quotations in the notes. There are a few exceptions, especially when a case is made for specific verbal techniques which are best presented untranslated. The texts of Boethius are L. Bieler, ed., *De Consolatione Philosophiae* (Turnholt: Brepols, 1957), and Richard Green, trans., Boethius, *The Consolation of Philosophy* (Indianapolis: Bobbs-Merrill, 1962). In choosing these texts, I have been guided by the goals of availability and scholarly accuracy. J. J. O'Donnell's review of the revised Loeb Library edition and translation (in *American Journal of Philology* 98 [1977], 77-79) has raised serious doubts concerning the usability of that otherwise readily available text. In spite of O'Donnell's objections, I have on occasion preferred the Loeb translators' at times overly literal renderings, in contrast to the occasionally loose and colloquial renditions of Green. Such uses are cited in the notes. On occasion, I have also substituted a translation of my own, especially in arguing for the continuity of an image or the structure of metaphors in Boethius' work.

In selecting other classical texts, I have tried to use those which are both reliable and readily available. Unless otherwise noted, all translations and quotations from Classical texts are from the Loeb Library editions. Quotations from Augustine are, when available, from the CCSL edition. In the case of the *Confessions*, my text is Skutella's as reprinted in the Bibliothèque Augustinienne edition. In spite of objections from some, I prefer the phrasing of R. Pine-Coffin's translation of the *Confessions* (Harmondsworth: Penguin, 1961). For Fulgentius, I have used Helm's Teubner edition and Whitbread's translation (Athens, Ohio: Ohio Univ. Press, 1971). For Seneca, I have followed the Loeb texts, with the exception of the *Agamemnon*, for which I have used R. J. Tarrant's new edition (Cambridge: Cambridge Univ. Press, 1976). I have also checked readings against F. Leo's edition (Berlin: Weidmann, 1878). For Boethius' mathematical and logical writings, the best texts are *In Isagogen Porphyrii*, ed. S. Brandt CSEL 48 (Leipzig: Freytag, 1906); *Commentarii in librum Aristotelis Peri Hermeneias*, ed. G. Friedlein (Leipzig: Teubner, 1867). For *De topicis differentiis*, I have used the text in PL, 64. When a text is quoted from another secondary source, I have cited it as such, but have also, as far as possible, checked the original quotation. All translations throughout this study are attributed, unless they are my own.

ACKNOWLEDGMENTS

It is my pleasure to thank those individuals and institutions who have supported the writing of this study. Jay Schleusener read many successive drafts of the manuscript and helped clarify its structure and argument. Michael Murrin supported the project from its inception and greatly influenced its scholarly approach. John V. Fleming offered advice and support instrumental in turning the manuscript into a publishable book. I am also indebted to Robert Kaster, J. J. O'Donnell, and Winthrop Wetherbee for help with the nuances of Late Latin language and literary history. Peter Brown generously read a late draft of the book, and his comments helped point me to the larger cultural contexts of Boethius' world. I am grateful also to Tom True, Patricia Halliday, and the staff of the Princeton Computer Center for their help in the preparation of the manuscript. A preliminary version of my chapters on the *Consolation*'s opening appeared as "Boethian Silence," *Medievalia et Humanistica* 12 (1984), 97-125, and I thank the editor and publisher for permission to reprint portions of the article.

Research for this study was conducted at the libraries of the University of Chicago, Princeton University, the Princeton Theological Seminary, the Institute for Advanced Study, and the New York Public Library. Financial support came from the National Endowment for the Humanities, the American Council of Learned Societies, and the Office of Research and Project Administration at Princeton. Finally, it is my pleasure to thank Mrs. Arthur Sherwood of Princeton University Press for the ease and grace with which this study has been considered and produced.

BOETHIUS AND

DIALOGUE

INTRODUCTION

This study's central purpose is to demonstrate the thematic and methodological coherence of the *Consolation of Philosophy*. In grounding the *Consolation* both in Late Antique literary history and in the corpus of Boethius' writings, the book first outlines a tradition of literary and philosophical dialogue through close readings of selected Latin authors from the first to the sixth century; second, it shows how Boethius established throughout his literary career—in his early commentaries, translations, and logical and theological works—a consistent persona of reader and writer beset by the impediments of cultural decline and the hindrances of a hostile audience. The major portion of the book shows how *The Consolation of Philosophy* charts a reader's progress through an engagement with poetic and prose texts, and how it consistently "rewrites" earlier portions of its text into new contexts to measure that progress. It is the purpose of this introduction to outline the scope and plan of the book, and to make explicit the theoretical and critical assumptions which underlie its method.

Chapter I opens with a review of the literary historical contexts of Late Antiquity. Drawing on the pioneering work of Erich Auerbach, and considering the bold, new studies of Brian Stock, this section presents a view of the literary public for the fifth and sixth centuries. It presents cultural explanations for Boethius' literary concerns. As the arena of literary studies moved from public declamation to private study, and as the exercise of language moved from forum to classroom, the contexts for the reading and writing of literature narrowed. Broadly speaking, literature began to lose its public, as works such as the *Aeneid* were read not as political poems celebrating a social and historical order, but rather as allegories of education, whose realm of action was not the world but the classroom. As literary study and literacy itself retreated into the school and private social circle, a set of tropes developed to express the writer's relationship to his audience. Images of ignorance, hostility, and overall difficulty characterize the prefaces to prose works of the time, and they appear throughout Boethius' writings. Boethius' own projected program of reading and commentary, expressed in the commentary on Aristotle's *Perihermeneias*, has both a cultural and a personal resonance. On the one hand, it expresses a culture's awareness of the decline in literary abilities, and the growing reality that the works of Aristotle, Plato, and Cicero were no longer guides to moral behavior or public eloquence, but rather set texts in the education of the individual. On the other hand, Boethius gives voice to a persona whose life was to be charted not through events experienced but rather through texts read. Boethius presents a life of books, in which what we are to know about him comes from his reading habits and his written responses to that reading. The early commentary *In Isagogen Porphyrii*—Boethius' only work, save the *Consolation*, written in dialogue form—presents the persona in nascent form, as the student closes the work desiring to spend a lifetime reading and studying the works of Aristotle with his teacher. The prefaces to the theological tractates also address problems in reading and writing. Boethius concretizes the difficulty of writing through a series of metaphors which will reappear throughout his work. He also addresses his work to individuals who represent to him the ideals of study and pedagogy later to be found in the figure of Lady Philosophy. Boethius' struggles with his text and with his audience in the tractates show us a writer obsessed with the problems of beginning a work; with placing it in the context of his previous reading and in the corpus of his existing works; and with finding an audience suitable for its expression.

Before Chapter I examines the *In Isagogen* and the tractates, it takes a chronological approach to outlining the methodological problems which will figure in Boethius' writings. Cicero's *Tusculan Disputations* is presented as a work which adopts the Academic Skeptical method of argument to produce a text whose content can only suggest possible approaches to truth. I will admit that I read the *Tusculans* somewhat pessimistically, arguing that its theme is the limitations of human language and the inabilities of written and spoken discourse to communicate fully the truths it aspires to claim. Augustine's *Soliloquia* and *De Magistro* are then explored as taking up the Ciceronian personae of student and teacher, while also confronting the same methodological problems as the *Tusculans*. Whether Augustine presents the discussion as a dialogue with the self or with his own son, the conversation frequently breaks down, with the dialogue moving to monologue, and the student and teacher pausing to reestablish the techniques of their method of inquiry. As a comic foil to this tradition, I see Fulgentius' *De Continentia Virgiliana*. Here, the student/teacher colloquy takes as its purpose the explication of a text. But in its elaborate stylistic quirks and exaggerated characterizations of its participants, Fulgentius' dialogue effectively parodies the literary and grammatical traditions which stand behind it. By deliberately rewriting Virgil's text into a new narrative and epistemological order, Fulgentius bears witness to the ahistorical bases of allegorical interpretation, while at the same time questioning the nature of literary *auctoritas*.

Such are the literary, historical, and cultural contexts in which I claim *The Consolation of Philosophy* took shape. The body of this study presents less a reading of the *Consolation*, in the usual sense of that term, than an attempt to chronicle the reader's progress through the text and its structures of literary allusion. By these features I mean that the *Consolation* presents the prisoner as a reader of his own and Philosophy's writings, and that the patterns of allusion to such authors as Cicero, Plato, Aristotle, and Seneca chronicle a reader's response to a syllabus of study. There are several themes and problems which form the core of the analysis, and they might briefly be isolated here.

First, there is the distinction between dialectic and philosophy. By these terms, I mean what Boethius meant in his treatise, *De topicis differentiis*. Boethius saw dialectic as a method of inquiry which drew on probable or readily believable arguments, and which sought not necessarily to prove a point but rather to convince an audience. Philosophy, however, was narrowly conceived as demonstration. Its method was primarily syllogistic, and it could admit lines of reasoning which, while seemingly unbelievable to the ordinary listener, were in fact based on necessary truths. In the early books of the *Consolation*, the prisoner appears as an orator and dialectician concerned more with the effects of his words than with their philosophical weight. He seeks not truths but opinions. The prisoner repeatedly calls for Lady Philosophy's arguments to be rephrased into the language of the common man, and she soon realizes that before she can introduce him to the matter of Platonic thought, she must first educate him in a method of argument. Their dialogue frequently breaks down, and she must exhort the prisoner not to accede to her authority but to sustain discussion. The basis of this education is the Aristotelian method of debate as expressed in his *Topica* (a work Boethius translated) and filtered through Cicero's own *Topica* (a work on which Boethius wrote a commentary). By Book Three, the prisoner has progressed sufficiently to sustain the momentum of the dialogue. Yet, his willing assents to Philosophy's arguments, and his repeated answers that her remarks "appear" to be true, rather than are demonstrably true, again reveal the fundamental difference between himself and his teacher: for Philosophy, things are; for the prisoner, they seem to be. It is not until Book Four that the prisoner gains enough in confidence and technique to understand her explanations and to anticipate her objections. By Book Five, for reasons I will explain presently, the dialogue moves finally to monologue, as Philosophy lectures, using the techniques of philosophical demonstration. The dialogue of the *Consolation* thus chronicles the growth of a debater coming to terms with the limits of his own language and method in the attempt to articulate philosophical truths.

Second, there is the role of the prisoner as reader and writer and, in turn, his relationship to the reader outside the *Consolation*'s text. In Chapter I I show how Boethius cultivates a persona who exists only for books and who survives only in the written responses to books: e.g., the voice of the commentator or theologian. Chapter II opens with the *Consolation*'s beginning, where the prisoner writes of his past life in terms of the other works he has written. In addition, the deeply allusive nature of his opening poem—drawing so heavily on Virgilian and Ovidian echoes—further reinforces the impression that the prisoner can only express himself in the borrowed tropes and forms of his reading. In other words, the prisoner creates himself as a reader and writer: what we as readers can know of him comes less from the details of Boethius' biography (i.e., extra-textual information) and more from the traditions which he adopts and addresses. In the course of the *Consolation*, the prisoner is reeducated as a user of language. Philosophy leads him away from forensic, dramatic, and dialectical forms of expression towards a purely philosophical mode of discourse. In turn, she replaces the earlier texts he had read with poems and prose tracts of her own making. The poetry, especially the three mythological *metra* on Orpheus, Ulysses, and Hercules, are designed to be interpreted as literary texts. These poems are built out of complex structures of literary allusion: to the traditions of Homeric epic, antique allegoresis, and Senecan tragedy. Lady Philosophy effectively rewrites her sources, and in the case of Seneca she uses earlier, tragic scenes as a foil for her own inspirational message. Philosophy's prose speeches also rewrite themselves, as Boethius establishes patterns of metaphor and imagery which reappear throughout the *Consolation* as a series of benchmarks against which the prisoner and reader can assess his progress. One aspect of my approach involves establishing these parallels in the *Consolation*'s text to show how passages in the later books recast earlier phrasings from the prose and the poetry. Finally, towards the work's close, Philosophy's prose speeches can be approached as authoritative treatises which can be read and commented upon. The

with a belief in the interiority of understanding and an awareness of the Forms. The language of the *Consolation*'s prose, as well as its poetry, is remarkably figurative, and I argue in the course of this study that the dialogue's progress often works through structures of imagery as well as argument. In the case of the poetry, I show how the elaborate figurative diction and rhetorical control of the great metra display Philosophy as a master of verse as well as prose, and how they serve to equate her creative and organizing skills in poetry with the figure of God as an *artifex*. In the Timaean hymn, in particular, Philosophy's rhetorical structures mime the subject of her prayer.

In these ways, *The Consolation of Philosophy* enacts the notion of a *gradus* of study expressed in Boethius' other writings and within the *Consolation*'s opening moment itself. The prisoner moves from silence, through vacuous oratory, through limited dialectic, to philosophical demonstration, and finally to the silence of a reader engaging fully with intellectual texts. This progress charts itself not only through the forms of discourse the work employs, but also through the patterns of reading, revising, and rejecting outside literary sources such as Seneca's plays.

To avoid misapprehension, let me say what this book does not do. It does not attempt a comprehensive account of all of Boethius' writings, nor does it attempt to explain his career in terms of the recoverable historical details of his education, professional life, and death. It does not try to reevaluate the massive body of Greek Neoplatonic source material for the *Consolation*, nor does it try to reassess Boethius' own experience of Greek thought and literature. The study also tries to avoid polemic or apology concerning the status of Boethius' Christianity or of the possibly religious texture of the *Consolation*'s diction. Finally, it does not chronicle the fate of the *Consolation* at the hands of later readers, commentators, and poets, although I hope that by refocusing attention on the work's methodological concerns this study will provoke a new look at the "Boethianism" of such medieval writers as

Chaucer, Dante, and Jean de Meun. My choice of sources and analogues has also been selective. On the one hand, I have tried to cast a new light on Boethius' well-known debts to Cicero, Augustine, and Seneca. On the other hand, I have suggested for the first time, as far as I am aware, Fulgentius' *De Continentia* as a useful analogue for the *Consolation*'s method and mythography. In short, I have tried to stay within a tradition which would have provided Boethius with a diction in Latin and with an attitude towards Roman literary life and history.

This book grounds itself in a variety of historical studies and in a certain set of attitudes taken from twentieth-century literary theory. The researches of Pierre Courcelle and Winthrop Wetherbee on the Neoplatonic heritage and afterlife of Boethius' work provided some of the original impetus for my study. Joachim Gruber's line-by-line commentary on the *Consolation*'s text has been invaluable. Gruber's method, however, treats the work as an assemblage of literary borrowings and philosophical inheritances. By amassing all possible sources of a phrase, argument, or word in the *Consolation*, Gruber, I feel, ultimately denies much of the originality of Boethius' technique. These recent works of scholarship, while diverse in their techniques and goals, share a critical attitude which slights the possible Christian content of the *Consolation*. The studies of C. J. De Vogel, Christine Mohrmann, and Henry Chadwick have sought to find Biblical and liturgical references throughout the *Consolation*'s text, and Chadwick's recent book on Boethius successfully establishes his place in early church history. In addition to these studies, and the many others I have consulted on points of history and interpretation, the fifteen-hundredth anniversary of Boethius' birth saw the publication of a collection of articles edited by M. Gibson. This collection conveniently gathers important primary source material, especially on Boethius' logical works. The readings of Jonathan Barnes have helped my own articulation of Boethius' intellectual goals, while the studies of Helen Kirkby and J. M. Matthews have provided clear read-

ings of historical contexts. Anna Crabbe's elegant essay on
the *Consolation* in this collection happily confirmed some of
my original assumptions, while at the same time taking a line
of approach to Boethius' literary heritage which is much different from my own.

Critics of *The Consolation of Philosophy* have long seen it as
a work of epistemology, a work about knowledge and understanding. My approach seeks that epistemological focus
expressed in the ways Boethius makes method his theme and
the importance he places on the reader's presence in his text.
This perspective may make Boethius into a writer whose
literary concerns seem close to our own, an association which
raises critical problems on the place of contemporary theory
in reading older literatures. While the purpose of my study
is primarily historical, I am aware of adapting certain idioms
of twentieth-century theory to explore features of the Late
Antique dialogue and the articulation of the *Consolation*'s
method. Briefly put, these approaches focus on the theme of
"textuality" in fiction; on the critical weight given to the
concept of "silence" in discourse; and on the notion that a
writer's career self-consciously concerns itself with the production of written texts. For my purposes here, Edward Said
has persuasively synthesized a variety of traditions in contemporary literary theory which address these issues (see *Beginnings* [Baltimore: Johns Hopkins Univ. Press, 1975]). He calls
attention to the beginnings of careers and of individual texts
as those moments when a writer establishes his persona and
sets himself apart from the body of works he has written and
read. Thus, when I address the theme of "textuality" in a
written work, I am concerned with the ways in which a text
becomes a private transcription of a life charted through a
course of reading. When I turn to the theme of silence in
Boethius' writings, I am also developing some of Said's implications about the goal of a writer's task. Silence functions
not only as a moment of linguistic transcendence, as Said's
reading of Barthes implies (*Beginnings*, p. 328), but also as an
ideal environment in which reading and writing can transpire.

In my readings of Augustine and Boethius, I have thus tried to move away from narrowly historical evaluations of silent reading, to address the ways in which scenes of the writer's and the reader's silence dramatize the themes of interpretation for their texts. I have, however, not felt bound by all the terms of Said's analysis, nor by the traditions he rehearses. The fact, too, that I argue that the *Consolation* narrates the education of its pupil, while at the same time providing an education for its reader, renders my approach apparently indebted to the work of Stanley Fish. Fish argues for the reader's presence in the text, and for the text as a dialectical chronicle of reader response which successively employs levels of argument only to kick them away in the pursuit of truth. The heritage for this view clearly lies in the dialogues of Plato, and Fish's own work draws heavily on the characterization of Platonic dialogue presented in R. Cushman's *Therapeia* (Chapel Hill: Univ. of North Carolina Press, 1957). I have also turned to the idioms of a "rhetorical" body of modern criticism in expressing Boethius' creation of an audience with his works. The most relevant to my discussion include Walter Ong, "The Writer's Audience is Always a Fiction," *PMLA* (1975), 9-21, and M. Corti, *An Introduction to Literary Semiotics* (Bloomington: Indiana Univ. Press, 1972). Finally, after this study was accepted for publication, I was pleased to find many of its critical intuitions confirmed in the variety of studies in *New Literary History* 16 (1984), "Oral and Written Traditions in the Middle Ages" (especially Brian Stock, "Medieval Literacy, Linguistic Theory, and Social Organization," pp. 13-29).

My study, then, has two broadly defined purposes. First, as a work of historical scholarship, it brings the corpus of Boethius' writings to bear on an understanding of his literary achievement. It reassesses the place of such outside sources as Augustine and Seneca, while articulating a tradition of literary dialogue from Cicero to Fulgentius. Second, as an exercise in criticism, the book implicitly assesses the potential usefulness of a modern critical vocabulary in the exploration of older literatures. Its view of the reader's role in the text, and of the patterns of rewriting and rereading inscribed within it, attempts to express the verifiable details of a literary work in a theoretical idiom. In the end, the book's fidelity is to the books it studies, and its criticism bases itself in the data of historical texts. It is, too, a preliminary study, whose conclusions will point beyond the close reading of a single work to stimulate further research on the history of the literary dialogue in the Middle Ages.

CHAPTER I

READERS AND WRITERS: TRADITIONS
OF THE LATIN DIALOGUE

A Reader's Life

Years before his imprisonment prompted the writing of *The Consolation of Philosophy*, Boethius characterized his own program of study in his commentary on Aristotle's *Perihermeneias*. In these now famous lines, Boethius outlined a lifetime project of reading, translating, interpreting, and reconciling the works of Aristotle and Plato.

> I shall translate into Latin every work of Aristotle's that comes into my hands, and I shall write commentaries on all of them; any subtlety of logic, any depth of moral insight, any perception of scientific truth that Aristotle has set down, I shall arrange, translate, and illuminate by the light of a commentary. And I shall also translate and comment upon all Plato's dialogues and put them into Latin form. Having completed this not unworthwhile project, I shall bring the thought of Aristotle and Plato somehow into harmony, and show that these two philosophers are not at odds in everything as a great many people suppose. . . .[1]

[1] Boethius, *Comentarii in Librum Aristotelis Perihermeneias*, ed. C. Meiser, secundam editionem (Leibzig: Teubner, 1880), pp. 79-80 (hereafter referred to as Meiser, II). The Latin reads: ". . . ego omne Aristotelis opus, quodcumque in manus venerit, in Romanum stilum vertens eorum omnium commenta Latina oratione perscribam, ut si quid ex logicae artis subtilitate, ex moralis gravitate peritiae, ex naturalis acumine veritatis ab Aristotele conscriptum sit, id omne ordinatum transferam atque etiam quodam lumine commentationis inlustrem omnesque Platonis dialogos vertendo vel etiam

Almost as soon as it was expressed, Boethius' enterprise
sparked comment and discussion. Cassiodorus commended
his official predecessor for the project of turning Greek
thought into Latin form.[2] Six hundred years later, John of
Salisbury remarked that Boethius was wasting his time trying
to reconcile two dead men who failed to agree on anything
when alive.[3] Since the nineteenth century, scholars have invariably used this passage to justify a variety of rewritings of
Late Antique intellectual history.[4] Kappelmacher found little
original in the project of commentary and reconciliation,
seeing in it a simple echo of the Neoplatonic syncretism of
Ammonius and Porphyry.[5] More recently, it has been shown
that Boethius echoes the bold assertions of Cicero's literary
enterprise in the *Tusculans Disputations*.[6] Others have argued

commentando in Latinam redigam formam. his peractis non equidem con-
tempserim Aristotelis Platonisque sententias in unam quodammodo revocare
concordiam eosque non ut plerique dissentire in omnibus, sed in plerisque
et his in philosophia maximis consentire demonstrem." My translation is
based on the renderings of Jonathan Barnes, "Boethius and the Study of
Logic," in M. Gibson, ed., *Boethius: His Life, Thought and Influence* (Oxford:
Blackwell, 1981), p. 74, and M.-D. Chenu, *Nature, Man, and Society in the
Twelfth Century*, ed. and trans., Jerome Taylor and Lester K. Little (Chicago:
Univ. of Chicago Press, 1968), p. 73.

   [2] On Boethius' translation and commentary on the *Perihermeneias*, see Cassiodorus, *Institutiones*, ed. R.A.B. Mynors (Oxford: Clarendon Press, 1937),
II.iii.18, p. 128; on the transformation of Greek thought in general to Roman
idioms, see *Inst.*, I.xiv.3, Mynors, p. 40; on the need to get Greek thought
translated into Latin, see *Inst.*, I.ix.5, Mynors, p. 34. See also Cassiodorus,
Variae, ed. A. Fridh, CCSL 96 (Turnholt: Brepols, 1973), I.45, p. 49.

   [3] John of Salisbury, *Metalogicon*, ed. C.C.J. Webb (Oxford: Clarendon
Press, 1929), II.17, p. 94. But William of Conches approved of the project,
and saw the synthesis of Platonic and Aristotelian systems essential (see
Chenu, p. 74, n. 49).

   [4] For a summary of nineteenth- and early-twentieth-century scholarship
on the shape of the Boethian logical corpus and its relationship to Late Antique
intellectual history, see L. M. De Rijk, "On the Chronology of Boethius'
Works on Logic, I," *Vivarium* 2 (1964), 1-6.

   [5] Alfred Kappelmacher, "Der schriftstellerische Plan des Boethius," *Wiener
Studien* 46 (1928), 215-225.

   [6] See the suggestions in Helen Kirkby, "The Scholar and His Public," in
Gibson, pp. 56-57 and n. 55. Kirkby focuses also on Boethius' statements in
his *In Categorias*, PL64, 201B, a passage I discuss in this section.

that Boethius' challenge represents one last encyclopaedic attempt in the face of a collapsing classical culture, and still others have found the origins of the *Consolation*'s own synthetic method in this early statement of harmonization.[7] The passage, too, has been used as evidence in the debate on the decline of Greek learning in the West: one side finds in it proof of a Hellenic Renaissance under the Ostrogoths;[8] another sees it as a purely conventional statement of acculturation which says little about the realities of intellectual life under Theodoric.[9]

More than simply voicing a response to culture or the classics, this statement presents a picture of Boethius as a scholar deeply and self-consciously concerned with the shape of his intellectual life. It matters little that the program of translation and commentary was never finished. What does matter is that Boethius felt the need to place his present work in the context of a career. By announcing a plan of reading and writing, he gives shape both to the corpus of his existing works and to the yet unwritten additions to the corpus. But to understand this career and the place of Boethius' works within it involves an understanding of the literary culture of his time. Because of the paucity of evidence from sixth-century sources, and because of the polemic tone of much of the scholarship, I

[7] For the scholar in a decaying world, see James Shiel, "Boethius the Hellenist," *History Today* 14 (1964), 678-686, and H. Chadwick, *Boethius: The Consolations of Music, Logic, Theology, and Philosophy* (Oxford: Clarendon Press, 1981), p. 69. For the synthetic method of the *Consolation*, see the arguments of Chenu, "The Platonism of Boethius," in *Nature, Man, and Society*, pp. 72-79.

[8] The fullest statement of the idea of a Hellenic Renaissance in the sixth century can be found in Pierre Courcelle, *Late Latin Writers and their Greek Sources*, trans. H. E. Wedeck (Cambridge: Harvard Univ. Press, 1969), pp. 273-330, especially the remarks on p. 277. Courcelle holds that Boethius' project was original and had the official sanction and support of Theodoric.

[9] See Kirkby, "The Scholar and His Public," pp. 55-59, adducing evidence from Cassiodorus on the continuity of the study and translation of Greek writings from Cicero through Victorinus. Cassiodorus, she argues, praises Boethius, not for the novelty of his project, as Courcelle implies, but rather only for its excellence.

intend here simply to suggest the outlines of a set of attitudes. Focusing on attitudes towards reading and writing, I hope to place Boethius in an historical environment which was self-consciously literate and literary. In short, I propose that Boethius creates the persona of a reader and writer constantly challenged by the difficulty of his intellectual task; that he assembled this persona out of the tropes and conventions of the literature he read; but also that there are cultural explanations for his choice of tone and purpose.

Erich Auerbach has argued that the disintegration of Roman civic and political life towards the close of the Empire paralleled a decay in the teaching and practice of literature. "Latin literature on the ancient model lost its public and its function."[10] Auerbach makes the point that the Latin which did survive in Late Antiquity survived purely as a written language. As differences between learned and local language widened, the literary forms of Latin became fossilized; they appeared consciously removed from everyday usage. The study of Latin thus became the study of texts rather than of public poems or orations.[11] Building on Auerbach's arguments, Brian Stock has shown that the Latin of the time of Boethius had become "a learned bookish tongue," and that Boethius himself needed, in his commentaries, "to take account of the

[10] Erich Auerbach, *Literary Language and Its Public in Late Antiquity*, trans. Ralph Manheim (New York: Random House, 1965), p. 197.

[11] On the complex and long-term shift from the oral, public study of literature to the private and scholarly engagement of texts, see Auerbach, pp. 237-258 and E. R. Curtius, *European Literature and the Latin Middle Ages*, trans. W. R. Trask (Princeton: Princeton Univ. Press, 1953), pp. 149-150. More detailed studies of the relationship between literature and its public at different periods of the Empire include K. Quinn, "Poet and Audience in the Augustan Age," in W. Haase, ed., *Aufstieg und Niedergang der Römischen Welt*, Principiat, II.30.1 (Berlin: De Gruyter, 1982), pp. 140-166. For the educational backgrounds to the literary public, see, S. B. Bonner, *Education in Ancient Rome* (Berkeley and Los Angeles: Univ. of California Press, 1977), pp. 212-249. For the role of education in Late Antiquity, see H. Marrou, *A History of Education in Antiquity*, trans. G. Lamb (London: Sheed and Ward, 1956), pp. 314-350, and P. Riché, *Education et Culture dans l'Occident Barbare* (Paris: Seuil, 1962), pp. 55-64, 78-90.

growing distance between spoken and written forms."[12] Stock
has rewritten the history of the age in terms of the conflict
between oral and written cultures, where the philological
splits between proto-Romance and classical Latin articulate a
fundamental intellectual tension between a world defined by
speech and one defined by books.[13] In addition to the con-
tractions of a literary public and the linguistic changes in Vulgar Latin, a second, and perhaps more vital, transformation
of literary culture was under way. Greek was beginning to
die out as the language of educated discourse. Auerbach has
characterized the place of Greek in cultivated Roman life: "An
educated public almost always takes a particular foreign literary language as a model for the development of its own."[14]
As the educated public disappeared, so did its borrowed idiom, and regardless of how seriously we take the claims for
a Hellenic Renaissance under Boethius and his circle, the bulk
of the evidence suggests that the status of the Greek language
by the close of the fifth century was radically different from
its place in the young Augustine's education one hundred
years before.[15]

---

[12] Brian Stock, *The Implications of Literacy: Written Language and Models of
Interpretation in the Eleventh and Twelfth Centuries* (Princeton: Princeton Univ.
Press, 1983), p. 365.

[13] See Stock's discussions on pp. 19-30, 30-87. On the stylistic implications
of the development of Latin, see Auerbach, *Literary Language*, pp. 85-88; on
the period from Vulgar Latin to Romance, see pp. 251-253, with emphases
on the tensions between the written, literary language and the rapidly changing forms of spoken discourse. For the philological underpinnings to much
of this argument, see E. Löfstedt, *Late Latin* (Oslo: H. Aschehoug, 1959),
esp. pp. 11-38, 59-67.

[14] Auerbach, *Literary Language*, p. 249. On the place of Greek in Late
Antique studies, see Riché, *Education*, pp. 83-84; Marrou, *History*, pp. 255-
264, 345-347; Courcelle, *Late Latin Writers*, pp. 410-413. On the influence of
Greek on Late Latin, see Löfstedt, *Late Latin*, pp. 88-119.

[15] Debate is still lively on Boethius' knowledge of Greek and the details
of his education. Courcelle has argued for the Alexandrian school of Ammonius as the source of Boethius' education; his remarks are conveniently
summarized in *Late Latin Writers*, pp. 278-295. For arguments that Boethius
studied in Athens, see C. J. De Vogel, "Boethiana, I," *Vivarium* 9 (1971),

Taken together, Auerbach and Stock postulate a sixth-century literary and linguistic environment in which educated pursuits became increasingly identified not with public recitation—either in Latin or Greek—but rather with private reading and commentary.[16] The locus of such activity moved progressively inward: from the open declamations in the forum, to the closed disputations in the classroom. Fulgentius' *De Continentia Virgiliana*, a work roughly contemporary with *The Consolation of Philosophy*, portrays a schoolroom colloquy between a master and student which is the fictionalized encounter of the commentator with Virgil's spirit. That Fulgentius should present his engagement with the *auctor* as an imaginary classroom disputation reveals a fact of literary history for the early Middle Ages: the business of reading the classics was no longer a public one. No longer were the poems of Virgil read before an audience or even made the subject of friendly symposia.[17] More important, the reading of the *auctores* had now become an experience limited to the professionally educated; the prov-

---

49-66. For arguments on Boethius intimacy with the Greek commentary tradition, see James Shiel, "Boethius's Commentaries on Aristotle," *Medieval and Renaissance Studies* 4 (1958), 217-244; Shiel argues that Boethius' commentaries are simply translations from the scholia of a certain Aristotelian manuscript, and that they do not represent any original contribution to the commentary. For Shiel's new evidence for this position, see now "A Recent Discovery: Boethius's Notes on the Prior Analytics," *Vivarium* 20 (1982), 128-139. On the place of the Greek Neoplatonic schools in Boethius' culture, see Chadwick, *Boethius*, pp. 16-22. For a rigorous reassessment of the evidence on Boethius' Greek learning, his goals in the commentaries, and his techniques of translation, I am indebted to an unpublished paper by Sten Ebbesen, "Boethius as an Aristotelian Scholar."

[16] See Auerbach, *Literary Language*, pp. 243-246, on the Imperial habit of presenting works first through public recitations and only afterwards as "published" copies.

[17] As late as the turn of the fourth and fifth centuries, Macrobius could structure his *Saturnalia* as a symposium, where Virgil's text becomes the subject of discussion among several friends. But, already, the tensions between earlier "classical" norms and the newer ethos of the *grammaticus* are made evident. For a full discussion of these issues see Robert Kaster, "The Grammarian's Authority," *Harvard Studies in Classical Philology* 84 (1980), 219-262.

ince of learning was left to the future teachers and what one might call "professional students" who would populate the later Middle Ages. The encounter reported by Auerbach between Tacitus and an educated Roman equestrian would have been unthinkable in a later century where the King of the Ostrogoths reportedly signed his edicts with a stencil.[18] But the issue here is not simply literacy. Rather it is a complex set of attitudes, both historical and cultural, which delimited the activities of literary study to a small elite. Auerbach's sense of the disappearance of a "literary public" is given weight by the example of Cassiodorus. A figure virtually unique at the Gothic court, he eventually would carry on the task of reading and writing in the seclusion of a monastery. He is a transitional

---

[18] Auerbach, *Literary Language*, pp. 237-238, retells an anecdote of Pliny the Younger's to indicate the "wide range of the literary public after the republic." The story of Theodoric and the stencil appears in Anonymus Valesianus, Pars Posterior, 14.79, where it is reported that the King possessed a gold plate with the letters *legi* (meaning, "I have read it") cut out. Chadwick, *Boethius*, p. 3, doubts the story's truthfulness for several reasons: Procopius tells a similar story of the Greek emperor Justin; there is little else to indicate his illiteracy in the workings of his administration (see p. 286, n. 10, for sources and citations). Other arguments about Theodoric's literacy, and his possible patronage of learning, are rehearsed in H. Grundmann, "*Literatus—Illiteratus*," *Archiv für Kulturgeschichte* 40 (1958), 27-30 (who, while reporting in full the accounts of Anonymus Valesianus and Procopius, concludes that an independent and unambiguous account of the issue is essential before one can conclude that Theodoric was illiterate); C. P. Wormald, "The Uses of Literacy in Anglo-Saxon England and its Neighbors," *Transactions of the Royal Historical Society*, Fifth Series, 27 (1977), 97-98 (who argues that there is a distinction between the facts of Theodoric's possible literacy and the need he might have felt to appear less than literate to his warriors); Franz H. Bäuml, "Varieties and Consequences of Medieval Literacy and Illiteracy," *Speculum* 55 (1980), 240-241 (who argues that the absence or substitute of the signature is no evidence for illiteracy, but rather a convention of Medieval royal charters). While the story of Theodoric and the stencil may be less than fair, it nevertheless stands along with Pliny's anecdote as a useful cultural barometer of attitudes towards public literacy and learning. The question for future historical studies, I believe, will be, not whether these stories are objectively true, but rather why they were told in the first place.

figure, a man who began by juggling the careers of courtier, diplomat, and scholar, and who later abandoned public life for private study.[19]

The example of Cassiodorus, however, adds another historical issue to the heritage of Boethius. This was the tradition of *otium*, the leisure granted the intellectual nobleman for the pursuit of the life of the mind. The harried official, beset by daily dilemmas but longing for the refuge of his books, becomes a trope in Latin writing from Cicero through the sixth century.[20] John Matthews has demonstrated that the late imperial Senate sustained this attitude and expressed it in personal letters.[21] Such an attitude of "formal quietism, of a professed disinterest in political office and preference for the intellectual pursuits of learned leisure," certainly stands behind Boethius' further comments in the *Perihermeneias* commentary.[22] He will complete the project, "si vita otiumque suppetit" (Meiser, II, p. 80), that is, if life and leisure allow. Perhaps the clearest statement of Boethius' ambivalence towards his professional life is to be found in another well-known digression in one of the commentaries, this one on Aristotle's *Categories*.

> Even though my duties as consul prevent me from devoting all my time and energy to these studies, I still think it belongs to any public office to instruct the citizens by teaching them of the subject one has studied. The pristine valor of the Romans transferred to this one republic supreme authority over other cities.

[19] For Cassiodorus in his many roles, see the recent study by J. J. O'Donnell, *Cassiodorus* (Berkeley and Los Angeles: Univ. of California Press, 1979). O'Donnell's analysis of the man and his historical context has been challenged by Averil Cameron, "Cassiodorus Deflated," *Journal of Roman Studies* 71 (1981), 183-186.

[20] For the backgrounds to the concept, see Jean-Marie André, *L'Otium dans la Vie Morale et Intellectuelle Romaine* (Paris: Presses Univérsitaires de France, 1966).

[21] J. M. Matthews, "The Letters of Symmachus," in J. W. Binns, ed., *Latin Literature of the Fourth Century*, pp. 75-78, and his restatement in "Anicius Manlius Severinus Boethius," in Gibson, *Boethius*, pp. 25-26.

[22] Matthews, in Gibson, *Boethius*, p. 25.

So I shall deserve well of my fellow-citizens if I undertake what still remains, if I instruct the habits of our people in the arts of Greek wisdom. A consul's task must not omit this.[23]

Such a statement returns us to the problems of the *Periher-meneias* remarks, and, taken together, these two passages point towards an understanding of the place of Boethius in the literary culture of his time. The Boethian persona which emerges from these and other remarks is that of a scholar beset by impediments of time, audience hostility, and the difficulty of the scholarly task. His asides in the commentaries present not the man of political savvy, but the critic of textual sensitivity. He creates a private life for himself—a life lived through the written documents of a culture long since dead. This persona seems to contrast sharply with the few known historical facts of Boethius' life. A professional politician in a crumbling world, Boethius followed a career characterized by the intrigue and displays of power which are the code of politics.[24] When, for example, we read Cassiodorus' letter asking Boethius to recommend a harpist for Clovis the Frank, we see a man valued not simply for his knowledge, but a man marked by the political sagacity to complete the mission successfully.[25] Nor is Boethius a public educator, after the fashion of his model Cicero. Certainly, Boethius' works on arith-

---

[23] "Et si nos curae officii consularis impediunt quo minus in his studiis omne otium plenamque operam consumimus, pertinere tamen videtur hoc ad aliquam reipublicae curam, elucubratae rei doctrina cives instruere. Nec male de civibus meis merear, si cum prisca hominum virtus urbium caeterarum ad hanc unam rempublicam, dominationem, imperiumque transtulerit, ego id saltem quod reliquum est, Graecae sapientiae artibus mores nostrae civitatis instruxero. Quare ne hoc quidem ipsum consulis vacat officio. . . ." PL, 64: 201B. My translation is based on Shiel, "Boethius the Hellenist," p. 680.

[24] For Boethius' public life as written through the institutions (Church, Senate, Empire) he served, see Chadwick, *Boethius*, pp. 1-16, 22-68. For the backgrounds to Boethius' political life found in the culture of Late Imperial Rome, see John Matthews, "Anicius Manlius Severinus Boethius," in Gibson, *Boethius*, pp. 25-43.

[25] Cassiodorus, *Variae*, II.40, ed. Fridh, pp. 87-91.

metic, music, and dialectic would—and ultimately did—provide a young man with the basic grounding in the public arts. But his present plan is far different from any attempt to offer a syllabus for the education of an official.

Boethius' ambitions are private. They write the autobiography of a literary artist in terms of the texts he has read rather than the things he has seen. His monuments will remain documents rather than deeds. There are two consequences to this view of a literary career. The first sees texts as the bearers of tradition, and in turn views the processes of reading and interpreting as an engagement with the world through books. The second sees the processes of reading and rewriting as intimately linked together. The urge to write on what one has read, however, is more than a personal problem. The act embodies a principle of acculturating old texts into new contexts. At one level, it is an attempt to seek not what the *auctor* meant but rather what he means; thus there is translation over time. At another level, it is an attempt to make Greek thought at home in a Roman world; there is also translation over space. Boethius' phrasing in the *Perihermeneias* commentary, "in Romanum stilum vertens," implies that he read virtually with pen in hand and that the process of translation was a process of transformation. Aristotle will not simply be rendered into Latin, but will, in effect, be Romanized into the intellectual life of Boethius' own time. The very physicality of this process is emphasized not only by the etymological resonances of the moving stylus behind the words "stilum vertens," but also in the root metaphor of "in manus venerit": whatever works of Aristotle come into his hands. This process of acculturation motivates Cassiodorus' famous letter of recommendation.

In your hands Greek teachings have become Roman doctrine. . . . Thanks to your translations, Pythagoras the musician and Ptolemy the astronomer may be read as Italians; Nichomachus the arithmetician and Euclid the geometer are heard as Ausonians; Plato the theologian and Aristotle the logician dis-

pute in the language of the Quirinal; Archemedes the physicist
you have restored to the Sicilians as a Latin.[26]

The quadrivium becomes uniquely and even locally Italian in
Cassiodorus' version of Boethius' achievement. By scattering
the Greeks throughout the Latin world, Cassiodorus creates
a kind of empire of thought. But he brings to an Italy long
fragmented and under siege a unity only within a syllabus of
study, only within the classroom.

If Boethius was to be praised as having brought Greek
civilization to Rome, it was a civilization which lived in the
school. The classification according to the disciplines of study
renders Boethius' accomplishment the making of a syllabus
rather than the reshaping of a culture. To this extent, Cassiodorus appears to grasp fully the implications of Boethius'
Perihermeneias commentary: the commitment to treat the logical, moral, and scientific works of Aristotle embodies a statement of Late Antique paedeia. As Helen Kirkby rightly points
out, there is nothing in Cassiodorus' claim—here or elsewhere—which refers to the novelty of the enterprise and
which could be used as evidence for a Hellenic Renaissance.
"It is clear," she writes, "that Cassiodorus saw Boethius, as
Boethius saw himself, as part of the long Roman tradition of
translators and commentators on Greek philosophy, of which
Cicero and Marius Victorinus formed a part."[27]

---

[26] ". . . ut Graecorum dogmata doctinram feceris esse Romanam. . . .
Translationibus enim tuis Pythagoras musicus, Ptolemaeus astronomus le-
guntur Itali: Nicomachus arithmeticus, geometricus Euclides audiuntur Au-
sonii: Plato theologus, Aristoteles logicus Quirinali uoce disceptant: me-
chanicum etiam Archimedem Latialem Siculis reddidisti." *Variae*, 1.45, ed.
Fridh, p. 49. Translation based on that of Barnes, in Gibson, *Boethius*, p. 73.

[27] Kirkby, in Gibson, *Boethius*, pp, 56-57. On the continuing traditions of
Greek translation, Cassiodorus speaks of certain "countrymen" who have
transferred Aristotle "to the Latin language by means of translation and
exposition" (". . . quem nostri non perferentes diutius alienum, translatum
expositumque Romanae eloquentiae contulerunt"). From *Inst.* II.iii.1, ed.
Mynors, p. 109; English rendering from L. W. Jones, ed. and trans., *Cassiodorus: An Introduction to Divine and Human Readings* (New York: Columbia
Univ. Press, 1946), p. 158.

But we may not even take this statement at face value, for the differences between Boethius' and Cicero's literary enterprises hinge on both the personal and cultural changes outlined by Auerbach and Stock. In Boethius, schooling and culture become equated, as they were for most Late Antique writers, and the tone as well as the purpose of his project differs radically from Cicero's apparently similar objectives in the *Tusculan Disputations*. For Cicero, the motivation to study bears upon the "right conduct of life."[28] He praises his contemporaries as abler than the Greeks, while Boethius seems to condescend to his reading public. The genius and genesis of Cicero's program of translation comes from the people; for Boethius, it comes from within. When he turns to the technical arts of mathematics, for example, Cicero does not offer the Boethian kind of engagement with the author, but tries rather to serve his public in making mathematics an applied art.

> With the Greeks geometry was regarded with the utmost respect, and consequently none were held in greater honor than mathematicians, but we Romans have restricted this art to the practical purposes of measuring and reckoning.[29]

One may compare this sentiment with the ambitions Boethius laid out in the preface to his *De Arithmetica*. He intends, he writes Symmachus, to make the Romans familiar with the riches of Greek literature.[30] He takes the study of arithmetic far more seriously than Cicero seems to take the pursuit of mathematics, and scholars have shown in great detail Boethius' debt to Greek mathematical thought. In this work, too, Boethius is acutely conscious of arithmetic's place in the quad-

[28] "ad rectam vivendi." All quotations and translations from Cicero, *Tusculan Disputations*, ed. and trans., J. E. King, Loeb Classical Library (Cambridge: Harvard Univ. Press, 1927); here, pp. 2-3.

[29] "In summo apud illos honore geometria fuit, itaque nihil mathematicis illustrius: at nos metiendi ratiocinandique utilitate huius artis terminavimus modum" (*Tusc. Disp.*, I.ii.5, p. 6).

[30] *Boetii De Institute Arithemtica* . . . , ed. G. Friedlein (Leipzig: Teubner, 1867), p. 3.

rivium; it is the first of his translations because the subject is the first to be mastered.[31] In the opening of the text itself, probably Boethius' first completed scholarly treatise, he announces his plan of a coherent syllabus of study, a plan which anticipates the scope and tone of the plan in the *Perihermeneias* commentary.[32]

The central distinction between Boethius and Cicero involves an attitude towards the relationship of culture and learning. Cicero attempts to apply Greek learning to Roman ways of life, without any explicit attempt to Hellenize the Latins. Boethius, however, tries to acculturate Greek thought into his Latin culture. Both writers admit to the technical subtleties of Greek thought and expression; but, while Boethius tries to preserve and recreate it, Cicero seeks simply to appropriate it. Boethius seems fascinated with learning for its own sake, and his plan of translations is motivated by a coherent course of study. Cicero seeks only the practical applications of art, apparently motivated by no plan save pragmatism.

In a similar manner, Boethius and Cicero part company on their attitudes towards their audience. For Cicero it is essential that public fame accompany intellectual achievement: "Public esteem is the nurse of the arts, and all men are fired to application by fame whilst those pursuits which meet with general disapproval always lie neglected."[33] Boethius' audience, however, is invariably a hostile one, and his efforts can rarely

---

[31] "Cum igitur quattuor matheseos disciplinarum de arithmetica, quae est prima, perscriberem, tu tantum dignus eo munere videbare, eoque magis inerrato opus esse intellegebam" (Friedlein, p. 5, 6-9). See, too, the passage where Boethius calls this work "laboris mei primitias" ("the first of my labors") (Friedlein, p. 5, 22).

[32] See Boethius' remarks in Friedlein, pp. 7-12, and the characterization of his plan as a *quadrivium*: "Hoc igitur illud quadruvium est, quo his viandum sit, quibus excellentior animus a nobiscum procreatis sensibus ad intellegentiae certiora perducitur" (Friedlein, p. 9, 28 to p. 10, 1). For discussions of this plan, see Courcelle, p. 276; Chadwick, *Boethius*, p. 73.

[33] "Honos alit artes omnesque incenduntur ad studia gloria iacentque ea semper, quae apud quosque improbantur" (*Tusc. Disp.*, 1.ii.4., p. 6).

be seen as ever redounding to his personal glory. His statements of anger and impatience with his ignorant public pose
problems for the modern reader. Are we meant to take them
at face value, as Courcelle did, and from them posit a hostile
reaction to Boethius' Hellenic goals?[34] Or are we to assert
simply, along with Helen Kirkby, that these asides are purely
conventional *topoi*, almost a reflex for any Late Antique
writer?[35] I think we must give Boethius more credit than either
of these viewpoints allows, for we may see his comments as
participating in the larger structure of imagery he used to
create the persona of a writer struggling with his task. Boethius reveals a conscious need to justify the projects of his
reading and his writing to a skeptical public. His works on
topics theory counter the criticism of "insolent men" and
"savage minds,"[36] and he seems torn between the needs for
precise translation and the demands of a critical public.[37] The

[34] *Late Latin Writers*, pp. 322-323, noting how in his prefaces, Boethius
tries to enlist the aid of John the Deacon and Symmachus, "to support him
in the great philosphical program that he had outlined." On Boethius and
Symmachus as "antiquarians," attempting to combine "a genuine Christian
faith with a devotion to all that was pagan in Roman tradition," see
A. Momigliano, "Cassiodorus and the Italian Culture of his Time," *Pro-
ceedings of the British Academy* 46 (1955), pp. 210-214.

[35] Kirkby, in Gibson, *Boethius*, pp. 58-59.

[36] E.g., *In Topica Ciceronis*, PL, 64: 1152A: "Nec me saevae hominum mentes
arrogantiae notent, . . ."; 1157A: ". . . quis ferret insolentium hominum
temeritatem provectus suos culpare volentium quibus provectibus proficer-
ent. . . ." See Chadwick, *Boethius*, p. 120 and p. 299, n. 33, for further discussions and citations.

[37] For Boethius' remarks on the stylistic infelicities made at the expense of
precise translation, see *In Isagogen*, ed. S. Brandt, CSEL, 48 (Leipzig: Freytag,
1906), p. 135, and the discussions of this passage in Barnes, in Gibson, *Boethius*, p. 77, and Chadwick, *Boethius*, p. 136. Sten Ebbesen has, however,
advanced the argument that Boethius' translations are deliberately "un-
Latin": that they, at times, translate Greek morpheme by morpheme; that
they attempt to mime Greek syntax; and that this fidelity stems from Boethius' goal of writing low-level, "pedestrian" works for schoolroom use.
Thus, Boethius sets out to give only the most rudimentary trots to Greek
texts, and his stylistic peculiarities have an apparently pedagogic purpose
(Ebbesen, "Boethius as an Aristotelian Scholar").

prefatory letter to Symmachus which introduces *De arithmetica* chronicles the "sleepless nights" and massive labors needed to complete the translation.[38] He depends on the authority of Symmachus to still the voices of public detractors.[39] Certainly these are tropes, and the exordial conventions Boethius uses can be found in a variety of Late Antique writers.[40]

But Boethius has selected very carefully from the store of *topoi* available to him. Taken together, his remarks on unresponsive readers and difficult texts concretize the difficulty of writing and they reemphasize the fundamental inadequacy of his tools to his task. The length of the *Perihermeneias* commentary; the several versions of the text we know Boethius struggled to compose; and the very massiveness of the project as a whole—all these features combine to reveal a writer faced with insurmountable tasks. The perfect translation of Porphyry or Aristotle, "word for word," is an impossibility in the context of the competing desire to acculturate Greek ideas into Latin forms. The proposed plan of translation, commentary, and harmonization is almost an intentional impossibility. The Boethian enterprise itself becomes only a propaedeutic to the proper task of study. The endlessness of the project points to a literary career concerned primarily with beginnings and fresh starts: with setting plans, opening books,

[38] "Quod nobis quantis vigiliis ac sudore constiterit, facile sobrius lector agnoscet" (Friedlein, p. 5, 4-5). On "sleepless nights" as a trope, see Eusebius, *Life of Constantine*, 1.19, where he states that he was so eager for learning that he "sometimes passed sleepless nights furnishing his mind with divine knowledge." Quoted in Glanville Downey, "Education in the Christian Roman Empire," *Speculum* 32 (1957), 51.

[39] "Qua in re mihi alieni quoque iudicii lucra quaeruntur, cum tu utrarumque peritissimus litterarum possis Graiae orationis expertibus quantum de nobis iudicare audeant, sola tantum pronuntiatione praescribere" (Friedlein, p. 4, 23-27). For comparisons with Boethius' later dedications to Symmachus and his relationship to a hostile audience, see the later section of this study on the theological tractates.

[40] See Tore Janson, *Latin Prose Prefaces* (Stockholm: Almquist, 1964). On the benevolence of the dedicatee at the expense of the ill-will of a hostile audience, see pp. 142-143; on the epistolary preface as a convention, see pp. 116-120.

and renewing the past in the light of the present. As I will argue later, the theological tractates and the *Consolation* itself struggle with the problems of beginning a written work, and with the literary pressures to relate that beginning to the corpus of writings which has preceeded it. From this perspective, Boethius' preoccupation with beginnings is an issue of literary criticism and a problem in the development of his persona.

For the present, one might argue that in Boethius' ambitions lies the historical consciousness of his culture's decline and of the near futility of his role as the last contributor of insight into the Latin West.[41] "I shall perform the task that remains and instruct our state in the arts of Greek wisdom," and the ironies of his response should not be missed. In them lie the sad echoes of Cicero's once bold task:

> I shall encourage all, who have the capacity, to wrest from the now failing grasp of Greece the renown won from this field of study [i.e., Philosophy] and transfer it to this city, just as our ancestors by their indefatigable zeal transferred here all the other really desireable avenues to renown.[42]

In his attitude towards past learning and its place in the present, Boethius seems to invert Cicero's claims: Cicero aimed to initiate a movement, Boethius, to close it.

To this point, I have argued that Boethius' prefaces and digressions sketch the life of a reader and writer, and one might therefore seek an example of Boethius manipulating a text to focus on the problems of writing and "textuality" central to the personal and cultural contexts of his task. Just such an example has been provided by Brian Stock, whose reading of the *Perihermeneias* commentary itself shows the commentator concerned with the relationship of speech to writing, and in turn, with the problems of producing a written

---

[41] As does Chadwick, *Boethius*, p. 69.

[42] "Quam ob rem hortor omnes, qui facere id possunt, ut huius quoque generis laudem iam languenti Graeciae eripiant et transferant in hanc urbem, sicut reliquas omnes, quae quidem erant expetendae, studio atque industria sua maiores nostri transtulerunt" (*Tusc. Disp.*, 11.i.5., p. 150).

text.[43] According to this version, Boethius argues that forms of speech (*locutiones*) rely on their ability to be both heard *and* read. Stock paraphrases: "In order for there to be speech, first the tongue must strike the air and then the emitted sounds must be transcribable in written characters" (Stock, p. 367). Speech and writing thus function as inextricably linked systems of meaningful communication. Throughout the commentary, writing becomes the measure of meaning.[44] Written forms, Boethius argues, help establish the meanings of words, and he postulates a sequential relationship of world and word. First, an object exists; then, it is perceived and understood; then, it can be expressed verbally; and finally its name can be written down.[45] Boethius remains deeply interested in the problems of writing and in the relationship of thought and speech to written forms. His definition of *littera* as "inscriptio atque figura partis minimae vocis articulatae" (an inscription or figure of the smallest expressible part of speech),[46] focuses on the physical act of inscribing texts, and in the commentary *In Porphyrium* Stock also sees written language as the vehicle for Boethius' notion of intellectual engagement. "In *descriptio* he sees not only 'description' but 'de-scribing,' that is, the making of a copy or a transcript."[47] The point of Stock's summary is that Boethius reworks the emphases of Aristotle's text into a concern with the written letter, and we can apply these observations to the autobiographical digressions in the commentaries and the technical works. The metaphors through which Boethius expresses his acts of reading and writing; the apparent need he has to create a hostile audience for his project; the impediments he announces for his task; and the continual desire to place each work within a larger plan of study and transcription—these asides inscribe into

[43] Stock, *Implications of Literacy*, "Boethius on Aristotle," pp. 366-372.

[44] E.g., see Stock's discussion, *Implications*, pp. 368-369, paraphrasing the *Perihermeneias* commentary, Meiser, II, p. 20, 29-31.

[45] See Stock, *Implications*, p. 369, n. 204, quoting Meiser, II, p. 21, 25-29.

[46] Meiser, II, p. 23, 16-18.

[47] Stock, *Implications*, p. 390.

Boethius' texts a certain literary persona whose major task involves surmounting the difficulties of writing. Boethius' concern with *litterae* makes acts of thinking and reading acts of writing as well: theoretically, the *Perihermeneias* commentary made writing the natural end point of verbal cognition; practically, his works demonstrate that the business of interpretation is both the understanding of *locutiones* and the inscription of new texts.

To pursue these links between reading and writing, I turn to several works which may be considered preliminary to the writing of *The Consolation of Philosophy*. They are not, strictly speaking, to be seen as sources, but rather as illustrations of how earlier writers, and the early Boethius himself, confronted the problems of linguistic expression and understanding and presented their explorations in the form of philosophical dialogue. They share features of structure, method, and theme, although they are widely different in their ostensible purposes. I have already mentioned Cicero's *Tusculan Disputations* as a work which tries to assimilate Greek thought. I turn to it now as an enactment of Greek method: the Aristotelian system of argument combined with the Academic Skeptical format of *disputatio in utramque partem*. The *Tusculans* offers to compete with Greek literary texts which are its model, as Cicero gears his energies to record precisely the dialogue which transpired; he is out to write literature. Augustine's *Soliloquia* and *De Magistro* present the mind in conversation with itself, and display the Saint's application of classical methods to Christian theology. Fulgentius *De Continentia Virgiliana*, already mentioned as a document of cultural history, will be treated as a comic foil for the colloquy genre and as an analogue to the *Consolation*'s engagement with literary and intellectual authority. Boethius' own early *In Isagogen Porphyrii* comments upon and explicates Porphyry through a discussion between Boethius and a friend, and it is in this friend's role that Boethius presents, in nascent form, the persona of the student which will motivate the *Consolation*'s dialogue. Finally, I will consider the theological tractates

as exploring the limitations of language in expressing philosophical wisdom, and show how Boethius transforms the
dialogue structure into a series of internal meditations which
take Augustine as their model.

The goal of these dialogues is always the production of a
text. For Cicero, it is the compendium of Greek learning
which would become a Latin monument of literature to stand
beside the Greeks. For Augustine, it is the production of a
document of study and reference. For Fulgentius, it is a usable
allegorical commentary on Virgil. All of these authors direct
their energies self-consciously to commiting the dialogue to
writing. In so doing, they render the dialogue process itself
as inseparable from the writing of a text. Such activities imply
not only that the authors engage a future reading public, but
also that they conceive of an imaginary audience, outside the
circle of friends or students for whom the text was written.
These texts thus explore the development of the writing persona, while at the same time embodying within them an imagined reader's expectations. Whether the audience is presumed
to be hostile or favorable, it is at the very least fictional. In
these ways, the dialogues I will discuss enable their readers
to measure themselves against both the student figure within
the text, and the imaginary reader the text itself inscribes.
Cicero, Augustine, and Fulgentius anticipate Boethius in that
they all postulate a mind in conversation with itself; that they
express this conversation between the figures of student and
teacher; and that their conversations always produce a readable
work which will engage a future imaginary audience in constant colloquy with its authors. To a certain extent, the literary
dialogues explored here will recreate the processes of reading
and understanding, and in so doing, they take as their theme
the methodology of literary education.

Cicero

"Let it now be the birthday of Philosophy in Latin Literature,
and let us lend it our support and submit to contradiction and

refutation."[1] In opening the second book of the *Tusculan Disputations* Cicero announces the goal of transforming Greek thought into Roman form. I have already suggested some ways in which Boethius adapted this stance to his own literary project; but the *Tusculans* hold more than polemic for the reader of the *Consolation*. Scholars have long recognized the specific debts Boethius owes to the dialogue, from the possible suggestions for the personification of Philosophy to the five-book structure which governs the work.[2] Central to Cicero's reasons for composing the *Tusculan Disputations* are also an explication of a philosophic method and a justification of a literary form. To celebrate Philosophy's Latin birthday through "contradiction and refutation" is to engage in the precise method of Greek inquiry. I intend to show here that the *Tusculans* are as much about technique as they are about doctrine, that Cicero puts the method of *disputatio in utramque partem*, outlined in his earlier works, into practice in this text. The dialogue presents the dramatic possibilities of debate, and it demonstrates Cicero's awareness of the literary uses of philosophical argument. Throughout the discussion, Cicero establishes a tension between *disputatio* and *oratio*, or between dialogue and monologue. Debate threatens to collapse, either through the student's unwillingness to argue or his ready willingness to concede. Frequently, Cicero resorts to an extended monologue to sustain the argument; in effect, he de-

---

[1] "philosophia nascatur Latinis quidem litteris ex his temporibus eamque nos adiuvemus, nosque ipsos redargui refellique patiamur" (*Tusc. Disp.*, II.i.5, p. 150).

[2] For the image of Philosophy as "medicina animi," see *Tusc. Disp.*, II.iv.11, p. 156, and these other citations: III.iii.5-6, p. 230; III.vi.13, p. 240; IV.xxii.58, p. 392. For discussion of these passages in relationship to the *Consolation*, see De Vogel, "Boethiana, II," *Vivarium* 10 (1972), 10. For the sources for Philosophy as *magister* in the *Consolation*, see *Tusc. Disp.*, II.vi.16 ("magistra vitae philosophia"), and the citations discussed in Gruber, *Kommentar*, p. 101. For the five-book structure of the *Tusculans* and its possible influence on the *Consolation*'s composition, see Anna Crabbe, "Literary Design in the *De Consolatione Philosophiae*," in Gibson, *Boethius*, pp. 244-245, also adducing the *De finibus* and Ovid's *Tristia* as structural influences.

bates with himself. By calling attention to these problems in disputation, he underscores a deeper problem in human communication, and he reinforces an essentially skeptical view of language and argument. Before detailing the dialogue's progress in the *Tusculan Disputations*, we must first explore the work's origins in Cicero's philosophical plan. His literary goals that I suggested earlier will then make more sense within the tradition of writings which stand behind *The Consolation of Philosphy*.

Cicero's literary disputations are frequently seen as the heirs to the Platonic dialogue, and Cicero himself lends some credence to this genealogy. He opens nearly all his major works with a review of Greek philosophy, but his history is directed towards a specific goal: a defense of Academic Skepticism. Cicero found the teachings of the New Academy to provide the terms and general outlook for his proposed union of *ratio* and *oratio* in public life.[3] Both the orator and the skeptic, he noted, train their minds through the practice of deliberative skills; both are prepared to argue persuasively all sides of an issue.[4] Their goals are not to determine certainty but rather to assess probabilities, for the Academy of Cicero's day offered the kind of moderate skepticism which, unlike the goals of the Pyrhonnic skeptics, claimed that healthy disputation could explore probable moral and epistemological alternatives, and thus formulate reasonable grounds for action. When

---

[3] For Cicero and the Skeptics, see the following: A. Weische, *Cicero und die neue Akademie* (Münster: Aschendorffsche Verlagsbuchhandlung, 1961); W. Burkert, "Cicero als Platoniker und Skeptiker," *Gymnasium* 72 (1965), 175-200; C. B. Schmitt, *Cicero Scepticus: A Study of the Influence of the Academica in the Renaissance* (The Hague: Nijhoff, 1972); O. Gigon, "Cicero und die griechische Philosophie," in H. Temporini, ed., *Aufstieg und Niedergang der Römischen Welt*, I, 4 (Berlin: De Gruyter, 1973), pp. 226-261.

[4] In the *Brutus* Cicero commends the Peripatetic and Academic schools as good grounding for the novice orator (119-120). The skeptically trained orator posed a formidable opponent, and in *De Natura Deorum*, Velleius praises Cotta, and in turn Cicero, "I am indeed a rash person . . . to attempt to join issue with a pupil of the Academy who is also a trained orator" (II.i.1, p. 123).

Cicero finds the origin of this method in Socrates, however, he appears unclear both in his purpose and in the details of his understanding of the so-called "Socratic method."[5] In *De finibus* he implies that Socrates aimed at eliciting truth, whereas in the *Tusculan Disputations* he stresses his purpose in defining probabilities.[6] What remains clear is that Cicero saw Socrates as the originator of a technique of ceaseless questioning adopted by the Academy. Arcesilias, the founder of the New Academy, developed the ability to argue against all positions equally. By withholding assent, he established a principle of uncertainty central to Skeptical thought. Carneades, according to Cicero, modified this earlier position; by claiming to argue both for and against any issue, he emphasized the probability of all assumptions and perceptions.[7] It is this moderate skepticism Cicero favors, and he characterizes its end and method in the *Academica*. Through argument *in utramque partem*, "all things are inquired into and no certain statements are made."[8]

To the Socratic and Academic heritage Cicero added Aristotle as the other source of his philosophic method. He credited Aristotle with founding "the practice of arguing both for and against every topic" (*De finibus*, v.iv.10). Unlike Arcesilias, Aristotle did not merely controvert propositions, but set all arguments on every side (*ibid*). Cicero presents a history of skepticism, then, by conflating the Socratic and Aristotelian (or what he also calls the Peripatetic) methods into the Academic school. From Aristotle, too, Cicero took a conception

[5] For a selection of views on Cicero's interpretation of Socrates' method, see Jerrold E. Seigel, *Rhetoric and Philosophy in Renaissance Humanism* (Princeton: Princeton Univ. Press, 1968), pp. 3-30; Michael J. Buckley, "Philosophic Method in Cicero," *Journal of the History of Philosophy* 8 (1970), 143-154.

[6] *De finibus*, II.i.2-3; *Tusc. Disp.*, I.7.

[7] See *De Natura Deorum*, I.11; Buckley, "Philosophic Method," pp. 143-148.

[8] *Academica*, I.xii.46. See also Cicero's remarks at *Acad.*, II.iii.7: "The sole object of our discussion is by arguing on both sides (*in utramque partem dicendo*) to draw out and give shape to some result that may either be true or the nearest possible approximation of the truth" (Loeb ed., p. 475).

of dialectic fundamentally at odds with the earlier, Platonic definition, and this Aristotelian approach informs the form and purpose of Cicero's literary dialogues.[9] Unlike the Platonic discussions, which sought ideals and absolutes, Cicero's move primarily among beliefs and opinions.[10] A Ciceronian debate is characteristically open-ended, with the argument turning on what appears most probable, or "verisimilar," to the speaker and his audience. As F. M. Cornford has illustrated, Plato's texts pursue knowledge rather than belief. While Cicero's dialogues find the dynamic of disputation an end in itself, Plato's take these suggested arguments as "mere stepping-stones which are kicked away in the ascent to correct definition."[11] For Aristotle, debate moved according to probabilities rather than truths, and the participants exercised their judgment and opinion to persuade and be persuaded. Aristotle's dialectician convinces through *endoxa*, or opinions, while Plato's demonstrates according to proofs. Friedrich Solmsen paraphrases Aristotle's view of dialectic and characterizes Cicero's method: "By habituating ourselves to look at a question from two opposite sides, we sharpen our eyes for truth."[12] Thus dialectic stands in relationship to philosophy only as a propaedeutic, and this relationship is markedly different from that in Plato. Dialectic for Plato has a greater philosophical power, for its exercise can disclose truth it-

[9] For Aristotelian vs. Platonic dialectic, see: Friedrich Solmsen, "Dialectic without the Forms," in G.E.L. Owen, ed., *Aristotle on Dialectic* (Oxford: Clarendon Press, 1968), pp. 49-68, esp. p. 52; Gilbert Ryle, "Dialectic in the Academy," in Owen, pp. 69-79; Eleonore Stump, "Dialectic in Aristotle's Topics," in her book, *Boethius's De Topicis Differentiis* (Ithaca: Cornell Univ. Press, 1978), pp. 158-178.

[10] For the difference between Platonic and Ciceronian dialogue, see the arguments in Joel Altman, *The Tudor Play of Mind* (Berkeley and Los Angeles: Univ. of California Press, 1978), p. 69; Buckley, "Philosophic Method," p. 146.

[11] F. M. Cornford, "Mathematics and Dialectic in the Republic, vi–vii," *Mind* 41 (1932), 173-190; the quotation is from pp. 181-182.

[12] Solmsen, "Dialectic without the Forms," p. 54; see Aristotle *Topica*, 163a29-163b3, which is the text under discussion.

self.[13] Dialectic becomes a means of understanding the nature of the Forms, and, methodologically, it leads its student through a process of conversion to new belief and knowledge.[14]

Cicero's dialogues appear substantially different in their intention and method from their Platonic ancestors. Yet, Cicero does not want to abandon the Platonic heritage, and his apparently confusing synthesis of Plato, Aristotle, the Academics, and, at times, the Stoics appears throughout his writings.[15] On the one hand, works such as the *Topica* and *De finibus* argue for Aristotelian theory at the expense of Stoic dialectic.[16] In his letters, Cicero claims to follow the "model of Aristotle" in presenting his philosophical works as dialogues and discussions.[17] On the other hand, the *Tusculan Disputations* appears written in the tradition "immortalized in Plato's literary masterpieces" (*Tusc. Disp.*, v.iv.11). When he announces that his dialogue will procede in *Graecorum more*, we may be left with little sense as to what he really means. Some sense can be made of Cicero's eclecticism by seeing it as an early analogue to Boethius' own attempted synthesis. Cicero seems to seek the best in a variety of schools of thought; he conflates "all of the ancients" into a corpus of texts from which he

---

[13] Robert Cushman, *Therapeia: Plato's Conception of Philosophy* (Chapel Hill: Univ. of North Carolina Press, 1958), p. 167, discussing *Republic*, 532d, 533b.

[14] Cushman, *Therapaeia*, p.167. See too, Stanley Fish, *Self-Consuming Artifacts* (Berkeley and Los Angeles: Univ. of California Press, 1971), pp. 2-3. For a summary of the historical developments of Plato's theories of dialogue and dialectic, see the section by E. L. Burge, "Dialectic," in W. H. Stahl, *Martianus Capella and the Seven Liberal Arts* (New York: Columbia Univ. Press, 1971), pp. 104-115.

[15] For extended treatment of Cicero and the Stoics, see Lisa Jardine, "The Origins of Humanist Dialectic," *Journal of the History of Philosophy* 15 (1977), 143-164, and Seigel, *Rhetoric and Philosophy*, pp. 3-30. For Cicero's eclecticism, and for the Academic method itself as eclectic and pragmatic, see Jardine, p. 157.

[16] *Topica*, 6; *De finibus*, IV.iv.8-9.

[17] See the Letter to Atticus, III.xiii.19; *ad Familiares*, I.ix.23 (to Lentulus).

picks and chooses.[18] His methods of translation and imitation
are selective rather than cumulative. He attempts, in the prefaces of his dialogues, to trace a common thread of argument
in all these different writers. He sees himself as a kind of artist,
and from his youthful *De Inventione* on, he envisions the goals
of rhetor and artist as similar. To take but the earliest example,
Book II of *De Inventione* opens with the story of Zeuxis selecting the best of five models to paint a picture of Helen.
Cicero compares the writing of his work with Zeuxis' principle of selection and representation. He too does not set before himself a single model, whose every detail he reproduces.
Rather, he will choose the best of many examples; his principle
of imitation is a selective one.[19]

When Cicero opens the *Tusculan Disputations* with an appeal
to the tradition of Latin philosophy and a brief history of
Greek and Roman oratory, he is characteristically reflecting
on the intellectual heritage of his work. He offers the persona
of a reader and writer acutely aware of the texts which have
gone into the making of his composition. He sees the dialogue
as a written, literary genre, not merely as a record of spon-
taneous events.[20] Cicero's stated intentions to write within a
literary as well as a philosophical tradition articulate the pri-
macy of producing a new text with every act of inquiry.[21] As

[18] For Cicero's use of the term *antiqui* and his conflation of "Aristotle and
other disciples of Plato," see the discussion in Seigel, *Rhetoric and Philosophy*,
p. 21.

[19] *De Inventione*, II.i.1–ii.5.

[20] For different views of Cicero's understanding of his dialogues' literary
nature, see P. Levine, "Cicero and the Literary Dialogue," *Classical Journal*
53 (1957), 146-151; M. Ruch, "Vérité historique, véracité de la tradition,
vraisemblance de la tradition, vraisemblance de la mise en scène dans les
dialogues de Cicéron," *Revue des Etudes Latines* 26 (1948), 61-63. For a large-
scale overview of many of the issues raised by this section, and for a
collection of primary source materials which supplements the ones adduced
here, see Wesley Trimpi, "The Quality of Fiction: The Rhetorical Trans-
mission of Literary Theory," *Traditio* 30 (1974), 1-118, especially pp. 43-51.

[21] The *Tusculans* concludes with these sentiments: writing becomes a way
of filling the time left by *otium*; writing is an act of inquiry and interpretation,
a form of spiritual consolation; writing is an act of imagining an audience in
terms of one's self (*Tusc. Disp.*, v.xli.121, p. 546).

a writer, Cicero too must conceive of his audience, and he contrasts the goals of orator and philospher in these terms. In his capacity as speaker, he sets out to win the approval of the multitude; in his role as writer, he attempts to address only the worthy. "Philosophy is content with few judges" (II.i.4.), he writes; while she avoids the multitude, they too are suspicious of her followers (*ibid*). But writings should speak not just to competing schools and in a jargon of one selective community. There are books enough, he complains, and to add one more to already crammed libraries may seem pointless. Even Cicero cannot claim to read the lot of them (II.6-8). Instead, he writes:

> Our opinion is that everything committed to writing should approve itself to the taste of all educated readers, and if we ourselves are unable quite to succeed in this, we do not for that reason think we should abate our efforts to do so.[22]

From here, Cicero immediately moves to an implied link between the method of Academic disputation and the success of writing philosophic dialogues. His syncretism in philosophical models is matched by his variety of literary models, and he sees the goal of his enterprise as contributing to a body of texts. His claims for an educated readership reflect not only on his intended audience but on the persona he wishes to create. Cicero portrays himself as a reader; his own studies apparently prompt the form and matter of his dialogues, and his surveys of Greek and Latin literatures offer, in effect, a syllabus of study for the public man in the leisure of his country retreat. Finally, it is vital to recognize that Cicero directs the presentation of his works towards their accessibility to his readership. He chooses to reproduce the dialogue's structure, and his preliminary remark in Book I is representative of the view he echoes throughout the *Tusculans*: "But in order that the course of our discussions may be more con-

---

[22] *Tusc. Disp.*, II.iii.8, p. 154: "Nobis autem videtur, quidquid litteris mandetur, id commendari omnium eruditorum lectioni decere; nec, si id ipsi minus consequi possumus, idcirco minus id ita faciendum esse sentimus."

veniently followed, I shall put them before you in the form of a debate and not in narrative form."[23]

In addition to establishing a literary method, this statement also affirms the debate's commitment to the forms of Aristotelian argument outlined in Cicero's *Topica*. Cicero had considered debate (*contentio*) to originate from a "question at stake" (*qua de re agitur*) (*Topica*, 95). The dialogue in the *Tusculan*'s first book grows from an issue posed by the questioner (here, whether death is a great evil), and the discussion seems to begin in answer both to Cicero's commitment to report the discussion as it transpired (the idiom *quasi agatur res*) and to his initial invitation to suggest any subject as a theme. This preliminary invitation is characteristic of the topical method of argument and the Socratic form of inquiry. He explains to his partner:

> The procedure was that, after the would-be listener had expressed his view, I opposed it. This, as you know, is the old Socratic method of arguing against your adversary's position; for Socrates thought that in this way the probable truth was most readily discovered.[24]

The disputants' procedure mirrors the Academic method of arguing all points of an issue, and it shares with the skeptics a goal of verisimilar conclusions. By using topical discovery (*inventio*) the participants will draw out probabilities.

But the text's primary concerns appear most clearly when the dialogue threatens to break down. Scarcely has the discussion been underway, when the questioner seems confused. He is anxious to hear a definitive answer and is impatient with the debating process. He asks Cicero to "explain more fully; for your last remarks are somewhat intricate and compel me

---

[23] *Tusc. Disp.*, I.iv.8, p. 10: "Sed quo commodius disputationes nostrae explicentur, sic eas exponam, quasi agatur res, non quasi narretur."

[24] *Tusc. Disp.*, I.iv.8, p. 10: "Fiebat autem ita, ut, cum is, qui audire vellet, dixisset quid sibi videretur, tum ego contra dicerem. Haec est enim, ut scis, vetus et Socratica ratio contra alterius opinionem disserendi. Nam ita facillime quid veri simillimum esset inveniri posse Socrates arbitrabatur."

to agree before I am convinced."[25] He wishes to hear a "continuous speech" (*oratio*), and in apparent disbelief, Cicero exclaims: "What? If I put a question to you, will you make no reply?" Clearly, the student has violated the rules of inquiry, for he prefers that Cicero ask him no more questions. Cicero realizes that if their argument is to move anywhere, he must argue with himself to try to preserve the probable goals of skeptical investigation. "I shall humor you and explain what you wish as best as I can, . . . following out a train of probabilities."[26] *Disputatio* has become *oratio*, but, even here, Cicero's main task is the establishment of probability. When the questioner replies, "We are ready to hear," he seems to speak not only for himself but for the readers as well; they too have become a willing audience. Now, the force of Cicero's authority rather than his arguments begins to convince his listener and his reader, and our position is anathema to the Academic who holds that, "In discussion it is not so much the weight of authority as the force of argument that should be demanded. . . . Those who desire to learn . . . cease to employ their own judgment, and take what they perceive to be the verdict of their chosen master as settling the question."[27] This is precisely the situation as the dialogue collapses. The *Tusculan Disputations* dramatizes the problems of pedagogical authority in a way which looks forward to the dialogues of Augustine and Boethius. At stake is not simply the inability of the student to sustain discussion, but also the willingness of the teacher to let the colloquy turn into a lecture. In the *Tusculans* the student fears that he is losing the ability to suspend judgment and pursue debate for its own ends; in turn, he prefers to break off dialogue. But Cicero also demonstrates the problems which beset a teacher whose *oratio* must become the mode of probable argument.

[25] *Tusc. Disp.*, I.viii.16, p. 20: "Uberius ista, quaeso. Haec enim spinosiora prius ut confitear me cogunt quam ut adsentiar."

[26] *Tusc. Disp.*, I.viii.17, p. 20: "Geram tibi morem et ea, quae vis, ut potero, explicabo . . . probabilia coniectura sequens."

[27] *De Natura Deorum*, I.v.10.

Cicero begins by presenting differing views on the soul. He notes that to decide among them is for the gods alone, for man can only select among probable choices (I.xi.23). Cicero tries to resume dialogue, but only to reestablish the original problem of authority. The questioner cannot find answers by reading Plato, for when he reads he concedes to the author's presence rather than to his proofs. He again asks for an explanation from Cicero, who proceeds with a speech he himself agrees is longwinded (I.xlvi.111). But the questioner recognizes the implied Academic principles even here, and notes how Cicero arranged his speech in two parts to argue both sides of the issue (I.xlvii.112). With a lengthy rhetorical epilogue, Cicero acknowledges his pupil's observation and closes Book I with the prospect of future discussions. This summary reveals Cicero's concern with the limits of human argument and the practical difficulties of debate. While his character may combine philosophy with oratory in his ability to argue every view, he is at times as guilty as his novice in impeding the debate. While his student opts for silence, the master chooses verbosity. Both partners play a part in developing the tension between dialogue and monologue.

The succeeding books bring out the methodological and thematic problems of the first. Book II elaborately prepares the reader for the ensuing discussion. Cicero again pleads for a Latin expression of the Greek tradition (II.ii.5): the *Tusculan Disputations* will revive the Academic method. He reaffirms his commitment to arguments directed only towards verisimilitude, and he restates his adherence to the method of the *Peripateticorum Academiaeque*. The written text, he asserts, will preserve *utramque partem dicendi*, for "in our house at Tusculanum I thus employed the time at our disposal" (II.iii.9). The work will appear presented not in narrative form, but as close as possible to the exact words of the actual discussion. Throughout the remaining books, too, there is a constant tension between disputation and oration: between the method of discovery through suspension of belief and the capitulation to unfounded belief. Failure to suspend judgment kills debate. Cicero must repeatedly argue with himself to pursue probability. In Book III he launches a long *oratio* on temperance by claiming to argue both from experience and authority (III.viii.17). By attempting to maintain the open-ended nature of the investigation whenever monologue occurs, he seeks, in Book IV, "the most probable solution to every problem" (IV.iii.7), and it is in the opening movements of this book that he foregrounds the tension between monologue and dialogue. He asks his pupil:

> Which course do you prefer, then? Shall we at once spread our sails or like sailors working out of harbor use the oars for a bit . . . ? My question meant, should I spread the sails of eloquence (*orationem*) at once, or push on first a little with the oars of dialectic (*dialecticorum*)?[28]

His questioner replies:

> This last way, to be sure, for all sides of the question I raise will be more completely dealt with by the use of both methods.[29]

His consent enables Cicero to lay out the views of differing philosophical schools; by thus opposing Stoic and Peripatetic theories, in this passage, he preserves *utramque partem dicendi* by himself. When he attempts to revive debate after his exposition, Cicero highlights the prevailing tension of the entire work: now that his *oratio* is finished, they may return to disputation (IV.xiv.33). But the student remains overwhelmed and chooses silence.

Book V takes up the historical polemic which opened the entire work. Cicero traces the history of the word *Philosophia* and the biographies of its earliest followers. He stresses how

---

[28] *Tusc. Disp.*, IV.iv.9, p. 336: "Utrum igitur mavis? statimne nos vela facere an quasi e portu egredientes paullulum remigare? . . . quaerebam igitur utrum panderem vela orationis statim an eam ante paullulum dialecticorum remis propellerem."

[29] *Ibid.*: "Isto modo vero; erit enim hoc totum, quod quaero, ex utroque perfectius."

literature serves thought, for Plato's literary masterpieces have preserved the Socratic method. When he chooses to follow their example, both in the actual debates at Tusculanum and in the texts which supposedly reproduce them, Cicero takes his stand as the heir to Plato, Socrates, and Carneades. He makes claims for the philosophical status of his method and the literary quality of his writings. In attempting to relieve his audience from deception, he echoes the skeptical idea of disputation as a way out of error. His text conforms to Carneades' practice, for it offers a wise man guidance through truth and falsehood (v.iv.11). He will, as he restates later, suspend his own judgment in order that others may decide the issue on its own merits rather than on his (or anyone else's) authority (v.xxix.83). Unlike Carneades, whose temper was apparently legendary, Cicero will pursue his inquiry with a calm mind, and here he echoes his earlier association of orator and actor, having claimed the former superior in his ability to argue *cum mente tranquilla* (iv.xxv.55). Cicero thus presents himself as a model of forensic conduct and as an exemplar of the method in practice.

The local impediments to debate which Cicero presents point to problems at the global level. In its emphasis on the tenuous nature of discussion, the *Tusculan Disputations* challenges successful communication in society. It raises anew the original question of *De Inventione*: what is the role of eloquence in civilization? There, Cicero answered that rhetorical study and practice fostered a civic consciousness. In the *Tusculans*, however, he points towards epistemological issues underlying his early optimism. Now, the disputants seclude themselves in the Tuscan villa; the characters, unlike those of the earlier, historical dialogues, have neither name nor rank, and their arguments do not carry the weight of historical personae. Cicero labels them simply *A* and *M*. This anonymity complements the condition of *otium* in which the dialogue transpires in order to free Cicero to explore problems of finding meaning and conveying knowledge. In its setting and its drama, the dialogue anticipates the fictions of Augustine and

Boethius, where we witness former public men—rhetorician and senator—now stripped of their familiar selves. In these three writers, the detached setting offers, in the words of one recent scholar writing on its later history, a place where "men find occasion to make ideal projections of themselves."[30] In their movements away from public judgment and opinion, the literary dialogues free the disputants from the condescension of the multitude. The Tuscan villa, Cassiciacum, Boethius' Aurelian retreat in the *In Isagogen*, or the *Consolation's* library/prison become states of mind as well as geographical locations, and in succeeding pages I will explore the ways in which this dynamic of withdrawal stimulates the production of literary transcripts of private meditations.

The *Tusculan Disputations* may therefore be considered a convenient initial statement of the thematic and methodological issues which stand behind *The Consolation of Philosophy*. In his commitment to produce a readable text and in his awareness of audience response, Cicero anticipates the kinds of tensions Boethius will establish between himself and his readership. By seeing the compositon of the *Tusculans* within a lifetime of intellectual and literary activity, Cicero offers a model of the career in action. Within the disputation itself, Cicero explores the ways in which authority figures impede free discussion; he presents himself as a model disputant who must carry on "dialogue" with himself in the face of a taciturn student; and he shows that the moments when dialogue breaks down can afford the opportunity for critical reflection on the techniques of communication. Cicero's attempted synthesis of the Platonic literary form with an Aristotelian disputational technique, moreover, looks forward to Boethius' own project in the commentaries, and to the movement of *The Consolation of Philosophy* itself.

---

[30] Daniel Javitch, *Poetry and Courtliness in Renaissance England* (Princeton: Princeton Univ. Press, 1968), p. 25. See also Trimpi, "Quality of Fiction," pp. 81-83, on the secluded setting of the classical and medieval debate.

Augustine

Ever since E. T. Silk argued for the influence of Augustine's dialogues on *The Consolation of Philosophy*, scholars have attempted to resolve Boethius' debt to the Saint.[1] The only clear reference to Augustine by name appears in a theological tractate.[2] Parallels from the *Consolation* appear present, but difficult to attest, and even the apparent similarity between the openings of Augustine's *De Ordine* and Boethius' *In Isagogen* may be due more to the tropes of exordia than to direct influence.[3] For Courcelle, who saw the relationship of the two writers purely as a theological issue, Silk's association was unfounded. Commenting on Silk's notion of the *Consolation* as a "sequel" to the dialogues, Courcelle argued:

> It is difficult to conceive how this writer can adopt such a title, as he does not establish any doctrinal relation between the *Consolation* and the *Dialogues*, but only a formal and external connection.[4]

One cannot, of course, prove the direct influence of Augustine, doctrinally or otherwise; even if Boethius knew first-

---

[1] E. T. Silk, "Boethius's *Consolatio Philosophiae* as a Sequel to Augustine's Dialogues and Soliloquia," *Harvard Theological Review* 32 (1939), 19-39. Reviving many of Silk's arguments, with special reference to the *De Ordine* and added attention to the *Confessions*, is Anna Crabbe, "Literary Design in the *De Consolatio Philosophiae*," in Gibson, *Boethius*, pp. 237-274. Gruber, *Kommentar*, however remains unconvinced that the "christliche Dialog" as exemplified by Augustine had a definite influence on the *Consolation*'s form (p. 32 and n. 218). See, too, Chadwick, *Boethius*, p. 250.

[2] "Vobis tamen etiam illud inspiciendum est, an ex beati Augustini scriptis semina rationum aliquos in nos venientia fructus extulerint," *De Trinitate*, preface, p. 4.

[3] Silk, "Sequel," p. 22, n. 10: "It is an interesting coincidence that both Boethius's first commentary on Porphyry and Augustine's *De Ordine* begin with an unusual night scene." Silk goes on to compare the two scenes in limited detail. Brandt, the editor of the *In Isagogen*, however, considers the work's opening to rely more on the literary conventions of *otium* as found in Cicero, and he also adduces the preface to Aulus Gellius' *Attic Nights* as a distinctive parallel (S. Brandt, ed., *Boethii in Isagogen Porphyrii commenta*, CSEL, 48 [Leipzig: Freytag, 1906], p. viii).

[4] Courcelle, *Late Latin Writers*, p. 318, n. 1.

hand the dialogues, *Soliloquia*, or *Confessions*, it would be very hard for us to place these documents of late-fourth-century Catholicism in the confusing and schismatic environment of early-sixth-century Christianity.[5] Augustine's texts, I will argue here and elsewhere in this study, are useful as analogues to Boethius' works. The *Soliloquia* and *De Magistro* in particular offer parallels to Boethius' engagement with the forms of dialogue and dialectic, and they participate in the history of a literary form.[6] They will also provide the writer of the theological tractates with an idiom for private meditation and internal, silent disputation.

Later in life, Augustine was to characterize the *Soliloquia* as, "deliberations with myself when I was alone in your [i.e. God's] presence,"[7] and this view neatly summarizes the opening moments of the early dialogue. Augustine, turning things over in his mind, is confronted by the voice of Ratio, a figure who externalizes his inner, mental processes. The first thing Ratio does is to exhort Augustine to write down his deliberations. What is essential is that they not simply be dictated to another, but be composed in solitude. Moreover, Augustine should not worry about pleasing a large audience, but

[5] For analysis of the Catholic culture of Boethius' time, see V. Schürr, *Die Trinitätslehre des Boethius im Lichte des "skythischen Kontroversen"* (Paderborn: Schöningh, 1935). See too Chadwick, *Boethius*, pp. 174-222, on the tractates in their historical and dogmatic context, especially in their relationship to Augustine's thought. Chadwick in general finds strong thematic and theological links between Boethius and Augustine; e.g., "I think it [the *Consolation*] a work written with the consciousness of Augustine standing behind the author's shoulder, so to speak" (p. 249). On the differences between the two, see p. 251.

[6] For a discussion of Augustine's *Soliloquia* and *De Magistro* as part of the history of the "Christian Dialogue," see B. R. Voss, *Der Dialog in der frühchristlichen Literatur* (Munich: Fink, 1970). Voss divides the Augustinian dialogue into two classes: the "szenisch," in which the number of speakers varies and in which a physical locus is present; and "nichtszenisch," in which the number of speakers is limited to two and where the dialogue becomes essentially a student/teacher colloquy (p. 197). He considers the *Soliloquia* a hybrid form, while the *De Magistro* obviously falls into the second category (for *Soliloquia*, see pp. 233-245; for *De Magistro*, pp. 271-277).

[7] ". . . disputati . . . cum ipso me solo coram te," *Conf.*, IX.iv.7.

should care only to address his peers. The opening conversation runs as follows:

> R: Now then, suppose you had discovered something, to what would you consign it, in order that you might proceed to other matters?
>
> A: To memory, of course.
>
> R: Is memory of such virtue that it preserves all that has been thought out?
>
> A: That is difficult; in fact it is impossible.
>
> R: It must be written down then. But what are you going to do now that your poor health shirks the task of writing? These matters ought not to be dictated, for they demand real solitude.
>
> A: You speak the truth. Wherefore, I really do not know what I am to do.
>
> R: Pray for health and assistance in order to attain what you desire, and commit this to writing, so that you may be the more heartened by your achievement. Afterwards sum up what you discover in a few brief conclusions. Nor should you now concern yourself about winning a host of readers; these notes will be enough for a few of your fellows.
>
> A: That is what I shall do.[8]

A dialogue establishes itself between master and disciple. The persona of the disciple readily admits the authority of Ratio, while at the same time conceding his own methodological ignorance (i.e., "Verum dicis. Itaque prorsus nescio quid agam"). In the pressure to commit the work to writing, Augustine takes as his priority the making of a text—and this text will differ substantially from such items as a dictated letter in that it will record the mind addressing only itself.

The opening of the *Soliloquia* gives voice to an idiom characteristic of Augustine's mature work, what Joseph Mazzeo

---

[8] *Soliloquia*, I.i.I. All quotations from the work, in Latin and in translation, will be from *The Soliloquies of Saint Augustine*, trans. Thomas F. Gilligan (New York: Cosmopolitan, 1943), with the Latin text printed, with corrections, substantially from PL, 32.

has labelled the "rhetoric of silence."[9] While his reading of
Augustine has come under recent scrutiny, his work nonetheless conveniently illustrates how the ideal of silence became
for Augustine a method of communication, not only between
the spirit and the self, but between it and Christ. "For Augustine all dialectic, true rhetoric, and thought itself were but
attempts to reascend to that silence from which the world fell
into the perpetual clamor of life as fallen men know it" (Mazzeo, p. 192). Augustine also explored the processes of reading
and writing as activities which, at their best, transpire in silence. One need only recall those famous moments in the
Confessions when the young Augustine finds Ambrose reading
in silence (VI.3), and when, at the moment of conversion, he
takes up the Scriptures and reads silently to himself (VIII.3).
Writing, in the *Confessions*, has become a private experience,
and its composition records a process of turning away from
the voices of men to the inner voice of the self or God. The
structure of the *Soliloquia* presents this pattern in nascent form,
and its initial, brief discussion of memory looks forward to
the great exposition of the *Confessions* (X.8-21), where Augustine shows how, by withdrawing into the self, the confession becomes a document written without the need of verbal
or physical companionship.

But Augustine has not reached that point in the *Soliloquia*,
for he remains here more like Cicero's pupil than the writer
of the *Confessions*. Throughout the early dialogue, Ratio leads
her pupil along, frequently pausing to explain her method or
to ensure that Augustine follows her arguments. A clear ex-

[9] Joseph Mazzeo, "St. Augustine's Rhetoric of Silence," *Journal of the
History of Ideas* 23 (1962), 175-196. Mazzeo's work has come under close
scrutiny from, among others, Marcia L. Colish, *The Mirror of Language: A
Study in the Medieval Theory of Knowledge* (New Haven: Yale Univ. Press,
1968), chapter 1, and in her more recent study, "St. Augustine's Rhetoric of
Silence Revisited," *Augustinian Studies* 9 (1978), 15-24. For additional light
on the role of reading and silence in the *Confessions*, see Ralph Flores, "Reading and Speech in St. Augustine's *Confessions*," *Augustinian Studies* 6 (1975),
1-13.

ample of such breakdown and reflection occurs in II.7, where
the discussion turns to the true and the similar, and then
explains the title of the work itself. Ratio opens slowly, asking
for Augustine's attention while "we go over" (*recurrimus*) old
ground (II.7.13). Augustine himself eagerly consents to endure the roundabout course untiringly, so great is his hope
of reaching the end.[10] Such zeal contrasts sharply with his
earlier despair out of which he begged to be led along by some
shortcut ("ut me tentes per aliqua compendia ducere,"
I.xiv.26). Ratio now leads him through an argument on truth
and falsehood which hinges on distinguishing between an
object and its reflection. In his eagerness and haste, Augustine
replies that we recognize the mirror image as false, "by signs
without number which would take too much time to mention."[11] Recognizing his haste, Ratio offers another example,
based now on figures in dreams, to determine true from false
images. Augustine hesitates, she concludes her argument
flawlessly, and all he is left with is an embarrassed speechlessness ("Non habeo quid dicam, et pudet me tam temerariae
consensionis meae superioris," II.vii.13).

The point of this exchange is two-fold: to clarify the disputational abilities and failures of Ratio and Augustine; but
also to reflect on the emotional and methodological impediments to successful discussion. Here, Ratio assures Augustine
that there is no need to be ashamed—very simply because no
one is around to hear them. She praises the method of question
and answer, and notes that only in silence can such a method
be carried out.[12] The *clamor* of opinion and emotion only

[10] "Nam ego circumitum istum semel statui tolerare, neque in eo defatiscar
spe tanta perveniendi quo nos tendere sentio," *Sol.*, II.vii.13.

[11] "et caeteris innumerabilibus, quae prosequi longum est" (*ibid*).

[12] "Cum enim neque melius quaeri veritas possit, quam interrogando et
respondendo, et vix quisquam inveniatur quem non pudeat convinci dis-
putantem, eoque pene semper eveniat ut rem bene inductam ad discutiendum
inconditus pervicaciae clamor explodat, etiam cum laceratione animorum,
plerumque dissimulata, interdum et aperta," *Sol.*, II.vii.14.

hinders argument, and she concludes that it was her "pleasure to seek the truth with God's help in peace and propriety by questioning and answering myself."[13]

By pausing to restate the method and its goals, Augustine also makes a literary point. He claims to have invented a genre whose achievement was to internalize the process of dialogue by writing fictions of the mind in conversation with itself. The opening commitment to producing a written text now takes on a new focus, as Augustine makes claims for the production of literature. The later moments of the *Soliloquia* are peppered with the kind of remarks on fiction and artistry which strongly imply a literary goal to Augustine's project. Discussion of fables (II.ix.16), pictures (II.ix.17), actors (II.x.18), sculptures (II.x.18)—all suggest that Augustine was preoccupied with the problems of artistic representation, not simply as they bore on philosophical issues, but as they helped him understand his own attempts at writing literary representations. To this extent, the *Soliloquia* is a tentative, exploratory work in which something new is self-consciously attempted. Ratio names the work: "Because we are speaking to ourselves alone, I chose to call it by the title of Soliloquies, a name which is, to be sure, a new one and perhaps an awkward one, but one which is quite suitable to indicate its purpose."[14] The work's limitations are clearly recognized as Ratio looks forward to "another book" (*aliud volumen*) which will answer those questions raised by her pupil's new-found zeal (II.xix.33). These moments of self-conscious literary awareness combine with those sequences of the dialogue's collapse to thematize the problems of writing an educational treatise.

The methodological and dramatic issues of the *Soliloquia* develop in greater detail in Augustine's later work, *De Mag-*

---

[13] "pacatissime, ut opinor, et commodissime placuit, a meipso interrogatum mihique respondentem, Deo adjuvante, verum quaerere," *ibid.*

[14] "Quae quoniam cum solis nobis loquimur, *Soliloquia* vocari et inscribi volo; novo quidem et fortasse duro nomine, sed ad rem demonstrandam satis idoneo," *Sol.*, II.vii.14.

istro.[15] In this text, too, the key issues involve clarifying the techniques of disputation; articulating the personae of master and student; and taking language itself, written and spoken, as a theme. The dialogue opens with a clear statement of method:

AUG: But how do we learn?
ADEOD: How but by asking questions?[16]

The process of question and answer, defined structurally in the *Soliloquia*, and given a new moral resonance in *De Magistro*, is beset by impediments. Two contradictory movements emerge: one which sees dialogue as a linear progress towards truth; the other which sees it as a circuitous set of restatements whose goal is unclear.

The first movement is defined through images of order, linearity, and correctness. When Augustine asks Adeodatus to "review what we have discovered by means of this discussion" (VII.19),[17] he essentially asks his pupil to review not simply the arguments employed, but also the entire process of *inventio* as it applies to their dialectical method. Central to this process is the maintenance of linear progression, even at the expense of missing the subtleties of the issues. Adeodatus' survey reveals the criteria of order and clarity essential to the argument thus far. First, a principle was agreed upon and then clearly understood. Augustine's responses involve the use of humor to avoid matters too profound for the student. Even though, at times, Adeodatus fails to follow the details of Au-

---

[15] On the chronology of Augustine's dialogues, and the conclusion that *De Magistro* is the last, see Voss, *Dialog*, p. 239.

[16] AUG: discere autem quomodo?
   ADEOD: Quo tandem censes, nisi cum interrogamus? (I.I.8-9)
All English translations will be from *Concerning the Teacher*, trans. G. E. Leckie (New York: Appelton-Century, 1938). All Latin quotations will be from *De Magistro*, ed. K.-D. Dauer, CCSL 29 (Turnholt: Brepols, 1970), pp. 157-203. References to this edition will be cited by section, paragraph, and line numbers.

[17] "Iam quae sermocinando inuenerimus, uelim recenseas," *De Mag.*, VII.19.1-2.

gustine's train of thought, and even though he admits to his own error and forgetfulness, he nonetheless concludes his review with a defense of his own speech as well as a capsule summary of the dialogue's method: "Do you . . . see whether I have set forth these things well and in good order?" (VII.20).[18]

But, after this review, the dialogue seems to be in trouble. Augustine appears to weave circuitous arguments (VIII.21), whose questions appear to go nowhere at all. From the *ordo* Adeodatus finds in the first half of their discussion, Augustine now moves into the realm of *ambages*.[19] It may seem, too, that he is simply playing with his pupil,[20] and in the next several sections of the work Augustine leads his son through a complex series of arguments—arguments not apparently designed to stimulate his inquiry but simply to elicit his assent. For the next ten paragraphs Adeodatus' words are reduced to a chorus of agreements, until Augustine takes it upon himself to review their difficult path. "Do you recall by what great circumlocutions we at length reached this slight point?"[21] he asks, and he characterizes the discussion thus far as "an interchange of words which has occupied us for some time" (X.31).[22] They have, he states, "labored to discover" a few points, and Augustine's rhetoric stresses the difficulty of their task, as well as the apparent triviality of their goal.[23] But Augustine is certainly right not to entrust his son with such a review; not only does Adeodatus fail to grasp the goal of their procedure, but, when he finally does respond, it is with an insecurity which nearly vitiates their method of inquiry.

[18] "Tu iam uideris . . . utrum ista bene ordinateque digesserim," *De Mag.*, VII.20.84-86.

[19] "Sed quonam tantis ambagibus tecum peruenire moliar, difficile dictu est hoc loco," *De Mag.*, VIII.21.4-6.

[20] "Tu enim fortasse aut ludere nos . . . ," *De Mag.*, VIII.21.6 ff.

[21] "Quanto tandem circuitu res tantilla peracta sit, meministine quaeso?" *De Mag.*, X.31.54-55.

[22] "Nam ex quo inter nos uerba iaculamur, quod tam diu fecimus, . . ." *De Mag.*, X.31.55 ff.

[23] ". . . haec tria ut inuenirentur *laboratum* est," *De Mag.*, X.31.56-57, and see n. 21.

He is disturbed by his father's questions, and his disturbance precludes his agreement. Augustine's method seems beset with contradictions, and Adeodatus is reluctant to speak out of fear that something lies hidden from his mind (x.31).[24]

Dialogue begins to break down, as the level of argument rises beyond the student's ability, and as the student himself feels the pressing need to accede simply to the teacher's authority. From this point on, Augustine himself takes the burden of discussion; Adeodatus says nothing from paragraph 33 until the final words of the work. As Augustine, in turn, directs his presentation (for it is now simply a lecture) towards specifically spiritual themes, he challenges the very principles of public discussion on which the colloquy was founded. Instead of discussion, contemplation becomes the vehicle for enlightenment. The mode of question and answer seems restricted now to discussions of sensible objects, whereas those things perceived solely with the mind are discussed, in effect, by the mind in conversation with itself.[25] Augustine develops a theory of impression by which the truths of the spirit become both "images in the recesses of the memory" and "documents of things sensed before."[26] One learns about the contents of such documents not by listening to the words of some outside lecturer, but rather through private contemplation.[27] Verbal discussion can take Augustine and Adeodatus only so far, for if the respondent hears only the words of the questioner, then his response will be limited. The point of the dialogic section of De Magistro, then, was for Augustine to ask those kinds of

[24] See Adeodatus' reply, x.31.62-68, where he picks up the imagery of ambiguity, circuity, and of the *involucrum*.

[25] *De Mag.*, XII.39.7-17.

[26] *De Mag.*, XII.39.17-25, especially the phrases, "sed imagines ab eis impressas memoriaeque mandatas loquimur," and "Ita illas imagines in memoriae penetralibus rerum ante sensarum quaedam documenta gestamus."

[27] "Sed nobis sunt ista documenta; is enim qui audit, si ea sensit atque adfuit, non discit meis uerbis, sed recognoscit ablatis secum et ipse imaginibus; si autem illa non sensit, quis non eum credere potius uerbis quam discere intellegat?" *De Mag.*, XII.39.25-29.

questions which stimulate the student "to teach himself through his inner power according to the measure of his ability."[28]

By transcending the format of public discussion, Augustine moves into the arena of spiritual contemplation. His theoretical and practical goals dovetail at the *De Magistro*'s close as Adeodatus—and the reader of the work—prepare themselves to listen to the inner teacher in silence. Thus the dialogue's enterprise is propaedeutic to the higher dialogue with the self. Adeodatus' silence throughout his father's lecture illustrates the need for silent contemplation, and, in effect, silent reading. This section of *De Magistro*, in rejecting the explicit dialogue format, becomes a text or treatise designed to be read silently rather than engaged with verbally. In one sense, it looks forward to those moments of silent reading chronicled in Augustine's *Confessions*, and it reflects on the "textuality" of the dialogue as Augustine himself would later reflect on the problems of writing down the meditations which become the *Confessions'* text. The metaphors of inscription Augustine employs in *De Magistro* to characterize cognition further reinforce the impression that one of the work's themes is its own composition: the problem of producing written documents of educational value. There is, then, a double edge to the work's title. While ostensibly about the true, inner teacher—Christ— *De Magistro* also illustrates the problems of confronting pedagogic authority and the limitations of being a teacher constrained by words.

When Adeodatus is finally asked to speak, at the work's conclusion, he rightly summarizes the key moments of Augustine's monologue. His previous expressions of confusion now turn to self-effacement as he reports:

> I am most grateful to you for the discussion which you delivered without breaking the thread of your thought, because it antic-

[28] "sic ergo quaerere oportuit, ut tuae sese uires habent ad audiendum illum intus magistrum," *De Mag.*, XII.40.51-52.

ipated and dissolved all the objections which occurred to
me . . . (XIV.46).[29]

By anticipating and refuting Adeodatus' unspoken responses,
Augustine himself has sustained the process of dialogue. His
concluding speech, according to his son, effectively taught
not through words uttered but through ideas recalled. To this
extent the *De Magistro* looks forward to *The Consolation of
Philosophy*'s structure and method. By presenting a colloquy
between father and son, it dramatizes the problems of authority in the dialogue. Adeodatus' temptations to accede to
his father's wisdom and ability prefigure the prisoner's need
to concede to Philosophy's presence. *De Magistro* establishes
a tension between the demands of linear progression and the
need to present complicated arguments in all their apparent
circuity. In turn, as discussion begins to favor digression and
circumlocution, the student figure fades into undistinguished
assent, and dialogue soon cedes to monologue. Unlike Cicero's *Tusculans*, however, the monologues in *De Magistro*, and
in the later sections of the *Consolation*, capitalize on the student's silence to explore spiritual issues whose implicit epistemology hinges on meditation and silent reading. By exploring the problems of public discussion, and by finally
rejecting the format altogether, Augustine makes the techniques of understanding his true subject. It is the way in which
he makes method his theme which motivates the structure of
the *Consolation* and which directs the reader of Boethius back
to the earlier texts which stand behind the prisoner's silence
and his speech.

Fulgentius

The spirit of our age, most saintly of Deacons, has imposed a
broad censorship of silence, that the mind should both cease to

---

[29] "Verumtamen huic orationi tuae, qua perpetua usus es, ob hoc habeo
maxime gratiam, quod omnia, quae contradicere paratus eram, praeoccupauit
atque dissoluit . . . ," *De Mag.*, XIV.46.40-42.

reveal its learning and must pursue this forgetfulness of itself because its concern is only with what is contemporary.[1]

Thus Fulgentius opens the *De Continentia Virgiliana* with a lament for the loss of past learning to present doctrine. A new Christian ethos has replaced the old paedeia based on the classics, and Fulgentius characterizes a cultural problem in distinctly pedagogic terms. He speaks of the teachings of Christian love which inform his reading; he will bypass those mystical texts, such as Virgil's *Eclogues*, which do not lend themselves to clear instruction; and he seems concerned to present a new synthesis of Christian and pagan teachings based on a close reading of texts.[2] But Fulgentius is no Augustine. He seeks not the "Egyptian gold" buried in pagan eloquence, nor does he attempt to offer a Christian hermeneutic along the lines of *De Doctrina Christiana*. Fulgentius appears more interested in the closed, private world of the classroom and the study. Gone are the friendly symposia which, only a century before, had structured the reading of Virgil in Macrobius' *Saturnalia*. Fulgentius does, however, owe something to both Augustine and Macrobius, and the *De Continentia* offers, I suggest, a comic restructuring of the patterns of student/teacher colloquy fashioned by the earlier authors.[3] Moreover,

---

[1] L. G. Whitbread, trans., *Fulgentius the Mythographer* (Athens, Ohio: Ohio State Univ. Press, 1971), p. 143, n. 2. This is Whitbread's alternative translation of these lines from the Latin: "Expetebat quidem, Leuitarum sanctissime, nostri temporis qualitas grande silentium, ut non solum mens expromptare desisset quod didicit, quantum etiam obliuionem sui efficere debuit quia uiuit" (R. Helm, ed., *F. P. Fulgentii Opera* (Leipzig: Teubner, 1898), p. 83, 1-4). The passage, Whitbread also argues, may be read as a personal lament for old age and bad memory (p. 119). For an argument that the opening is in fact a lament directed against the anti-intellectualism of the times, and is consistent with the motives of the entire commentary, see Gabriele Rauner-Hafner, "Die Virgil-interpretation des Fulgentius: Bemerkungen zu Gliederung und Absicht der 'Expositio Virgilianae Continentiae,' " *Mittellateinisches Jahrbuch* 13 (1978), 10.

[2] Whitbread, p. 119; Helm, pp. 83-84.

[3] For approaches to the issues of comedy and parody in learned literature of Late Antiquity and the early Middle Ages, see Curtius, *European Literature*,

the work offers a foil to the *Consolation of Philosophy*, especially in its exaggerated description of Virgil's appearance and in its virtual parodying of the tropes of instruction. In what follows, I will first suggest some tentative lines of inquiry into the opening of the dialogue and some comparisons with the *grammaticus* figure of an earlier generation. Then, I will analyze in detail the movement of the discussion to show how the *De Continentia* presents a version of the literary dialogue which constantly undermines the conventions of reading, understanding, and teaching which were developed in Cicero and Augustine. Finally, Fulgentius offers something of the age: a sense of the irrecoverability of classical thought and literature in its antique forms and a need to make relevant the texts of the ancients to the world of the moderns.

Fulgentius announces the visionary appearance of Virgil at the opening of the *De Continentia*:

> Grant me now the very appearance of the Mantuan bard, whereby I may restore to light his clandestine meanings. Behold, he comes to me more resplendent than a draught of the fountain of Ascra, just as bards are wont to appear, with a preoccupied frown and notebooks held ready to start some new composition, as, the inspiration wailing forth from within, they mutter to themselves some secret thought.[4]

The commentator had, immediately before, invoked the shade with five hexameter lines written "with the help of the Muses," and designed to satisfy Virgil's own muse. In its tone and diction, Fulgentius' opening tries to recapture something of the vatic mythology of an earlier era. In its arcane allusions and complicated syntax, the passage embodies the worst of a

---

pp. 417-420, and M. Bakhtin, *The Dialogic Imagination*, trans. Michael Holquist (Austin: Univ. of Texas Press, 1978), pp. 52-68, and, on parodies of the Latin grammatical tradition, p. 73.

[4] "Cede mihi nunc personam Mantuani uatis, quo fugitiuos eius in lucem deducamus amfractus. Nam ecce ad me etiam ipse Ascrei fontis bractamento saturior aduenit, quales uatum imagines esse solent, dum adsumptis ad opus conficiendum tabulis stupida fronte arcanum quiddam latranti intrinsecus tractatu submurmurant," Helm, p. 85, 11-16.

baroque Late Latin. This paradox of styles, attempting to synthesize the ancient and the contemporary, looks back to the initial hesitations of the work's first lines, and it informs the larger scope of Fulgentius' project.[5] The rhetorical excesses are set in sharp relief against their cultural setting. Like his older contemporary Sidonius, Fulgentius is deeply mannered and self-consciously pedantic. The Hellenisms and mythological allusions have an almost eerie sound coming from Vandal Africa, and Auerbach's comments on Sidonius in his context have a definite place here. "A public which expresses itself in such a way," he writes, "or takes pleasure in such expression when its very existence has become threatened has become hopelessly cut off from reality."[6] The implications of Auerbach's argument are that this kind of diction removes the literary work from a public at large and places it in a limited coterie of readers and scholars. In effect, Fulgentius writes a private language, a language shaped by the excesses of pedantry rather than the barbarisms of the public.

Virgil thus enters not as some bardic prophet of antiquity, but as an all-too-familiar crotchety schoolmaster.[7] The tone of the poet's appearance in this and the following scenes seems to take the tropes of visionary poetics and of the master/student colloquy to the extremes of parody. Fulgentius' Virgil is neither Ratio nor Magister, but a *grammaticus* confronting a brash fathead. Virgil enters as a writer and a reader; his *tabellae* are ready for inscription, and his goal will be a reading of his own *Aeneid*. And yet the subject of his discourse, we are told, will be limited "to the slight things that *grammatici*

---

[5] Curtius, *European Literature*, p. 420, remarks on the "specifically late-Antique mixture of serious and comic styles which can be exaggerated to the point of burlesque." This "mixed style" informs "the fictional background of Fulgentius' allegorical interpretation of Virgil."

[6] Auerbach, *Literary Language and Its Public*, pp. 257-258. See his discussion of Sidonius' styles and their cultural implications on p. 258.

[7] For Virgil as a contemporary schoolmaster, see J. W. Jones, "Virgil as Master in Fulgentius," in C. Henderson, ed., *Classical, Medieval and Renaissance Studies in Honor of B. L. Ullmann* (Rome, 1964), pp. 273-275.

expound for monthly fees to boyish ears."[8] This is what Fulgentius wants, but it certainly is not what he gets—and part of the humor here lies in just this confounding of the grammarian's role.[9] This role, in the fourth and early fifth centuries, consisted primarily of explicating the details of usage and diction. The figure of Servius in Macrobius' *Saturnalia* portrays an idealized grammarian, sensitive to the usages of *antiquitas* and *novitas*. His manner is self-effacing, his tone rarely condescending. In a larger sense, he is presented as the custodian of language and culture: a man who ensures continuity of an educational tradition and, with it, a sensitivity to literary history. We now know Macrobius' work to be a fiction, and his portrayal of Servius to have only a little to do with the historical commentator. His portraits of the grammarians, are, in fact, perhaps deliberately backward looking, for, seeking to recreate an earlier *aetas Praetextati*, Macrobius takes as his goal an educational polemic rather than the writing of cultural history.[10] But, of course, Fulgentius' Virgil is a fiction, too, and when his student asks for the minutiae of grammatical instruction, the irony of his request devolves to two interrelated points. First, the fact remains that instead of giving a narrow, grammatical commentary on Virgil's text after the manner of Servius, the poet offers a moral allegory. He has little concern for the fact that the *Aeneid* begins *in medias res*; he reads it as a straight chronology from beginning to end. Second, Fulgentius establishes a tension between the constraints of the ethos of his age and the demands of Virgil's art. His response to the disjunction between *antiqui* and *moderni*

[8] "sed tantum illa quaerimus leuia, quae mensualibus stipendiis grammatici distrahunt puerilibus auscultatibus," Helm, p. 86, 4-6. English in Whitbread, p. 121.

[9] For much of what follows on the history of the grammarian in antiquity and on Servius and Macrobius, I am indebted to two studies by Robert Kaster: "Macrobius and Servius: Verecundia and the Grammarian's Function," *Harvard Studies in Classical Philology* 84 (1980), 219-262; "The Grammarian's Authority," *Classical Philology* 78 (1980), 215-245.

[10] Kaster, "Macrobius and Servius," pp. 251-252.

is not, as in Servius and Macrobius, a linguistic issue.[11] It focuses rather on a Christian present confronting a pagan past. Virgil answers this issue in his first response.

> Insofar as your own fatheadedness and the distrust of your age in dangerous doctrine do not act as barriers to what can be taught, I shall pour out from the rushing torrent of my intellect a short measure which cannot make you sick with a mammoth hangover.[12]

The exaggeration and sarcasm of this response confound the image of the grammarian pointed by the earlier writers. Virgil apparently shows neither great wisdom nor, that key quality, *verecundia*. He has none of the self-effacement of a Servius; even the condescending smiles which cross the faces of Macrobius' other friends never break this Virgil's scowl.[13] Fulgentius' teacher becomes a foil for the whole tradition of commentary, and the problems of reading and writing will also function differently here than in the earlier dialogues I have examined. While the goal of producing a new text is present, the imagery of literacy is undercut. Virgil appears cloaked in the trappings of the book: his wax tablets stand ready for inscription, and his fingers form the shape of a capital *I*. His appearance is thus palpably similar to Lady Philosophy's entrance in the *Consolation*. Her book, however, is the *liber* of knowledge, and her symbolic letters are not the erect fingers of the orator, but the *pi* and *theta* of philosophical inquiry embroidered on her gown. I will develop these images in

---

[11] Kaster, "Macrobius and Servius," on Avienus' remarks on solecism and barbarism and Servius' response, pp. 242-247; "The Grammarian's Authority," on the difference between Virgilian and fourth century usage, pp. 223-238.

[12] Whitbread, p. 121. "Quatenus, inquit, in his tibi discendis non adipata grassedo ingenii quam temporis formido periculosa reluctat, de nostro torrentis ingenii impetu breuiorem urnulam praelibabo, quae tibi crapulae plenitudine nausiam mouere non possit," Helm, p. 86, 14-18.

[13] See Kaster, "Macrobius and Servius," pp. 238-239, and n. 59. Virgil does, though, smile once, at Fulgentius' objections to his assertive paganism, "Ad haec ille subridens . . . ," Helm, p. 103, 7.

greater detail in discussing the *Consolation*'s opening. It may suffice to say here that these visions become emblems of textuality and interpretation, and that it is also the figure of Fulgentius who, somewhat like the opening picture of the *Consolation*'s prisoner, calls attention to himself as an *auctor*. Boethius opens his work with a poem lamenting his past literary achievements; Fulgentius interrupts his master's exposition to call attention to his own writings, and the implications of his interjection are dramatically un-Boethian.

About a third of the way into their dialogue, Virgil asks the student to describe the contents of the *Aeneid*'s first book, and the student's answer gives a bare outline of the plot. Virgil then responds with the beginnings of his allegorical and etymological reading of the work, and he is about to explain the significance of Aeneas' seven ships when the student interrupts. He has already discussed numerology in another book, Fulgentius claims, and "it would be a sign of discursiveness if I insert in one book what I have already discussed in others."[14] Whoever cares to learn about the subject can read that book. Fulgentius' response seems to throw the entire fiction of literary dialogue into confusion. True, his interjection may be a simple act of sarcasm, directed at Virgil's condescension: he too is an *auctor*, and Virgil should not lose sight of the accomplishments of this *homunculus*. But this Virgil is a fiction, a figment of the narrator's mind who must obey the narrator's laws. Fulgentius drops the fictive persona of student to assert historical fact. The whole pretense of the dialogue breaks down as bibliographic reality intercedes. Fulgentius appears as a writer in his own right to reassert the written character of the very dialogue in which he speaks. He seems to owe something to *his* readers: he will not tire them with repetition from other works, but still will try to educate them. This interjection also makes the work's fictional disputants aware of a potential readership and of the authorial

[14] Whitbread, p. 125. ". . . eritque perissologiae nota si, quae in uno libro descripsimus, etiam aliis inseramus," Helm, p. 92, 3-4.

responsibilities due an audience. In effect, it draws the reader into the fiction by making audience judgment a criterion for the text's organization and progress.

Fulgentius' self-conscious awareness of himself as a writer, together with his concern for an imaginary readership, combine with the symbols, themes, and methods of the *De Continentia* to produce a work fundamentally about education. The dialogue takes the form of a lesson in the art of reading. The text of the *Aeneid* becomes the subject of study, and the commentary itself becomes a new text inscribed after the old. These methodological issues complement precisely what virtually all readers of the commentary have taken as its primary purpose: to produce an allegory of the life of man from birth through death and afterlife.[15] Aeneas confronts his own ignorance through a variety of teachers, and his development as a human being follows an educational path laid out by Virgil in the work's opening moves. The poet outlines the progression of his *fabula* based on a close reading of the epic's opening "arma virumque." In summary, he states that "in the guise of *historia*," he has presented a *gradus* of life and study.[16]

As I said before, first there is given by nature that courage of the soul which may serve for advancement, for no creature is taught that is not born capable of being taught; second, there is the learning which adorns nature as it advances. . . . It is indeed inborn by nature, taught by learning, and disciplined by experience.[17]

---

[15] See the bibliography cited in Whitbread, p. 115, and the arguments throughout G. Rauner-Hafner, "Die Virgil-interpretation des Fulgentius," pp. 7-49.

[16] Whitbread, p. 124. For the use of the term *gradus*, see Helm, p. 89, 18, 20; p. 90, 3.

[17] Whitbread, p. 124. ". . . quo sit ut supra diximus prima uirtus animi naturaliter data quae proficiat—neque enim eruditur nisi quod erudibile nascitur—secunda doctrina quae naturam ornat cum proficit . . . nascitur quidem ex natura, eruditur ex doctrina, cogitur ex utilitate," Helm, p. 90, 3-7; 16-17.

In this interpretive context, Virgil's injunction to his pupil now takes on an added significance.

> But to make sure that I am not explaining my *fabula* to ignorant ears, describe the contents of my first book; and then, if it is accurate, I will explain it to you.[18]

Fulgentius' work is therefore deeply self-reflexive. By restating the moral plot of the *Aeneid*, the speakers actively engage in that same educative process which the fiction of Virgil's poem supposedly chronicles. As a text about learning, the *Aeneid* comes culturally to life only in the schoolroom. No longer does Virgil's poem celebrate the civic values of an imperial Rome; no longer is its hero to be praised as a public man. It is now fit only for the private dialogue of *grammaticus* and student, as its meaning becomes the method of their discussion.

Aeneas' journey maps mental growth in geographical terms, and each book witnesses a series of confrontations with authoritative figures. He is born in Book I, where we find him speechless, like an infant before his mother. In Books II and III he is diverted by the stories at Dido's court. Book IV finds him swayed by passion, until Mercury, the god of intellect, redirects his course. Book V presents Aeneas honoring his father and his lineage in games and deeds of valor. By Book VI he is ready for formal instruction from the Sybil and the shade of Anchises. The concluding books, briefly summarized at the commentary's close, portray the tempering of the hero through experience. Thus, the poem's allegory recapitulates the tripartite *gradus* of nature, learning, and experience Virgil outlined at the work's opening. This, in short, is Fulgentius' reading, and much has been made of its individual details as well as of its influence on later allegorists

---

[18] Whitbread, p. 124. "Sed ut sciam me non arcaicis expromtare fabulam auribus, primi nostri libri continentiam narra; tunc demum haec tibi, si uisum fuerit, reserabimus," Helm, p. 90, 19-21.

from the ninth through fifteenth centuries.[19] More vital to my purpose, however, is the way in which Fulgentius unifies the progress of his hero, the development of his student, and the education of his reader.

His emphasis on Book VI, already established by the sixth century as the most philosophically important of the books, solidifies the pedagogical emphases of the commentary.[20] Fulgentius is less interested in the arcane symbolic and lexical problems which had fascinated Servius, and is concerned more with the method of instruction that Aeneas undergoes. The temple of Apollo, the *doctrina studiis*, becomes the classroom (see Whitbread, p. 128; Helm, p. 95). His instruction will be in the "obscure and secret mysteries of knowledge" necessary to a future moral life. There is a literary side to Aeneas' tuition. The golden bough symbolizes both *doctrina* and *littera* (see Whitbread, p. 129; Helm, pp. 96-7). Offering a Greek source, Virgil claims that the phrase *apo tes rapsodias* means "a scriptura" (from writings). When Aeneas finally enters Hell itself he confronts Cerberus, and in glossing this figure Fulgentius himself takes over from the master. In a way similar to his own interjection on numerology—but now speaking in Virgil's rather than his own voice—Fulgentius recalls his earlier treatment of Cerberus in the *Mitologiae*. Cerberus becomes a figure of legal contention: a representative of the misuse of eloquence in public life (see Whitbread, p. 130). So too, the later figure of Rhadamanthus will point to the proper use of words. His name synthesizes two Greek elements which translate as "ruling the word" and "understanding" (see

[19] For the history of the allegorical reading, see the surveys of E. G. Schreiber and T. Maresca, trans., *The Commentary on the Six Books of Virgil's Aeneid Attributed to Bernardus Silvestris* (Lincoln, Neb.: Univ. of Nebraska Press, 1978), "Introduction"; Michael Murrin, *The Allegorical Epic* (Chicago: Univ. of Chicago Press, 1980), pp. 27-46; G. Mazzotta, *Dante: Poet of the Desert* (Princeton: Princeton Univ. Press, 1979), p. 173.

[20] See P. Courcelle, "Les Pères de l'Eglise devant les Enfers Virgiliens," *AHDLMA* 22 (1955), 5-74, and the discussion in Murrin, *Allegorical Epic*, pp. 30-34; 39-44.

Helm, p. 101). The lesson here is that he who can control his words can denounce pride. Before meeting his final teacher, Anchises, Aeneas must perfect his memory and gain release from that "fear of teachers" (*magistrorum timor*, Whitbread, p. 132; Helm, p. 101), which could only hold him back from liberation.

Not only in its content but in its form, Fulgentius' treatment of Book VI pinpoints problems in linguistic education. It is at this moment in the *De Continentia* that Fulgentius revives the dialogue between master and pupil. The *humunculus* interrupts Virgil's exposition to comment on the Christian resonances of his readings, and to recognize that behind pagan philosophy may lie the seeds of Christian truth (Whitbread, pp. 128-129). Fulgentius couches his interjections, though, in the rhetoric of praise familiar to the student/teacher colloquies. He is not belligerent or proselytizing, but rather approving.

> I fully approve, Doctor, of your explanation . . .
> This is wisdom sure and manifest.
> . . . .
> You say truth, most learned Maro. . . .[21]

Even when Christian dogma conflicts with Virgil's authority in Fulgentius' mind, he still summons up a line of commendation: "O Roman spokesman for Bards, should you really obscure your illustrious intellect in the fog of so foolish a line of defense?"[22] There is, thus, a tension between the pupil's need to accede to pedagogical authority and the theologian's desire to preserve religious orthodoxy. The pupil never really resolves this confusion, for the *De Continentia* is hardly an explicit Christianization of the *Aeneid*'s moral allegory.

---

[21] Whitbread, pp. 128-129. "Certior ego hanc tuam comprobo doctor sententiam. . . . Quae uere certa manifestaque est sapientia," Helm, p. 96, 14-15; 17-18. "Uerum, inquam, dicis, Maro doctissime," Helm, p. 97, 18-19.

[22] Whitbread, p. 132. "O uatum Latialis autenta, itane tuum clarissimum ingenium tam stultae defensionis fuscare debuisti caligine?" Helm, p. 102, 19-20.

Nor does Virgil come off as a total failure. He seems to dismiss the pupil's charges by simply admitting that, as a pagan, he is incapable of explicating revealed truths (Whitbread, p. 133). "I have not come as an expositor well-versed in your book of scripture,"[23] and this is precisely the point. Virgil's role is to explicate and to enact a system of pedagogy rather than of philosophy. His role as grammarian enables him only to address issues in the method of teaching. He directs his explications, "So that what has been said may flow to you more surely and manifestly."[24] He remarks on the obviousness of his symbolism (Whitbread, p. 131). He introduces another scheme of learning in the allusion to the myth of Hercules and the Hesperides (Whitbread, p. 129). Finally, when we see Anchises instruct his son at the end of Book VI, we also witness the figure of Virgil instructing his pupil: "Here you see that, as befits God the creator, he teaches the secret mysteries of Nature. . . ."[25] The scenes of Aeneas' education become scenes of the pupil's instruction. Virgil becomes most openly didactic here, as the theme of his own poem is itself concerned with education in the liberal rather than the liturgical arts. The process of learning for the epic's hero parallels the progress of the epic's reader, and when Virgil turns from Book VI to VII, he shows how the specifics of an education can be applied to the life lived: "Although the discipline of learning dies with the student, yet it passes on the eternal seed of memory."[26]

As we trace the moral and intellectual development of Aeneas, we ourselves are educated, and we witness the scenes of explicit learning in Book VI as an allegory in little of the

---

[23] Whitbread, p. 133. "Neque enim hoc pacto in tuis libris conductus narrator accessi . . . ," Helm, p. 103, 11-12.

[24] Whitbread, p. 129. "Ut certius tibi planiusque liquescat quod dictum est . . . ," Helm, p. 96, 18-19.

[25] Whitbread, p. 132. "Uides ergo quia sicut Deum creatorem oportuit et de secretis naturae mysteriis docet . . . ," Helm, p. 102, 16-17.

[26] Whitbread, p. 133. ". . . disciplina doctrinae quamuis studendo desciscat, aeternum tamen memoriae semen hereditat," Helm, p. 104, 1-2.

homunculus' education at the hands of Virgil. When the student and the reader reach the end of the *De Continentia*, they reach the end of the *Aeneid* and the end point of their moral education. Fulgentius' final words pinpoint this activity, and they break the visionary fiction by returning the reader to the world of the commentary's opening. Following Virgil's exposition of Book XII the major manuscripts have a conclusive "Finit," and then this valediction: "Uale, domine, et mei tribulos pectoris cautius lege" (Helm, p. 107). The *dominus* is clearly no longer Virgil but "the most saintly of deacons" addressed in the work's dedication. The word *lege* can mean both "pick" and "read," and we can see this conclusion as an appeal to the reader of the newly written commentary to use it judiciously in understanding Virgil's fiction.[27] But in returning to the dedicatory mode, Fulgentius sustains another fiction: the notion that the work is a kind of letter, written at the request of its addressee.[28] These opening and closing remarks bracket the entire commentary within a larger dialogue between Fulgentius and his audience. Such bracketing complements those moments in the dialogue itself when the authorial Fulgentius breaks the flow of argument to refer to one of his own historically verifiable works. Readers exist both inside and outside the commentary's fiction: there are the imaginary readers of the *De Continentia* and the persona of the *homunculus* reading the *Aeneid*; but there are also readers, in a sense, outside the text, individuals like ourselves reading Virgil and Fulgentius from an almost equal distance.

Fulgentius' achievement is, in the end, both parodic and constructive. While he humorously exaggerates the heritage of the *grammaticus* and the commentary tradition, his accomplishment lies in subtly readjusting the place of classical literature in an insecure Christian world. Fulgentius begs many questions; yet, by placing the burden of moral interpretation

[27] See Whitbread's remarks, p. 153.
[28] On the "Briefform" of the work, see Rauner-Hafner, "Die Virgil-interpretation," pp. 9-10.

and selection on his reader, rather than blaming his author, Fulgentius individualizes the act of reading. The *De Continentia* may have value less for what it says explicitly about the *Aeneid* than for the method it provides for moral allegory. The figure of Virgil shies away from the many philosophical and historical claims he could make for his poem; he offers, instead, a way of teaching the *Aeneid*. Beyond the gongorism of the Latin and the extremities of the allegory lies an education in the arts of interpretation. By placing this education in a uniquely comic framework, Fulgentius avoids the censorship of his peers. He confounds the opposition of his dedicatees: his mind *does* reveal its learning, and a real, if somewhat shaky, synthesis of ancient and modern takes shape. In effecting this synthesis Fulgentius unites the form of the student/teacher colloquy with the subject of the allegory of education; he confronts problems of pedagogic and literary authority; and he shows how the reading of an *auctor* can produce a new text whose own theme explores methods of interpretation. Through these achievements, Fulgentius provides a literary and cultural foil for the education of *The Consolation of Philosophy*'s prisoner.

Boethius

Save for *The Consolation of Philosophy*, Boethius' only attempt at dialogue is the early, forced colloquy which structures the *In Isagogen Porphyrii*. It is arguably Boethius' first work, written just after the turn of the sixth century and perhaps soon after the completion of his Greek education.[1] While it is deeply significant that Boethius opens and closes his intellectual career with dialogues, the commentary cannot compare with the fluid interchanges of the *Consolation*. It remains a close kin of Fulgentius' *De Continentia*, where the student seldom appears except to read a passage, ask an irrelevant question,

---

[1] For the date of *In Isagogen* see L. M. De Rijk, "On the Chronology of Boethius' Works on Logic, II," *Vivarium* 3 (1965), 125-129, 159. De Rijk dates the work c. 504-505.

or praise his master. Unlike Fulgentius' work, though, Boethius' commentary shifts the emphases of the dramatis personae. Fulgentius had taken a form of himself as the student, and the literary problems of his chosen mask are evident. Fulgentius must play both *homunculus* and *auctor*, and when the one intrudes on the other the pretense of dialogue breaks down. Boethius prefers to speak as master in the first person and to relegate the questioner's role to a friend, Fabius. To this extent, his plan may resemble Cicero's *Tusculan Disputations*, but the similarity ends there. As in Augustine and Fulgentius, the student is seldom up to the master's standards. The text's editor sees him as full of "stupid admiration" for his teacher, and it has long been recognized that Fabius is a literary fiction designed only to advance the exposition of Porphyry's text.[2] The work's opening is in fact so littered with reminiscences of Cicero and Aulus Gellius that the literary status of the commentary seems very self-conscious.[3] In the context of Boethius' own career, however, the figure of Fabius offers, in nascent form, the Boethian persona of the later works. In his praise of the teacher, his insecurity with complex arguments, and his zeal for knowledge, Fabius anticipates the voice of the commentator, as well as the writer of the Tractates and the prisoner of the *Consolation*. The figure of Boethius, in turn, becomes the praiseworthy *magister* who will later appear as the Symmachus of the prose prefaces and as Lady Philosophy herself.

The *In Isagogen* opens with the kind of autobiographical attempt at dramatic verisimilitude familiar from the works of Cicero and Augustine. When the winter weather drives Boethius and his friends into the mountains and keeps them up

[2] S. Brandt, ed., *A.M.S. Boethii In Isagogenn Porphyrii Commenta*, CSEL 48 (Leipzig: Freytag, 1906), pp. viii-ix. On Fabius as a literary fiction, see De Rijk, p. 128, "Chronology," and Brandt, p. ix.

[3] Brandt cites Hirzel, *Der Dialog* (Leipzig: Teubner, 1895), vol. II, p. 363, on the Ciceronian heritage of *otium* in which philosophical dialogues were composed. He also calls attention to Aulus Gellius' Preface to *Attic Nights* for parallels to the winter setting (Brandt, p. viii, n. 2).

at night, the Romans find pleasure in reviewing Porphyry's commentary on Aristotle.[4] As at Cicero's Tusculanum or Augustine's Cassiciacum, Boethius' Aurelian retreat offers an escape from the demands of public life. Such a removal facilitates the exercise of that learned *otium* which had long been a Roman ideal. But while Cicero and Augustine had let their written works grow out of the dialogues themselves, Boethius has his dialogue develop from the reading of a specific text. By beginning with a book, Boethius, much like Fulgentius, chronicles a reader's progress; the text of the commentary becomes a new reading. Like the *De Continentia*, too, the *In Isagogen* has its student recount passages from the work at hand. Fabius' role in the dialogue devolves mainly to a simple recitation of both Porphyry's text and Victorinus' fourth-century commentary on it. If he seems superfluous to the commentary enterprise, it is his presence which reifies the act of interpretation as a dialogue between reader and *auctor*. Fabius and Boethius together dramatize what is otherwise a purely inward, mental process, much as Augustine and Ratio externalized acts of reflection into written conversations.

The *In Isagogen* remains, however, not simply a commentary on Porphyry, but, as scholars have long noticed, a deliberate recasting of Victorinus' commentary.[5] Boethius' relationship to the earlier commentator is somewhat ambivalent: while he praises Victorinus early on, he frequently quibbles with his renderings from Greek, and he disagrees flatly with his definition of philosophy.[6] Throughout the *In*

[4] "Hiemantis anni tempore in Aureliae montibus concesseramus atque ibi tunc, cum uiolentior auster eiecisset noctis placidam atque exturbasset quietem, recensere libitum est ea quae doctissimi uiri ad inluminandas quodammodo res intellectus densitate caliginantissimas quibusdam quasi introductoriis commentariis ediderunt" (Brandt, pp. 3-4).

[5] See Brandt, pp. xv-xviii. Jonathan Barnes, "Boethius and the Study of Logic," in Gibson, *Boethius*, p. 75 and nn. 9-11, surveys recent scholarship with an eye towards the problems of precise translation Boethius faced.

[6] For Boethius' retranslations of Victorinus, see Brandt, pp. 34-35 (on problems arising from translating the concept of *genera* from the Greek *schemata*); Brandt, p. 64 (on the problem of the concept of species); and, for other

Isagogen, Victorinus' text dominates, and it is so frequently quoted and cited that modern scholars have been able to reconstruct much of this lost work.[7] Victorinus mediates between Boethius and Porphyry. The existence of his commentary, with its faults and infelicities, apparently goads Boethius into the composition of his own work. Unlike Fulgentius, Boethius responds to a text not simply according to the problems it poses, but also according to the ways in which it has been read previously. It would be as if Fulgentius wished to quibble with Servius. Boethius thus sees his initial enterprise in commentary as part of a continuing tradition of study and writing: the fiction of the text's opening places it in a continuum of personal activity; but it also places it in a sequence of literary history. The *In Isagogen* is thus a work which addresses many different texts and in so doing, tries to establish a vocabulary for the praise of rational argument and literary explication. This vocabulary will operate through Boethius' later writings to characterize his relationships to his texts and readers.

Central to this idiom is the idea of *subtilitas*.[8] A word with a variety of connotations, it appears in the *In Isagogen* to refer to a quality of thought rather than a feature of style. Fabius uses the word to characterize the completeness and precision

---

citations and discussion, Brandt's preface, pp. xviii-xxix. Boethius disagrees with Victorinus' definition of philosophy (Brandt, pp. 7-9); he divides philosophy into theoretical and practical wisdom, and argues that its source is the divine mind and its goal is the illumination of the human mind with the light of truth. Implicit here is an objection to Victorinus' classification of philosophy as just another type of discourse. For a survey of the literature on the topic, see E. Reiss, *Boethius* (Boston: Twayne, 1982), p. 31 and n. 7.

[7] See Pierre Hadot, *Marius Victorinus* (Paris: Etudes Augustiniennes, 1971), pp. 366-380.

[8] *Subtilitas* can mean "precision of argument, logical quality (as the characteristics of the 'dialectical style')," according to the *Oxford Classical Dictionary*, ed. P.G.W. Glare (Oxford: Clarendon Press, 1976), s.v. *subtilitas*, 5, p. 1853. Boethius elsewhere uses the form *subtilus* to translate Aristotle's *akribesteron* (*Anal. Prior.*, 46a28), and the root forms of the Greek word appear to mean investigation with minuteness, accuracy, and precision, or thorough understanding (see Liddell-Scott, p. 55, s.v. *akrib-*; cf., *di akribeias*).

of Boethius' exposition, and Boethius himself uses it to describe Aristotle's habit of mind. Early on in the dialogue, Fabius responds to Boethius' arguments: "Most subtle, and lucid."[9] He praises one set of explanations as, "More subtle, by Hercules, than I have ever heard the matter treated before."[10] Boethius too will remark that he treats the force and subtlety of a certain concept,[11] and he claims that he discusses the issues of Porphyry's text rationally and subtly.[12] These and other moments keep the colloquy moving through a sequence of mutual admirations of explicator and text. Through these tropes of praise, Fabius gives but the appearance of following the discussion, for when he remains confused, he must, like Augustine's son, stop the exposition cold to query his teacher's method of argument. Here, the diction shifts from expressions of subtlety to demands for clarity.

At one point, unsure about the notion of incorporeables, and lost in the discussion's terminological distinctions, he asks: "What is it that you said just now when you were talking about incorporeables?"[13] Boethius' response reveals much about the goals of the dialogue and his own position as teacher.

> It would take a long time to treat this matter, and it would be of little profit to us in the line of reasoning we are pursuing. But I will say briefly this: that I called those extremities of those figures which are in geometry boundaries, but concerning the incorporeality which surrounds the boundaries, you may find plainly and completely treated if you can get a hold of the first book of the learned Macrobius' *In Somnium Scipionis*. But now, let us turn to what follows.[14]

[9] Brandt, p. 16, 10: "Subtillissime, inquit, et lucide . . ." (10).

[10] "Subtiliter mehercule et quod numquam fere ante haec audiuimus" (Brandt, p. 44, 6)

[11] "Sed quoniam plene de definitione tractatum est, *probationis uel diuisionis* uim subtilitatemque tractemus" (Brandt, p. 22, 13-14, emphases in text).

[12] "et quoniam ad definitiones quae pertinent quaedam dicta sunt, pauca etiam de his ipsis rationabilius subtiliusque colligemus" (Brandt, p. 21, 3-5).

[13] "Quid est, inquit, quod dudum dixeras, cum a te de incorporalibus tractaretur . . . ?" (Brandt, p. 31, 13-14).

[14] "Longus, inquam, tractatus est et nihil nobis ad hanc rem quam quae-

Boethius' response seems at once dismissive and explanatory. On the one hand, he does not wish to impede the exposition by reviewing the details of Porphyry's terminology. But on the other hand, he does direct his pupil—and his reader—to the proper place in another book where both can find the subject clearly treated. The response synthesizes the Augustinian and Fulgentian approaches: he is willing to sacrifice clarity for progress, but he also recognizes that no book should repeat discursively what another book says so well. In turn, Boethius applies the same criteria of understandability to his own work and to Macrobius'. Brevity becomes a goal of argument, while at the same time becoming an ideal of style.[15] The *In Isagogen* will aspire to be as clear and complete as the *Somnium Scipionis*. The phrasing *plenius uberiusque* applied to Macrobius' work is applied to the *In Isagogen* itself, as Boethius remarks how he tried to treat everything in Porphyry's work clearly and fully.[16]

These moments when the discussants address each other directly call attention to the problems of reading and explicating texts, as well as to the impediments to learned discussion about those texts. The distinctions between brevity and clarity offer a rough analogue to the distinctions between circuitous and linear arguments in Augustine's dialogues, in that both writers recognize that, at times, clarity must be sacrificed to progress. In these exchanges, Boethius relies on the earlier traditions of literary dialogue while anticipating many of the tropes he will use in the tractates and the *Consolation*. Boethius' impatience with his pupil looks forward to

---

rimus profuturus. sed dicam breuiter terminos me dixisse extremitates earum quae in geometria sunt figurarum, de incorporalitate uero quae circa terminos constat, si Macrobii Theodosii doctissimi uiri primum librum quem de Somnio Scipionis composuit in manibus sumpseris, plenius uberiusque cognosces. sed nunc ad sequentia transeamus" (Brandt, pp. 31-32).

[15] For backgrounds and the heritage to this issue, see Curtius, "Brevity as an Ideal of Style," in *European Literature and the Latin Middle Ages*, pp. 487-494.

[16] "Sed iam tibi, mi Fabi, omnia quaecumque ad Introductionem Porphyrii pertinent, plenius uberiusque tractata sunt" (Brandt, p. 131, 20-22).

the tone of Philosophy. Fabius' statements of commendation and confusion prefigure the prisoner's rhetoric. These passages also resonate with the scenes of dedication in the later commentaries, and, taken together, they imply a unity to the voice of the commentator throughout Boethius' career.

In concluding the discussion of the *In Isagogen*, Fabius looks ahead to future colloquies and later studies. He praises Boethius as a teacher and judge, and his final words hold a special irony for readers of the later works.

> May you promise me this with paternal spirit: but may I never be found wanting in these studies, especially with you as my teacher from whom, perhaps, if I live long enough, I shall grasp the entirety of Aristotle's logic.[17]

There are two clear echoes of this sentiment in Boethius' later writings, echoes which suggest that even if Fabius' salutation is conventional, it is a deliberate arrangement of tropes to construct a uniquely personal voice. First, Fabius' words foreshadow the terms in which Boethius will praise Symmachus at the end of the prefatory letter to *De Arithmetica*. There, Boethius asks for Symmachus' approval of the project of translation and for his judgment on the text's finished form. That he writes, "Tu tantum paterna gratia nostrum provehas munus,"[18] may have less to do with the fact that he is addressing his father-in-law than with the conventions of dedicatory prose.[19] This sense of a shared, guiding spirit contributes to the impression gained from both works that Boethius is beginning something: they signal almost a rite of literary initiation. While we can assume the *In Isagogen* to be Boethius' earliest work, he nevertheless considers the *De Arithmetica* "laboris mei primitias." At stake is less the actual chronology of the texts and more the idioms of beginnings

---

[17] "Tu, inquit, paterno haec mihi animo polliceris, uerum ego numquam deficiam ab his studiis, te praesertim docente, a quo totam fortasse logicae Aristotelis, si uita suppetit, capiam disciplinam" (Brandt, pp. 131-132).

[18] Friedlein, p. 5, 21-22.

[19] See the references in the first section of Chapter I of this study.

which both works employ.[20] For Fabius the dialogue is but the initial step in a lifetime of literary study. For Boethius, the *De Arithmetica* is the first translation in a projected series of philosophical and scientific works. It will open his works on the *quadrivium* and will thus initiate the ascent to knowledge facilitated by the careful study of those disciplines. The letter to Symmachus closes with this appeal to authoritative judgment as a way of almost blessing the project.[21] Such deference to authority will mark the progress of the Boethian persona, as he asks his readers and his dedicatees to measure his existing works against a planned corpus of his writings. The urge to canonize texts gives voice to a goal of reading and study which is not just the acquisition of knowledge, but the publication of that knowledge in written form.

The second echo of the *In Isagogen* conclusion appears in the *Perihermeneias* commentary. Hoping to complete the mastery of Aristotle's logic, Fabius looks forward to the ambitions of Boethius' later project of translation and commentary. The fact that Boethius himself concludes the *In Isagogen* by also anticipating the conclusion of this course of study, "at a later time with more diligent consideration," has led some scholars to conclude that the project was already envisioned by his mid-twenties.[22] From a different point of view, Kappelmacher saw in the commentary only further confirmation that the "schriftstellerische Plan" imitated the encyclopaedic goals of Porphyry himself.[23] In addition to these purely historical claims is the recognition that Boethius begins his literary career explicitly, and that he does so through dialogue; that he

---

[20] Aulus Gellius, however, uses the word *primitias* not necessarily to mean that this is his first work, but rather that it is rudimentary. The word may thus refer more to the level of treatment rather than the chronological place of the work in the corpus: "Non enim fecimus altos nimis et obscuros in his rebus quaestionum sinus, sed primitias quasdam et quasi libamenta ingenuarum artium dedimus" (*Attic Nights*, Preface, Loeb edition, vol. 1, p. xxxii).

[21] "Ita et laboris mei primitias doctissimo iudicio consecrabis . . ." (Friedlein, p. 5, 22-23).

[22] See De Rijk, "Chronology," pp. 128-129.

[23] Kappelmacher, "Schriftstellerische Plan," p. 219.

develops the personae of student and teacher he will employ throughout his life; and that, at the work's conclusion, he looks forward to a life of reading and study which motivates the voice of the later works. If Fabius is Boethius in nascent form, they both hope to complete an intellectual project if life permits. Fabius begs, "si uita suppetit," and the Boethius of the *Perihermeneias* commentary, perhaps returning to the promise of leisure which opened the *In Isagogen*, revises, "si uita otiumque suppetit" (Meiser, II, p. 80). The tropes of the Latin prose preface take on a new resonance here as we witness Boethius constructing a reader's life out of the conventions of literature.

It has been said that Boethius abandoned the dialogue form because it was "not a suitable form for learned commentary," and that, in working in an inappropriate genre, "Boethius' treatment of it is frigid."[24] We have seen however, that Cicero, Augustine, and Fulgentius all adapted the conventions of the colloquy both to comment upon and produce texts. The personae of student and teacher sketched in the *In Isagogen* owe a great deal to the idioms of the *Soliloquia* and the *De Continentia*. It has also been implied that Boethius abandoned the dialogue form until he revived it in the *Consolation*. In the prefaces to the theological tractates, however, Boethius preserves the dialogue format, but with a difference: he feels compelled to sustain a conversation in the absence of an interlocutor. His dialogues now become purely internalized conversations with himself on philosophical and theological issues. Like Augustine, Boethius focuses on the necessary silence in which such mental disputations must transpire. In addition, he self-consciously reflects on the problems of transcribing these imaginary colloquies, and the prefaces look back over the tradition of the literary dialogue, while at the same time foretelling the problems of reading and writing which the prisoner confronts at the *Consolation*'s opening.

There is a structural relevance of the tractates to this study

[24] Barnes, in Gibson, *Boethius*, p. 78.

as well. In discussing Boethius' commentaries, his first dialogue, and the key texts in the traditions upon which he drew, I have concentrated mostly on beginnings and endings: the *termini* which bracket the fictions and which demarcate the openings and closings of books. The problems of beginning with a text to read, and closing with a newly written work, motivate the composition of the *In Isagogen* and the *De Continentia*, and they stand behind the conclusions to the *Tusculan Disputations* and *Soliloquia*. The dialogue format also permits the engagement with authority figures in a variety of constructive ways: one may criticize an *auctor* and his work within the fiction, and thus be free of the potential censure of public debate; but one may also confront within the fiction figures of authority whose own statements are to be taken as readable texts. In such cases as the monologues of the *Tusculans* and *De Magistro*, the student figure changes from speaker to reader; their master's orations become, in essence, philosophical treatises whose length and complexity necessitate reading and study. They stretch the credibility of verisimilar dialogue to its limits. These works suggest that reading and dialogue are similar processes, and that within fictional dialogues, the figure of a reader develops in response to the authoritative master. The form of dialogue lends itself to many uses—from commentary, to meditation, to instruction—uses which Boethius will explore in his theological tractates.

Method in the Tractates

This chapter has attempted to outline the literary and historical contexts of Boethius' work through a close analysis of key texts. The dialogues and commentaries articulate what will be the main lines of inquiry for the study of the *Consolation*: the creation of a reading and writing persona; the problems incumbent on beginning a work; and the need to transcribe the dialogue between pupil and teacher—whether dramatized or imagined—into a written document. I focused, too, on those scenes when discussion or analysis seemed to break down, for it is at these moments that the text self-consciously reflects on its method and on the limitations of human language. Silence, then, becomes a strategy for argument. The pupil's silence may reveal something of his attitude towards pedagogic authority; the reader's silence, especially in Augustine, signals an engagement with sacred texts or divine wisdom. In the prefaces to the theological tractates, Boethius explores these problems in method and theme to reflect on the impediments to communication and on the difficulty of writing. He internalizes the processes of dialogue, while at the same time offering a defense of silence close to Augustine's. He also chronicles a process of philosophical writing which will explain the prisoner's difficulties with his own writing at the *Consolation*'s opening. These features of the tractates explain the persona's condition at the dialogue's beginning, and clarify his place at the end of the autobiography Boethius fashioned through his other works.

Boethius opens *De Trinitate* with an appeal to private, rather than public, judgment. The text he presents is very much a written structured document, "set forth in logical order and cast in literary form" ("formatam rationibus litterisque mandatam").[1] The word *mandare* signifies the formal presentation of a work, and it also appears at the beginning of texts to describe the physical activity of transferring thought into writing. At the opening of the *Contra Eutychen* and the *Consolation* as well, Boethius uses the word to bring to the reader's attention the role played by writing in the formation of a literary argument.[2] Boethius' concern with the linguistic character of

[1] All quotations and translations from the tractates will be from Boethius, *Tractates. De Consolatione Philosophiae*, ed. and trans. H. F. Stewart and E. K. Rand, rev. S. J. Tester, Loeb Library (Cambridge, Mass.: Harvard Univ. Press, 1973). This quotation is from pp. 2/3 (I use slash marks to signal facing-page Latin and English).

[2] *Contra Eutychen*, ". . . mando litteris quae coram loquenda servaveram . . ." (p. 72). In the *Consolation*, the prisoner announces that he has written down the events of his trial to be remembered: "Cuius rei seriem atque ueritatem, ne latere posteros queat, stilo etiam memoriaeque mandaui" (1.pr.4.25). Compare also the phrasing at 1.pr.1.1: "Haec dum mecum tacitus ipse re-

his tract—its status as a verbal argument—is also clear in his use of the two components of classical topics theory: invention and judgment. ("offerendam vobis communicandamque curavi tam vestri cupidus iudicii quam nostri studiosus inventi," p. 2).[3] The text subscribes to the ordering principles of dialectic as outlined, for example, in Cicero's *Topica*.[4] Discovery is subject to constant appraisal by writer and reader, and Boethius offers the products of his *inventio* to the public exercise of judgment.

The issue of writing is foremost in Boethius' mind. He is apparently uneasy about writing down any thoughts, not merely because of the material's difficulty, but because of its fundamentally private nature. He writes neither for fame, nor for applause, nor even for the elect, but primarily for the inner pleasure of discovery.[5] His text develops from long-pondered investigations; a work essentially composed in private, *De Trinitate* will address a comparatively limited, private circle of readers. Apart from Symmachus, Boethius seems surrounded by apathetic and jealous men, and to write for such readers, "would seem to bring discredit to the study of divinity" (p. 5).[6] The question of the vulgar reader is but one aspect of the nearly hermetically sealed discourse Boethius claims to write. Preservation of divine truth from the common or uninitiated had become, as is well-known, a frequently

putarem querimoniamque lacrimabilem stili officio signarem. . . ." See Joachim Gruber, *Kommentar zu Boethius De Consolatione Philosophiae* (Berlin: De Gruyter, 1978), p. 123, who fails to notice the special use of *mandare*, and Lewis and Short's *Latin Dictionary*, s. v. *mando*[1] which credits Cicero with the idiom *litteris scriptis mandare*, "to commit to writing."

[3] "I have caused it to be presented and communicated to you, being as much desirous of your judgment as zealous for my own discovery" (p. 3).

[4] "Cum omnis ratio diligens disserendi duas habeat partis, unam inveniendi alteram iudicandi," *Topica*, 6.

[5] "Neque enim famae iactatione et inanibus vulgi clamoribus excitamur; sed si quis est fructus exterior, hic non potest aliam nisi materiae similem sperare sententiam" (pp. 2-4).

[6] "Quocumque igitur a vobis deieci oculos, partim ignava segnities partim callidus livor occurrit, ut contumeliam videatur divinis tractatibus inrogare qui talibus hominum monstris non agnoscenda haec potius quam proculcanda proiecerit" (p. 4).

articulated problem in Late Antique thought.[7] It is at the heart of Macrobius' famous defense of fable and ultimately of the medieval term *involucrum*: the text wrapped in an allegorical cover.[8] Boethius also devotes some time and effort to concealing his truths.

> So I purposely use brevity and wrap up the ideas I draw from the deep questionings of philosophy in new and unaccustomed words such as speak only to you and to myself, that is, if you ever look at them. The rest of the world I simply disregard since those who cannot understand seem unworthy even to read them (p. 5).[9]

But this statement differs markedly from the Macrobian ideal of the mysteries of fabulous narrative. First, Boethius limits his readership to an apparent audience of one. Of course, this claim is not to deny the historical contexts in which the tractate was written, nor is it to assert, in the face of evidence advanced by Chadwick, Schurr, and others, that Boethius placed himself outside the vital theological debates of his day.[10] It is, however, to claim that the persona of the writer stretches to

[7] On this concept, see the remarks in Michael Murrin, *The Veil of Allegory* (Chicago: Univ. of Chicago Press, 1969), especially Chapter 2, "Allegory and Prophecy in the Ancient World."

[8] "Philosophers make use of fabulous narratives; not without a purpose, however, nor merely to entertain, but because they realize that a frank, open exposition of herself is distasteful to Nature, who, just as she has withheld an understanding of herself from the uncouth senses of men by enveloping herself in variegated garments, has also desired to have her secrets handled by more prudent individuals through fabulous narratives." From Macrobius, *Commentary on the Dream of Scipio*, trans. W. H. Stahl (New York: Columbia Univ. Press, 1952), p. 86.

[9] "Idcirco stilum brevitate contraho et ex intimis sumpta philosophiae disciplinis novorum verborum significationibus velo, ut haec mihi tantum vobisque, si quando ad ea convertitis oculos, conloquantur; ceteros vero ita submovimus, ut qui capere intellectu nequiverint ad ea etiam legenda videantur indigni" (p. 4).

[10] V. Schurr, *Die Trinitätslehre des Boethius im Lichte der 'skythischen Kontroversen'* (Paderborn: Schöningh, 1935), pp. 136-227 (for the context of *De Trinitate*). For a summary of Schurr's research and that of more recent writers, see Chadwick, *Boethius*, pp. 185-190; for a reading of the preface to *De Trinitate* as straight autobiography, see Chadwick, p. 213.

the limit the tropes of dedication and of concealment, and that he uses these conventions to highlight the difficulty of finding a suitable discourse for theological inquiry. Symmachus, Boethius implies, may never even read the tractate; and yet he is presented as the work's only truly qualified reader.

Boethius plays with the problems of writing for an audience by calling attention to the conspicuous absence of an interlocutor for his arguments. The problem of the absent addressee and of the development of a difficult, "private" discourse fit only for that addressee, can be made clearer by comparing the *De Trinitate* preface with those of two other tractates. The prefaces to the *Utrum Pater* and the *Quomodo Substantiae* begin with explicit questions. Boethius attempts to recreate the fiction of live conversation, as the writer appears to respond to arguments which have been posed with a certain immediacy. The *Utrum Pater* begins with the writer asking a fundamental philosophical question about the substance of the Trinity. In his attempt to preserve the dynamic of question and answer, Boethius articulates a dialogue with himself. The words *quaero* and *interrogo* in the preface's opening lines signal the pose of the teacher, while the word *respondebo* anticipates the student's reply.[11] The opening of *Quomodo Substantiae* dramatizes this process of inquiry; Boethius' initial word, *postulas*, announces a question asked and foretells a response.[12] John the Deacon's queries on Boethius' earlier *Hebdomads* engender a written reply, and the preface counterpoints the problems of *De Trinitate* in two ways. First, there is the problem of private meditation and the reflection on an argument or text in isolation.

> But I think over my *Hebdomads* with myself, and I keep my speculations in my own memory rather than share them with

[11] "*Quaero* an pater et filius ac spiritus sanctus de divinitate substantialiter praedicentur an alio quolibet modo. . . . Si igitur *interrogem*, an qui dicitur pater substantia sit, *respondetur* esse substantia. Quod si *quaeram*, an filius substantia sit, idem dicitur" (p. 32, emphases added).

[12] "Postulas, ut ex Hebdomadibus nostris . . ." (p. 38).

the pert and frivolous persons who will not tolerate an argument unless it is made amusing (p. 39).[13]

Here, Boethius anticipates the tone of the *De Trinitate* preface.[14] Public dialogue gives way to private meditation, and the opening scene in *De Trinitate*, with the writer pondering a question in solitude, shares with the tone of the *Quomodo Substantiae* a need for privacy in writing and reading. Second, the *Quomodo Substantiae* confronts the problem of brevity addressed in the *De Trinitate* preface. John the Deacon had apparently complained of the opacity of Boethius' text, and he responds:

> Wherefore do you not take objection to obscurities consequent on brevity, which are the sure treasure-house of secret doctrine and have the advantage that they speak only with those that are worthy (p. 39).[15]

Together with the *De Trinitate* preface, these assertions make a claim for brevity and obscurity as an issue not only of philosophy but almost of aesthetics. While his remarks may share something of Macrobius' desire to veil truths in strange terms, as the words of *De Trinitate* make clear, it also has two other points of reference, one within and the other outside the corpus of Boethius' writings.

Boethius' praise of brevity and obscurity in the tractates at first glance seems to contradict his impatience with these qualities in Aristotle's writings. Aristotle "muddles his meaning by a confusing brevity, and hides it in a cloud of obscurity"

---

[13] "Hebdomadas vero ego mihi ipse commentor potiusque ad memoriam meam speculata conservo quam cuiquam participo quorum lascivia ac petulantia nihil a ioco risuque patitur esse seiunctum" (p. 38).

[14] I say "anticipates" because it has been shown that the *De Trinitate* and the *Utrum Pater* were probably composed later than the *Quomodo Substantia* and the *Contra Eutychen* (see Chadwick, *Boethius*, pp. 180, 211).

[15] "Prohinc tu ne sis obscuritatibus brevitatis adversus, quae cum sint arcani fida custodia tum id habent commodi, quod cum his solis qui digni sunt conloquuntur" (p. 38).

(Barnes, p. 78; Meiser, II, p. 99).[16] At the beginning of the first *Perihermeneias* commentary, Boethius noted that Aristotle's method is difficult and hard to follow, and his present treatment will therefore deal "only with matters where Aristotle's brief and obscure statements impede the simple understanding of his argument" (Barnes, p. 78; Meiser, I, 31-32).[17] In referring to the "obscurities consequent on brevity" which John had found in the *Hebdomads*, Boethius, I think, equates his own work with Aristotle's: they are both difficult texts which demand commentary. Boethius characterizes his *Hebdomads* as belonging to *huiusmodi scriptionum*, "a certain class of writings," and he describes his own process of reviewing the work as an act of commentary ("Hebdomadas vero ego mihi ipse *commentor* . . . ," p. 38). That his own and Aristotle's texts are brief and obscure signals the need for explication, and it is the job of the commentator to tease out meaning for those worthy to receive it. The commentaries and the tractates address similar audiences: small, appreciative, and educated. In both sets of works, the *vulgi* are treated only with contempt, as a potential readership hostile to the method and goal of Boethius' intellectual pursuits.

The tractates differ from the commentaries, of course, in their overall theological and specifically Augustinian focus. The image of the divine spark which opens *De Trinitate*, to take but one example, remains a Platonic trope filtered through Augustine, and it suggests his concept of illumination and the doctrine of recall developed in the *De Magistro* and elsewhere.[18] We may view the preface to *De Trinitate* as Au-

---

[16] "volens Aristoteles distribuere dictionem . . . contradictionem sensum confusa brevitate permiscuit et nebulis obscuritatis inplicuit," Meiser, II, p. 99, 24-27; translation based on that in Barnes, in Gibson, *Boethius*, p. 78.

[17] "quocirca nos libri huius enodationem duplici commentatione supplevimus et quantum simplices quidem intellectus sententiarum oratio brevis obscuraque conplectitur, tantum hac huius operis tractatione digessimus," Meiser, I, pp. 31-32; translation based on that in Barnes, in Gibson, *Boethius*, p. 78.

[18] Among the many passages in Augustine's works where these ideas are expressed, see *De Magistro*, XI.36.16-18, XII.40.30-33. Compare also the remarks in *De Magistro* on the deception by "external light" (XI.38.51-55) with

gustinian in spirit, and the Saint's name in fact closes this section of the work.[19] Boethius' writing manifests Augustine's idea of the "internal silent words by which the inner teacher, Christ, teaches us the truth" (Mazzeo, p. 187).[20] By adumbrating a doctrine of illumination within his spiritual autobiography, Boethius also recalls those moments in *De Magistro* when Augustine calls upon "not the speaker who utters words, but the guardian of truth within the mind itself." Boethius chronicles the cognitive life of what Augustine called the "interior man" who deals in public words, only to remind him of the truth that teaches privately.[21] Yet, Boethius realizes that as long as he has chosen to communicate to the world of men, his method will be limited. With human language as his vehicle, he will be unable to express fully the spark of insight granted to him. Writing, like the other *artes*, is only one step on the ladder towards truth.

> We should of course press our inquiry only so far as the insight of man's reason is allowed to climb the height of heavenly knowledge. For in the other arts the same point is set as a sort of limit, as far as which the way of reason can reach (p. 5).[22]

the extended passage on the true light of Biblical revelation discussed on *Confessions*, x.xxxiv.51-52. Compare also Philosophy's remarks at III.pr.12.25, and Gruber's collection of Platonic source material, *Kommentar*, p. 307, 312.

[19] Again with a Platonic image—itself adopted by Augustine—of the seeds of thought: "Vobis tamen etiam illud inspiciendum est, an ex beati Augustini scriptis semina rationum aliquos in nos venientia fructus extulerint" (p. 4). See the similar phrasing in Philosophy's banishment of the Muses (i.pr.i.9). On the imagery of the seeds of thought and fruits of reason, and its sources in the Bible, Plato, and Augustine, see Gruber, *Kommentar*, pp. 67-68, and his remarks on III.m.11.11 (p. 307).

[20] Joseph Mazzeo, "St. Augustine's Rhetoric of Silence," p. 187.

[21] "De uniuersis autem, quae intellegimus, non loquentem, qui personat foris, sed intus ipsi menti praesidentem consulimus ueritatem, uerbis fortasse ut consulamus admoniti. Ille autem, qui consulitur, docet, qui in interiore homine habitare dictus est Christus . . ." (*De Magistro*, xi.38.44-48).

[22] "Sane tantum a nobis quaeri oportet quantum humanae rationis intuitus ad diuinitatis valet celsa conscendere. Nam ceteris quoque artibus idem quasi quidam finis est constitutus, quousque potest via rationis accedere" (p. 4).

The *via rationis* described here is but a formal method which may teach us what to write or say, but not to think. Boethius' phrasing echoes the metaphors of the "way" taken from the theory of dialectic, and the notion of study as an ordered progress through basic stages to a higher goal forms the framework to his own *De topicis differentiis*.[23] He uses the word *via* again to characterize the method of the *Utrum Pater*. The imagery of *ars* as a *via* and of the *gradus* of study will reappear in the *Consolation*'s opening passages to characterize Philosophy's attempt to develop the prisoner's language skills and to direct his reason.[24] The preface to *De Trinitate* thus draws on a variety of terms and images which characterize Boethius' reflections on method in his other works. He focuses on the strengths and weaknesses of using language to convey theological argument, and the last words of *De Trinitate* return to the central problems of his writing persona.

In submitting the work for Symmachus' approval, Boethius calls attention to the authority of his dedicatee. The preface had almost eliminated him from the intended circle of readers, wondering whether he would even look at Boethius' text. Now Boethius offers his argument to a judge whose authority alone "will decide whether it has been run through on a straight course or not" (p. 31).[25] He returns to the tropes of submission first articulated in the *De Arithmetica* preface and voiced too in the student figure of the *In Isagogen*. In so doing, he establishes a kind of dialogue between himself and the

[23] The use of *via* as a technical term, frequently in the phrasing "via et ratio" translating the Greek *methodos*, will be discussed in the following chapter. See the opening of *De topicis differentiis*, Book II, for Boethius' idea of the hierarchy of study.

[24] See the discussion in the following chapter for the use of *via* and *gradus* in the *Consolation*'s opening. For an early characterization of a course of study in these terms, see Boethius' *De Arithmetica*, ed. Friedlein, p. 9, and the discussion in Courcelle, *La Consolation de Philosophie dans la Tradition Littéraire* (Paris: Etudes Augustiniennes, 1967), p. 26, n. 2, and Chadwick, *Boethius*, pp. 72-73.

[25] "Nunc vestri normam iudicii exspectat subtilitas quaestionis; quae utrum recte decursa sit an minime, vestrae statuet pronuntiationis auctoritas" (p. 30).

reader; he revives the process of writing and revising; and he essentially leaves the work, itself a product of limited human ability, open-ended. The *Utrum Pater* had also concluded with a request for the dedicatee's authoritative judgment. Here, it is a matter of faith rather than method, but the petition remains the same: if the writer has left the work unfinished or flawed, it is the duty of the reader to correct it.[26] Taken together, these moments in the tractates present the figure of a writer preoccupied with beginning and ending a work. As in the *Perihermeneias* commentary or the end of the early *In Isagogen*, the persona Boethius creates concerns himself with initiating a course of study and transcribing the products of that study into written form. Relationships to dedicatee and wider audience are always at issue, and the tensions between silent meditation and public disclosure structure his texts. Nowhere, I think, are these concerns more explicit than in the preface to the *Contra Eutychen*.

Boethius' initial remarks in this tractate notice the absence of an interlocutor with whom he can argue. Unlike the *Utrum Pater* or *Quomodo Substantiae*, there is no immediacy to his response. Alone now, for whatever reasons, Boethius sets down in writing, "what I had been keeping to say by word of mouth" ("mando litteris quae coram loquenda servaveram," pp. 72/73). The process of writing is again a private one, but here it becomes a way of filling the space of silence with written words. Boethius' autobiographical explanation of his beliefs in the *Contra Eutychen* also explains the purpose of his solitary, silent thought. Now, however, it is the silence

---

[26] "Haec si re recte et ex fide habent, ut me instruas peto; aut si aliqua re forte diversus es, diligentius intuere quae dicta sunt et fidem si poterit rationemque coniunge" (p. 36). The preface to the *Contra Eutychen* also asks for the dedicatee's judgment and correction, though here he asks John the Deacon to correct the work only for Boethius to revise and send it again to Symmachus for final approval: "sin vero vel minuendum aliquid vel addendum vel aliqua mutatione variandum est, id quoque postulo remitti, meis exemplaribus ita ut a te revertitur transcribendum. Quae ubi ad calcem ducta constiterint, tum demum eius cuius soleo iudicio censenda transmittam" (p. 76).

of a man trapped in the babble of the ignorant. At issue is interpretation. He recalls how a letter expressing unorthodox belief was read before the assembly. This public reading engenders a flurry of vocal opposition, but the words of the mob are without insight into the complexity of the problem. In fact, they deny its obscurity, an act anathema to either Augustine's or Boethius' aesthetic and philosophical commitments to the pleasures of difficulty.[27]

> On that occasion all loudly protested that the difference was evident, that there was in this matter no obscurity, confusion or perplexity, and in the general storm and tumult there was found no one who really touched the edge of the problem, much less anyone who solved it (p. 75).[28]

The crowd expresses itself in a noisy tumult incapable of investigating truth. *Inventio*—the process of reasoned, rational discovery—is denied them. In abusing the techniques of public disputation, they violated the order of argument and appeal to the whim of emotion. For all their clamor, their words are hollow.

Only Boethius, he tells us himself, sat apart from them, far from the man (i.e., Symmachus) he watched.[29] Instead,

[27] On Augustine's notion of obscurity as an aesthetic issue, see Mazzeo and the earlier studies of Maurice Pontet, *L'exégèse de saint Augustin prédicateur* (Paris: Boccard, 1944), pp. 119-127, and H. I. Marrou, *Saint Augustin et la fin de la culture antique* (Paris: Boccard, 4th edition, 1958), pp. 478-484. For Augustine's view of obscurity and ambiguity in rational discourse, see his *De Dialectica*, ed. J. Pinborg, trans. B. D. Jackson (Dordrecht: D. Reidel, 1975), chapters 8-9 (pp. 102-113).

[28] "Hic omnes apertam esse differentiam nec quicquam in eo esse caliginis inconditum confusumque strepere nec ullus in tanto tumultu qui leviter attingeret quaestionem, nedum qui expediret inventus est" (p. 74). For the historical background to this scene, along with treatments of the substance of the bishop's letter, and the doctrinal controversies involved, see Schurr, pp. 108-136; Chadwick, *Boethius*, pp. 180-185.

[29] "Adsederam ego ab eo quem maxime intueri cupiebam longius atque adeo, si situm sedentium recorderis, aversus pluribusque oppositis, ne si aegerrime quidem cuperem, vultum nutumque eius aspicere poteram ex quo mihi aliqua eius darentur signa iudicii" (p. 74).

"I kept silent (*conticui*)." He meditates to himself on the issue,
and when insight comes to him, it is a totally private experience. He finds truth not by listening to the outer voices of
others, but to the inner voice of himself. His metaphor of
sudden revelation brings with it a complex of Biblical and
Augustinian images which help define the meaning of his
silence and point to a method of intellection which goes beyond human language.

> So I continued to ponder all the questions in my mind, not
> swallowing what I had heard, but rather chewing the cud of
> constant meditation. At last the door opened to my mind's
> knocking, and the truth which I found in my inquiry disclosed
> all the fogs of the Eutychian error (p. 75).[30]

The diction is highly metaphorical: the alimentary imagery
signals a process of private cognition in terms familiar from
Augustine and other Late Antique ecclesiastical writers;[31] the
figure of the mind as a door, however, alerts the reader to a
process of sudden revelation taken from the Bible and the
close of Augustine's *Confessions*. The phrasing of the Gospels,
"petite, et dabitur vobis; quaerite, et invenietis; pulsate, et
aperietur vobis," shares with the tractate a view of the accessibility of truth to the spiritually aware.[32] The Bible and
Boethius together advocate a diligence rewarded with knowledge. Seeking, asking, and knocking have their fulfillment in
finding, receiving, and opening. *Inventio* now becomes a term
of more than technical significance; it comes to represent the
kind of mental activity missing in the mob. The word's meaning transcends the arenas of public discussion to which it once
had reference. Unlike the *indocti*, who fail to understand

---

[30] "Meditabar igitur dehinc omnes animo quaestiones nec deglutiebam
quod acceperam, sed frequentis consilii iteratione ruminabam. Tandem igitur
patuere pulsanti animo fores et veritas inventa quaerenti omnes nebulas Eu-
tychiani reclusit erroris" (p. 74).

[31] See E. R. Curtius, *European Literature and the Latin Middle Ages*, pp. 134-
136.

[32] The Biblical passage appears at Luke: 11:9 and Matthew: 7:8.

through debate, Boethius comes to knowledge through silent meditation. His activity in the *Contra Eutychen* may be seen as parallel to the Augustinian process of purposeful writing which characterized his *Soliloquia*: "Deliberations with myself when I was alone in your [i.e., God's] presence" (*Conf.*, IX.5).[33] Boethius' phrasing also recalls the conclusion to the *Confessions*, as Augustine reflects on the inability of one man to teach the truth to another. "A te petatur, in te quaeratur, ad te pulsetur: sic, sic accipietur, sic inuenietur, sic aperietur" (XIII.38.53).[34] As a record of the individual's confrontation with itself through silent meditation, reading, and writing, the *Confessions* closes by denying the need for any interlocutor save God. In a similar manner, the meditation recorded in the *Contra Eutychen* is a disputation conducted without the need of human companionship, and the force of Boethius' imagery explains Symmachus' absence both from the remembered story of the debate and from the written text of the *Contra Eutychen* itself.

For Augustine, what fills this absence is the eternal presence of God. For Boethius, with more immediate concerns here, what fills the space left by silence is writing. "The pen is now to take the place of the living voice" (p. 77).[35] Boethius turns the process of composing back upon itself. As in the preface to *De Trinitate* and in Augustine, solitude and silence remove the writer in space and time from the noise of the multitude. Boethius turns away ("transeo," he states) from these external distractions to savor the eloquence granted by the mind alone. But somewhat differently from Augustine, Boethius appears preoccupied with the problems of beginning his texts, and his overriding concern with technique and method, combined with his autobiographical statements, makes the problem of recording, rather than recalling, foremost in the reader's mind. Edward Said's remarks on the relationship between an

---

[33] ". . . disputati . . . cum ipso me solo coram te," *Conf.*, IX.v.7.

[34] For discussion of the *Confession's* final line, see G. Mazzotta, *Dante, Poet of the Desert*, pp. 225-256 and n. 38.

[35] ". . . semel res a conlocutione transfertur ad stilum" (p. 76).

author's career and his attempts at beginning a new work express what I find to be the problems implicit in the prefaces to the theological tractates, and, as I will later argue, in the opening of the *Consolation*.

> [We may] take the author's career as wholly oriented toward and synonymous with the production of a text, especially if the author himself seems obsessively concerned with just that concern over technique or craftsmanship. A further implication is that the author's career is a course whose record is his work and whose goal is the integral text that adequately represents the efforts expended on its behalf.[36]

Boethius creates the image of an author facing either a long gestation period for his work, or of the writer as a frustrated speaker, waiting anxiously for the opportunity to express his thoughts. The writing of *De Trinitate* can only begin after a long period of investigation.[37] *Contra Eutychen* similarly begins after a lengthy time of reflection.[38] Both texts open with the decision to write down for the present those thoughts which have occupied the past.

Boethius begins each work by confronting anew the difficulty of writing, and by giving it a place in the implied autobiography which stands behind its composition. Not only does he make reference to the work's place in his life, but, like his asides in the commentaries, he also considers the present work's relationship to his other writings and to the plan of study which motivates his career. *De Trinitate*'s preface reviews its author's continual difficulty whenever he attempts to transcribe what he thinks. The *Quomodo Substantiae* develops from reflection on another work in the writer's corpus. The preface to *Contra Eutychen* begs the reader to measure the work against the body of Boethius' writings: "If you pronounce it to be sound I beg you to place it among the other

---

[36] Edward Said, *Beginnings: Intention and Method* (Baltimore: Johns Hopkins Univ. Press, 1975), p. 196.

[37] "Investigatam diutissime quaestionem . . ." (p. 2).

[38] "Anxie te quidem diuque sustinui . . ." (p. 72).

writings of mine" (p. 77).[39] Boethius' beginnings in the tractates establish what Said calls "relationships of continuity"
with works already existing.[40] The persona of the writer in
these texts expresses the same concerns with an authoritative
dedicatee, vulgar readership, and literary career which were
found in the commentaries and earlier works. Each new text
fits into a planned structure of the writer's life, whether that
structure is the "schriftstellerische Plan" voiced in the *Perihermeneias* commentary or the *In Isagogen* conclusion, or the
implicit body of theological writings Boethius claims Symmachus to know. To this end, I have explored those moments
in Boethius' writings where he initiates the plan of a literary
career and where he reflects on the problems of beginning an
individual text. It is this preoccupation with beginnings which
gives to the opening of the *Consolation* a new resonance for
Boethius' career. Unlike the earlier works, the *Consolation*
breaks with all other beginnings and makes itself something
new and different from anything which has gone before.
While the author of the tractates values the past, the prisoner
of the *Consolation* mourns it; while the commentator sees a
future of reading and writing, the prisoner laments that he
can no longer compose. Again the author addresses the present

[39] "Quod si recte se habere pronuntiaveris, peto ut mei nominis hoc quoque inseras chartis . . ." (p. 76).

[40] Said, *Beginnings*, p. 3: ". . . we can regard a beginning as the point at which, in a given work, the writer departs from all other works; a beginning immediately establishes relationships with works already existing, relation-ships of either continuity or antagonism or some mixture of both." Said also characterizes the writer's feeling of the "necessity at the beginning . . . to see [the] work as making reference, first, to other works, but also to reality and to the reader, by adjacency, not sequentially or dynastically" (p. 10). Concerning the troubles expressed at the opening of *De Trinitate*, we may turn to Said's phrasing: "Finally, and almost inevitably, for the writer, the historian, or the philosopher, the beginning will emerge reflectively and, perhaps, unhappily, already engaging him in an awareness of its difficulty" (p. 35). On the relationship between writing and speaking in the tractates—and the absence of any "real" interlocutor—we may take as relevant Said's view that "writing is capable of evoking the spoken voice, it revives life in all its complexity, . . . it permits the illusion of living presence" (pp. 21-22).

effort to all his previous writings, but now it is a relationship of contrast rather than continuity. Here, the writer's silence is the fallen counterpart to the insightful, Augustinian rhetoric of silence. Rather than listening to his inner teacher, the prisoner hears only the Muses. Before he can ascend to that higher silence, he must first find his true voice.

CHAPTER II

THE SEARCH FOR VOICE

Chapter I of this study began and ended with approaches to the Boethian persona from both historical and critical perspectives. As an intellectual in a decaying world, he read and wrote within the closed confines of the study and the literary circle. His attitudes towards dedicatee and public are couched in the idioms of Late Antique prose. There is also an individual unity to Boethius' work: creating the figure of a writer obsessed with beginnings, plans, and the shape of a career written through the texts he has produced and read. Parallels with the dialogues of Cicero, Augustine, and Fulgentius provide sources and historical analogues for the patterns in which Boethius expressed these concerns. In particular, these authors focused on the tension between active participation in debate and passive silence before the master. Such moments of silence signal the breakdown of dialogue, and they mark those moments in the works when the writer pauses to reflect on problems of method.

I propose here a reading of the *Consolation*'s opening which explains the prisoner's silence and his subsequent efforts at dialogue. While Augustine saw the fundamental spiritual movement as one of speech to silence, Boethius focuses on the essential propaedeutic to all philosophical speculation: public discussion. In the *Consolation*, silence can be a vice: it betrays an ignorance of the most basic methods of communication and understanding. Reasoned eloquence, the Ciceronian ideal, becomes the goal towards which Philosophy directs the prisoner's voice in the *Consolation*'s opening books.

My reading implies a notion of levels of discourse in the *Consolation*, a notion expressed both in the texts of Chapter I and in Boethius' own logical writings. Briefly put, rhetoric and dialectic, for Boethius, were only preludes to philosophy. Following Cicero and Aristotle, rather than Plato, Boethius posited a dialectician who persuaded through opinions rather than proofs.[1] As I have shown in Chapter I, Cicero's dialogues moved among beliefs and opinions and remained open-ended; Plato's in contrast sought to kick away the methodological preliminaries in the articulation of higher truths. For the first part of the *Consolation*, Boethius takes the Ciceronian and Aristotelian heritage, especially topics theory, as his model. Writing in the *De topicis differentiis*, Boethius provides the terms for the analysis of the prisoner's initial conversations with Philosophy. There, he had classed all forms of probable argument under the rubric of dialectic. He included the topics, which he considered "the starting point of necessary arguments."[2] Philosophical demonstration, however, was narrowly conceived as syllogistic reasoning. The philosopher, Boethius wrote, employs necessary proofs, and "he differs from the orator and dialectician in their areas of inquiry, namely that for them it consists in ready believability, and for him in truth."[3] The tension between belief and proof

---

[1] See the discussion in Chapter I of this study and the references cited there. Aristotle's dialectician convinced through *endoxa*, or opinions. Such opinions, however (as Boethius stresses in *De topicis*), must come from rational speculation and investigation of the world—they are the opinions of the wise man or specialist. They may, however, also gain currency by popular acceptance. Aristotle had considered dialectic a propaedeutic to philosophy, and Solmsen shows how the practice of the dialectical method may "sharpen our eyes for truth" ("Dialectic without the Forms," p. 54, working from Aristotle, *Topica*, 163a29–163b3).

[2] Stump, trans., p. 41. *De topicis differentiis*, PL, 64: 1182B: ". . . necessariorum quoque principia traditio ista contineat."

[3] Stump, trans., p. 41. *De topicis differentiis*, PL, 64: 1182A: "Patet igitur in quo philosophus ab oratore ac dialectico in propria consideratione dissideat, in eo scilicet quod illis probabilitatem, huic veritatem constat esse propositam."

Boethius establishes in this work characterizes the problems which beset the prisoner's initial confrontations with his master, and the following analysis illustrates how the rules of dialectic seldom meet the needs of philosophy. The prisoner must therefore begin at the beginning: from a lethargic speechlessness he will move through the excesses of rhetoric and the limitations of dialectic before Philosophy can introduce him to the methods of philosophical demonstration.

I

From its opening, the *Consolation* struggles with words and texts. Foremost in the prisoner's mind is not, as we would expect, his recognizable grief, but a deeper, less recognizable impediment: silence. He is no longer able to compose verses full of meaning and value; now his poem is but a hollow elegy for lost youth. He cannot invent his own words, but must silently take dictation from the Muses.

> I who once wrote songs with keen delight am now by sorrow driven to take up melancholy measures. Wounded Muses tell me what to write, and elegiac verses bathe my face with real tears.[4]

Reduced to a scribe, his role is passive, and the prisoner expresses a loss of moral and literary direction. He walks along a lonely *iter* of life (1.m.1.6) and his step falters: "Qui cecidit, stabili non erat ille gradu" (1.m.1.22). Behind his lament stand the idioms of Ovidian elegy and Virgilian epic. The exiled voice of the *Tristia* is here, and with it what one scholar has called the "programmatic" claims of reviewing a literary life and ordering its achievements generically.[5] Also present are

---

[4] Green, trans., p. 3. "Carmina qui quondam studio florente peregi, / flebilis, heu, maestos cogor inire modos. / Ecce mihi lacerae dictant scribenda Camenae / et ueris elegi fletibus ora rigant" (1.m.1.1-4).

[5] See the discussion of Anna Crabbe, "Literary Design in the *De Consolatione*," in Gibson, *Boethius*, pp. 246-824. For sources and citations, see Gruber, *Kommentar*, pp. 51-52.

the claims made at the end of Virgil's *Georgics* and in the pseudo-Virgilian opening to the *Aeneid*. Such remarks not only create a hierarchy of genres, which structures the literary career, but they emphasize that with the beginning of each literary work lies a new beginning for the author's life. Boethius' opening lines use these traditions against themselves, as they lament the writer's inability to continue the progress through higher genres and, more directly, to continue the literary career at all. Read in the context of the Boethian persona developed in his earlier works, these lines describe a life lived through texts coming to its silent end.[6]

The prisoner remarks how he sits in silence, ready to inscribe his lament, when the majestic figure of Philosophy enters.[7] Much has been made of the drama of her initial appearance, and even more has been said about the symbolism of her attire.[8] I want to stress the strong and repeated use of imagery taken from linguistic education. Philosophy's dress is certainly a symbol of philosophical learning, but it is more.

[6] The sources in question are Virgil, *Georgics*, IV, 559-566; *Aeneid*, I, 1a-d. For the notion of the literary career in Antiquity as defined through a hierarchy of genres, see Lawrence Lipking, *The Life of the Poet* (Chicago: Univ. of Chicago Press, 1981), pp. 76-93.

[7] "Haec dum mecum tacitus ipse reputarem querimoniamque lacrimabilem stili officio signarem astitisse mihi supra uerticem uisa est mulier reuerendi admodum uultus . . ." (1.pr.1.1).

[8] See the extended discussion in Joachim Gruber, "Die Erscheinung der Philosophie in der *Consolatio Philosophiae* des Boethius," *Rheinisches Museum für Philologie* 112 (1969), 166-186. Gruber argues that the scene is a classical Epiphany, and that the prisoner's silence is merely the dumbfoundedness of one confronted with a heavenly appearance. Gruber cites the *Odyssey*, XIX, 42, and the *Aeneid*, IV, 279. In describing Philosophy's gown, in the *Kommentar*, he adduces a plethora of Platonic and Neoplatonic sources, as well as the allegorical description of Philosophy in Cicero's *Tusculan Disputations*. For a discussion of the iconography which developed around the description of Philosophy, see P. Courcelle, *La Consolation de Philosophie dans la tradition littéraire* (Paris: Etudes Augustiniennes, 1967), pp. 17-28 (on the text and its sources), pp. 29-66 (on medieval readings and illustrations through the twelfth century), and plates 22-27 (for illustrations of Philosophy in the manuscripts).

It is an imaginary book on whose literal margins (*margine*) are inscribed the Greek letters *pi* and *theta*. "And between them were seen clearly marked stages, like stairs (*in scalarum modum gradus quidam*), ascending from the lowest level to the highest."[9] The flat, fallen *gradus* of the prisoner contrasts with the rising vertical *gradus* of philosophical education. The meaningful markings of Philosophy's gown (the word *insigniti*) echo the meaningless marks Boethius made in silence (the word *signarem*). Through these verbal echoes Boethius creates a unified structure of imagery which explains the prisoner's initial silence and prepares us for Philosophy's opening words.

The word *gradus* is, of course, a commonplace metaphor for the struggle through life or education.[10] Here, however, it signifies specifically a progress of verbal argument: the steps towards reason and belief effected through dialectical disputation and the mastery of invention and judgment. Its sources are clear. In the *Tusculan Disputations* Cicero summarized the Socratic habit of inquiry as a method of understanding through discussion, and his review of the *Meno* places the idea of the *gradus* in a specifically dialogic context.[11] In this passage,

[9] ". . . atque in utrasque litteras in scalarum modum gradus quidam insigniti uidebantur, quibus ab inferiore ad superius elementum esset ascensus" (I.pr.1.4). Green, trans., p. 4. For arguments that the *theta* on Philosophy's gown represents the mark of a condemned man, and thus mirrors the letter on Boethius' own clothing, see Chadwick, *Boethius*, pp. 225-226.

[10] Gruber sees in the prisoner's unstable step (*stabili non gradu*) a military metaphor taken from Plato and imbued with a newer Christian significance (*Kommentar*, p. 57). To Gruber, the word *gradus* signals an ethical instability: a lack of competence in performing decisive moral action against worldly temptation. The word *stabili* looks forward to the cosmic stability that is God (e.g., *stabilis manens*, III.m.9.3), and in Gruber's words, foreshadows "der Unterschied zwischen der Beständigkeit des Weltalls . . . und dem Wechsel der irdischen Dinge" (p. 57). In prosa 1, the word *gradus*, however, embodies the Pythagorean sense of the path of study towards truth, and Gruber appropriates Courcelle's suggestion (itself received from Fortescue) that the *gradus* is the progress of the quadrivium (*Kommentar*, pp. 64-65). See Courcelle, *La Consolation de Philosophie*, p. 26 and n. 2.

[11] ". . . ad ea sic ille respondet, ut puer, et tamen ita faciles interrogationes sunt, ut gradatim respondens eodem perveniat quo si geometrica didicisset" (*Tusc. Disp.*, I.xxiv.57).

the *gradus* comes to symbolize a path towards knowledge taken not through private speculation but through public argument. As verbal activity, this movement stands in sharp contrast to the silent passivity of the prisoner's *gradus*, and it foreshadows the steps by which Philosophy will lead him in her method of question and response. When Augustine appropriates this imagery in the *De Magistro* he gives a specifically Christian resonance to the epistemological goal. Yet, the terms in which he analyzes his own dialogue with Adeodatus are primarily methodological rather than theological. The path towards a blessed life may be directed, "by truth itself through the stages of a degree suited to our weak progress."[12] Here, the *gradus* represents a preliminary exercise, conducted at the comparatively low level of human discourse.[13] Finally, Fulgentius had employed the term to characterize the tripartite system of reading, remembering, and enacting which motivated the dialogue between himself and Virgil's shade, and between Aeneas and his various figures of instruction. In this specifically pedagogic context, Fulgentius signals the stages of study as the progressive engagement with different texts and the cultivation of an art of reading.[14]

In his own writings on dialectic, Boethius adopted the word to characterize the study of argumentative forms. At the opening of Book Two of *De topicis differentiis* Boethius reprimands those students who would skip the necessary, early stages of study and proceed directly to its more advanced levels. Of these impatient students he writes: "When they read the title

---

[12] Leckie, trans., p. 30. ". . . ipsa ueritate gradibus quibusdam infirmo gressui nostro accomodatis . . ." (*De Mag.*, VIII.21.16-17).

[13] Augustine states, "Dabis igitur ueniam, si praeludo tecum non ludendi gratia, sed exercendi uires et mentis aciem, quibus regionis illius, ubi beata uita est, calorem ac lucem non modo sustinere, uerum et amare possimus" (*De Mag.*, VIII.21.19-22).

[14] See the discussion in Chapter I. For Fulgentius' use of the term *gradus* as a course of study, see the following remarks: "Nam ut tuis saturantius aliquid adhuc satisfaciamus ingeniis, trifarius in uita humana gradus est, primum habere, deinde regere quod habeas, tertium uero ornare quod regis. Ergo tres gradus istos in uno uersu nostro considera positos . . ." (Helm, p. 89, 16-21); "Hos ergo gradus uiuaciter intuere . . ." (Helm, p. 90, 3).

of these Books—*De differentiis topicis*—they omit the stages of
the study and immediately direct their attention to the end of
the work. But to me it seems inevitable that the mind of the
student will be unable to achieve the higher stages of the study
unless the prior stages of the study have been previously
learned."[15] Boethius' point throughout *De topicis* is that the
topics are a system of argument rather than thought. They
are, like the *via rationis* described in *De Trinitate*, a limited set
of approaches to problems of judgment and belief. Such a
system is bound by the limitations of ambiguity and obscurity
in human language; yet, as a regimen of study, the topics can
lead to the threshhold of philosophy.[16] For Boethius and his
predecessors, the *gradus* comes to represent a system of the
study of language and the progress by which that study leads
to understanding. When the word appears in the *Consolation*'s
opening, it complements the repeated images of silence, writing, and speech. It highlights the failure and points towards
the success of verbal expression. This process becomes the
search for voice which is the controlling movement of Book
One.

When Philosophy herself speaks, however, it is with a loud
rhetorical flourish which banishes the Muses and which is
designed to rouse the prisoner from his silence and lethargy.
She understands his passive relationship to the Muses of poetry, and recognizes his silence for what it truly is: "When
she saw the Muses of poetry standing beside my bed and
consoling me with their words, she was momentarily upset

[15] Stump, trans., p. 43. *De topicis differentiis*, PL, 64: 1181D-1182D: "Nam
cum de differentiis topicis librorum titulum legerint, omissis doctrinae gradibus statim finem operis attendunt. Mihi autem necessarium videtur quod,
nisi sit praecognitum, ad ulteriora discentis animus pervenire non possit,
. . ."

[16] Implied in Boethius' statement, "Quid igitur est dicendum, patet via
rationi" (*De topicis differentiis*, PL, 64: 1210D). Stump translates, "The road to
reason therefore shows us what to say" (p. 86). Compare this statement with
Boethius' claims in the *De Trinitate* preface, where the *via rationis* represents
the path to limited understanding by following the *artes* of human discourse
(*De Trinitate*, pref., p. 4).

and glared at them with burning eyes."[17] Again, Boethius gives structural unity to the opening passages through a series of verbal echoes. Philosophy recognizes that the Muses are dictating to the prisoner as he himself confessed: her phrasing "verba dictantes" echoes his "dictant scribenda." Her first words boldly fill the empty silence in which the prisoner writes. In this context her banishment of the Muses can be read in a new way. Not only do they represent the vicious, vacuous music of a deranged mind; not only do they espouse the *musica effeminita* guiding the prisoner's opening carmen.[18] They are also a positive barrier to Boethius' search for his own voice. They render him passive and put words in his head, if not his mouth. They hinder the expression of his own self, that self he had forgotten. Philosophy's rejection focuses not on their absolute danger—for to a common man they do little harm—but on their effect on one of the learned, "educated in the philosophical schools of the Eleatics and the Academy."[19] Presumably, he was a man gifted with both reason and speech; yet, he lies here, wasting his time on irrational poetry and staying dumb. Such a man, Philosophy laments in her first poem, sought and understood the workings of Nature, and could give voice to his understanding: "This man used to explore and reveal (*reddere*) Nature's secret causes."[20] Her word *reddere* literally means the ability to give back in language, to translate or interpret from one language to another, or from symbols into speech.[21] The word suggests that

[17] Green, trans., p. 4. "Quae ubi poeticas Musas uidit nostro assistentes toro fletibusque meis uerba dictantes, commota paulisper ac toruis inflammata luminibus" (I.pr.1.7).

[18] See David Chamberlain, "Philosophy of Music in the *Consolatio* of Boethius," *Speculum* 45 (1970), 80-97, esp. p. 85.

[19] Green, trans., p. 5. ". . . hunc uero Eleaticis atque Academicis studiis innutritum" (I.pr.1.10).

[20] Green, trans., p. 6. I.m.2.23.

[21] Gruber does not remark on this word. See the quotations in Lewis and Short, *A Latin Dictionary*, s.v. *reddo*, def. 4: Cicero's wording, "cum ea quae legeram Graece, Latine redderem" (*De Orat.*, 1.155); Horace's usage, "verbo verbum reddere" (*Ars Poetica*, 133). The word also had the sense of reciting

active quality now missing in the prisoner's silent transcription. Moreover, Philosophy sees into the prisoner's mind as he himself could not. She finds him lying *effeto lumine mentis* (1.m.2.24). He had merely considered himself languishing *effeto corpore* (1.m.1.12).

The *Consolation*'s opening moves thus contrast the listlessness of the prisoner's laments with the power of Philosophy's eloquence. The emptiness of Boethius' opening poem is a foil for Philosophy's richly symbolic appearance. While the Muses have given the prisoner language, it is, strictly speaking, a "literal" language: it points only to human words. Philosophy favors a symbolic language: a language opaque to the uninitiated, one which must be interpreted and which ultimately points away from earth to heaven. The signs on her gown are not the kind of open, literal signs which explain themselves. They are the closed symbols which invite the mind's attention to a dimension of being which is not truly literal, not bound by words and letters. We cannot content ourselves with familiar explanations of Philosophy's appearance and her allegorical persona. Hers is an ostentatious symbolism which alerts us to its status *as* symbolism.[22]

The tensions between speech and silence develop further in the course of Book One. In prosa 2, Philosophy questions the prisoner's silence: "Quid taces" (1.pr.2.4). He appears stupefied by her appearance. But his silence is neither the dumbfoundedness of the visionary, nor the speechlessness of

---

or rehearsing a speech, and in the Middle Ages, in ecclesiastical contexts, the word still had the sense of verbal recitation (see. R. E. Latham, *Revised Latin Word List* [Oxford: Oxford Univ. Press, 1965], s.v. *reddo*, p. 396).

[22] The preface to Fulgentius' *Mitologiae*, with its visionary appearance of Calliope banishing the student's muses, has traditionally been seen as an analogue to Boethius' text (see Courcelle, *Late Latin Writers*, p. 296, and R. Helm, "Der Bischof Fulgentius und der Mythograph," *Rheinisches Museum* 54 [1899], pp. 120-121). The *I* which forms from Virgil's fingers in the *De Continentia* offers, however, a more effective parallel to the *pi* and *theta* inscribed on Philosophy's gown. Both appearances are described in terms of the written letter, and together with their symbolic books, Virgil and Philosophy become positive figures of writing in contrast to their student's literary impotence.

the awed.[23] Rather, as Boethius himself states, it is a complex state. He is *tacitum, elinguem, mutum*: stripped of language, he has lost the ability to communicate in any form. When he can speak, through Philosophy's grace, he does not know where he is. The voice which returns to him is the oratory of the Senate. "Are you a prisoner, too, charged as I am with false accusations?"[24] He considers himself still on trial for his crimes, still in the court rather than the library. When he finally gives vent to his anguish in prosa 4, it is through a classic, five-part oration defending himself against an imaginary accuser before a jury that is not there. The prisoner momentarily collects his thoughts only to let out a flurry of thoughtless speech.[25]

The prisoner's speech is pure oratory, replete with rhetorical questions and extended technical displays.[26] His speech is like his opening poem transcribed in silence: language without meaning, or more appropriately, eloquence without wisdom. The speech also treats a form of writing similar to the prisoner's opening transcription. Midway through his tirade, Boethius asserts that he has written down the details of his accusation to be remembered by future generations. "I have put this in writing so that posterity may know the truth and have a record of these events" ("Cuius rei seriem atque ueritatem, ne latere posteros queat, stilo etiam memoriaeque mandaui").[27] This writing, designed to preserve truth, merely perpetuates a lie. The truths of the affair are simply the facts, a bill of particulars in a case of law. This is not the *veritas* of the philosopher, but simply a record of human events. By

[23] As Gruber would claim, *Rheinisches Museum* 112 (1969), 166-186. See too, *Kommentar*, pp. 64-65, 91, and this remark on p. 75: ". . . das Schweigen ist die Voraussetzung für die Erkenntnis Gottes."

[24] Green, trans. p. 7. "An ut tu quoque mecum rea falsis criminationibus agiteris?" (I.pr.3.3).

[25] "Tum ego collecto in uires animo" (I.pr.4.2).

[26] See Kurt Reichenberger, *Untersuchungen zur literarischen Stellung der Consolatio Philosophiae* (Köln: Romanistische Arbeiten, 1954), p. 37. For an analysis of Boethius' speech as a classic, five-part oration, see pp. 35-76.

[27] Green, trans., p. 12; I.pr.4.25.

confusing truth with detail, the prisoner also confuses true memory with mere reportage. Boethius writes for public remembrance, and for vindication in the court of men rather than in the eyes of God. This kind of memory contrasts decisively with the proper philosophical or spiritual recollection which is one of the *Consolation*'s central goals. "If you can remember what your true country is," Philosophy enjoins after this speech, he will know that it is not, "as Athens was, ruled by many persons," but remains rather the *patria* of the soul ruled by God.[28] In his tirade, the prisoner travesties the Platonic relationship between remembering and forgetting which Philosophy had addressed in prosa 2.[29] He reveals his forgetfulness by thinking that truth and memory can be wholly bound in the written letter, and by believing that to commit something to writing (*stilo mandare*) is to commit it to eternity. In his overriding fidelity to *verba* rather than *res*, the prisoner admits that his case simply hinges on words. He claims to respond to the forgeries (the *falsa littera*) he is accused of writing (1.pr.4.26). While his opening carmen was an act of recording in silence, the prisoner's tirade becomes an act of recording performed through empty rhetoric.

That Philosophy is visibly unmoved by this bluster indicates the prisoner's misjudgment of his audience. After her broad, philosophical remarks on the prisoner's true forgetfulness and the condition of his spiritual exile, she returns to language. She analyzes the speech in terms taken explicitly from the theory of argument embodied in Boethius' own writings on the topics. Before she can engage the prisoner in

---

[28] Green, trans., p. 16. "Si enim cuius oriundo sis patriae reminiscare, non uti Atheniensium quondam multitudinis imperio regitur, . . ." (1.pr.5.4).

[29] See 1.pr.2.6: "Sui paulisper oblitus est. Recordabitur facile, si quidem nos ante cognouerit." See also her later remarks at III.m.11.15-16: "Quodsi Platonis Musa personat uerum, / quod quisque discit immemor recordatur." For the related literature on this subject, and its Greek sources, see Volker Schmidt-Kohl, *Die neuplatonische Seelenlehre in der Consolatio Philosophiae des Boethius* (Meisenheim am Glan: Anton Hain, 1965), pp. 18-20. The idea of learning as remembering which stands behind Philosophy's formulations may be found in the *Meno*, beginning at 81C.

a dialogue, she must descend to his level. The first indication of her shift in diction comes when she describes the library. As a *locus*, the library signifies the literal and figurative place of argument. She seeks a "storeroom of the mind" in which she has placed not physical books but the opinions they contain. The value of her writings lies not in their presence as objects, but in their ability to preserve philosophical truths.[30] By employing a diction taken from classical mnemnonic theory, with its emphases on the *loci* and *sedes* of argument, Philosophy moves metaphorically into the prisoner's rhetorical world, while at the same time emphasizing the existence of her own higher truths. She then summarizes his previous speech, separating and arranging the individual arguments by topic. She lists in order his accusations and comments on his forensic technique. Each statement is rhetorically signalled:

> De obiectorum . . .
> De sceleribus fraudibusque . . .
> De nostra etiam criminatione . . .
> Postremus aduersum fortunam . . .
> in extremo musae sauientis. . . .
> (1.pr.5.8-10)

Three sentences in a row open with the same *de*, and taken together with the following signals (*postremus, in extremo*) these devices call attention to Philosophy's deliberate display of her skill at *dispositio*. By organizing her remarks in this explicit manner, she offers herself as a model disputant. She is a master of both rhetorical forms and psychological calm.[31] Hers is an ordered response which manifests itself through verbal perspicacity and mental tranquillity. Philosophy highlights the prisoner's shortcomings and abilities as a debater

---

[30] "Itaque non tam me *loci* huius quam tua facies mouet nec bibliothecae potius comptos ebore ac uitro parietes quam tuae mentis *sedem* requiro, in qua non libros sed id quod libris pretium facit, librorum quondam meorum sententias collocaui" (1.pr.5.6, emphases mine).

[31] ". . . illa uultu placido nihilque meis questibus mota" (1.pr.5.1).

and, in this way, justifies her cure. Grief has twisted his words, and she must use "milder medicines" to effect her treatment.

   To correct his deficiencies as an arguer, Philosophy engages the prisoner in dialogue, and to do so she begins her arguments in a dialectically technical way. She realizes that to move him away from opinions and towards truths—to effect her cure— she must begin at the level of probable disputation. After announcing the formal plan of question and answer which motivates their argument, the prisoner accepts.

> "First, will you let me test your present attitude with a few questions, so that I can decide on a way to cure you?"
> "Ask whatever you like, and I will try to answer."[32]

Their discussion properly develops from this point, with a commitment to dialogue at its basic level. The contract Philosophy proposes suggests that the dialectical method will dictate the form and pattern of their exchange. Echoing Boethius' own remarks in *De topicis differentiis*, Philosophy had, immediately before (at 1.m.6), foreshadowed discussion along the correct way. The *via* here, although a metaphorical usage, implies a methodological rather than a moral way.

> Sic quod praecipiti uia
> certum deserit ordinem
> laetos non habet exitus.
> (1.m.6.20-22)

This passage embodies the classical view of topical argument as an ordered way or method towards a proper goal, and, while the subject of Philosophy's poem is cosmology, her final lines offer the kind of prescription Boethius himself had made at the opening of *De topicis differentiis*, II. The heritage for her diction lies most clearly in works of the rhetorical tradition. For the *ad Herennium*, technique (*ars*) was "prae-

---

[32] Green, trans., p. 18. "Primum igitur paterisne me pauculis rogationibus statum tuae mentis attingere atque temptare, ut qui modus sit tuae curationis intellegam?—Tu uero arbitratu, inquam, tuo quae uoles ut responsurum rogato" (1.pr.6.1-2).

ceptio, quae dat certam viam rationemque dicendi" (1.3), and this phrasing survives in Quintilian and Seneca.[33] *Via* and *ordo* were the key terms in all classical definitions of correct argument. In *De topicis differentiis*, Boethius claimed that the topics point debaters to the path of truth ("viam quodammodo veritatis illustrat"), and he asserted that the study of the topics promised "the paths of discovery" (*inveniendi vias*).[34] Book II of *De topicis differentiis* stresses how adherence to the proper

[33] Quintilian, *Institutio Oratoriae*, II.xvii.41: "Ars est potestas via, id est ordine, efficiens, esse certe viam atque ordinem in bene dicendo nemo dubitaverit." Seneca, *De Beneficiis*, IV.xxxiii.2: "Omne hac via procedit officium." For an extended discussion of the history of the word *via* to translate the Greek *methodos*, see Neal Gilbert *Renaissance Concepts of Method* (New York: Columbia Univ. Press, 1960), pp. 48-55. Interestingly, as Gilbert notes, Boethius translates Aristotle's *methodos* not into the Ciceronian circumlocution, *via et ratio*, but rather into a Latin coinage, *methodus*. Compare the opening of Boethius' translation of the *Topica* (100a20) with that of an anonymous, twelfth-century translation (perhaps the work of James of Venice), both printed in L. Minio-Paluello, *Aristoteles Latinus*, vol. 5, *Topica* (Leiden: Brill, 1969):

Boethius	*Anonymous translator*
Propositum quidem negotii est methodum invenire a qua poterimus syllogizare de omni problemate ex probabilibus, et ipsi disputationem sustinentes nichil dicemus repugnans.	Propositum quidem negotii viam invenire a qua poterimus colligere de omni proposita questione ex probabilibus, et ipsi rationem reddentes nichil dicemus contrarium.

Gilbert notes that earlier readers found in the one text's use of *methodus* an indication of a later, non-Boethian authorship. Given the overriding textual evidence for Boethius' authorship of this text in Minio-Paluello's edition, I think the usage of *methodus* demonstrates the author's sensitivity to Aristotle's vocabulary. By clearly and deliberately avoiding the common latin expression with *via*, Boethius calls attention to the metaphor of the way etymologically buried in the Greek term (the *hodos* or "way"). Moreover, Boethius' own use of expressions with *via* in his other works further points to the importance of his coinage in the *Topica* translation, and his awareness of its Greek etymology. For the literary and philosophical origins of the Greek term, see Otfrid Becker, *Das Bild des Weges und verwandte Vorstellungen im frühgriechischen Denken* (Berlin: Hermes Einzelschriften, 1937), Heft 4, pp. 15-22.

[34] Stump, trans., p. 42; PL, 64: 1182D.

order of study is essential before reaching the end.[35] In the tractate *Utrum Pater*, too, the term *via* signals a certain methodological commitment to a mode of philosophical inquiry. Behind Philosophy's words lies the method developed by Aristotle, praised by Cicero, and developed by Boethius into the techniques of dialectical discovery.[36]

The prisoner, however, still has problems with method. He stubbornly adheres to the attitudes of a dialectician faced with a philosopher. Two examples from prosa 6 stand out. First, when asked about the governance of the universe, the prisoner can only reply: "I don't quite get the point of your question, so I am unable to answer."[37] Aristotle had permitted an answerer, when he did not understand, to say, "I do not understand." "He is not compelled to reply yes or no to a question which may mean different things."[38] When faced with another, directly philosophical question, however, the prisoner's reliance on dialectical rules becomes his undoing. Philosophy questions his knowledge of himself as a man, and asks: "Well then, what is a man? Can you give me a definition?"[39] The prisoner replies, "Do you mean that I am a rational animal, and mortal? I know that, and I admit that I

---

[35] See n. 15 for text.

[36] The principles of ordering form the heart of Aristotle's view of proper debate. Boethius' Latin pointedly brings this out: "Post haec autem de ordine, et quomodo oportet interrogare, dicendum. Oportet autem primum quidem interrogare eum qui debet locum invenire unde argumentandum, secundo autem interrogationes formare et ordinare singula ad se, reliquum vero et tertium dicere iam ea ad alterum" (*Topica*, VIII, 155b3-5). Cicero, in his own *Topica*, credits Aristotle with developing a system (*disciplina*) for discovering arguments ("inveniendorum argumentorum"), "ut sine ullo errore ad ea ratione et via perveniremus" (*Topica*, 2). In his commentary on this passage, Boethius notes that Cicero preserved Aristotle's system, "ut sine ullo errore ad argumentorum inventionem via quadam et recto filo atque artificio veniretur" (*In topica Ciceronis*, PL, 64: 1043A).

[37] Green, trans., p. 18. "Vix, inquam, rogationis tuae sententiam nosco, nedum ad inquisita respondere queam" (1.pr.6.8).

[38] *Topica*, 160a15.

[39] "Quid igitur homo sit poterisne proferre?" (1.pr.6.15); Green, trans., p. 19.

am such a creature."[40] The question "what is man" had become, by Boethius' time, one of the classic examples of definition in dialectic.[41] In his treatise *De Dialectica* Augustine
had quoted the definition as if it were a commonplace, and
in *De Magistro* Adeodatus voices a confusion similar to the
prisoner's over the meaning of *homo*.[42] Augustine is concerned
here with the idea of a noun (*nomen*) and the concept of sig-
nification. His pupil mistakes the word for the object, and
describes *a* man. In Boethius' own *De topicis differentiis*, the
definition is held up as a more complete response than "two
legged animal capable of walking," just as in *De Magistro*,
"animal rationale mortale" is considered the *tota definitio*. "The
question," Boethius writes in *De topicis*, "has to do with
definition."[43]

But Philosophy's question has little to do with definition.
As Courcelle realized, Philosophy does hearken back to an
Aristotelian mode of argument: "Voilà donc le prix que Philosophie attache aux définitions logiques, telles que celle d'Ar-
istote!"[44] The point is not merely, as Courcelle would have
it, that Philosophy calls attention to the spiritual inadequacy
of the prisoner's response, nor that, in this dialogue, the author of the *Consolation* reveals himself to be more than "un
simple logicien."[45] In failing to develop his answer philosophically (e.g., that man has an immortal soul), the prisoner
responds with a textbook answer; the idea of responding as

[40] Green, trans., p. 19. "Hocine interrogas, an esse me sciam rationale
animal atque mortale? Scio, et id me esse confiteor" (I.pr.6.15).

[41] For sources in Aristotle and Porphyry, see Gruber, *Kommentar*, pp. 155-
156.

[42] "Nam definitio hominis est 'animal rationale mortale' " (*De Dialectica*,
p. 110). The argument in *De Magistro* is at VIII.24.123-136.

[43] Stump, trans., p. 55. *De topicis differentiis*, PL, 64: 1191A: "Nam si est
hominis diffinitio, animal gressibile bipes, cum id minus videatur esse
diffinitio hominis, quam animal rationale mortale, sitque diffinitio hominis
ea quae dicit alias gressibile bipes, erit diffinitio hominis animal rationale
mortale. Quaestio de diffinitione."

[44] Courcelle, *Cons. Phil.*, p. 26.

[45] Courcelle, *Cons. Phil.*, p. 27.

a philosopher does not occur to him, and he remains trapped in a rudimentary habit of thought and expression. The scene has moral and methodological significance. In the context of Philosophy's own preparation for a technically accurate dialogue, the prisoner's response is another example of misdirecting his voice. As in the speech of prosa 4, he has misjudged his audience.

From silence, then, the prisoner has progressed through florid rhetoric to a limited dialectic. He offers only examples of speaking and writing gone wrong, where silence is not a virtue but a vice. In the succeeding books, Philosophy will guide his expression through rhetoric and dialectic, but she must also educate him in the ways of writing. At best, writing can become the natural process of the mind's independent investigation of truth. The problems of the tractates and of Augustine's *Soliloquia*, for example, testify to the thinker's need to write his thoughts. At its worst, however, writing becomes the unthinking reflex of a man with no words of his own.

II

Book Two, with its detailed presentation of Fortuna, has appealed to virtually all generations of the dialogue's readers. It is this character and her attendant images which have seemed the uniquely Boethian aspect of the *Consolation*. For the purposes of this study, however, I will show how the book explores the various ways through which Philosophy directs the prisoner's voice into rational argument. Her claims for the relativity of fame and the mutability of human speech develop the tractates' ideal of philosophical silence. Book Two explicitly raises the question of good and bad uses of rhetoric. In turn, Philosophy's remarks gradually delimit the effectiveness of the *artes* in the progress towards truth. The central poems of Book Two, little noticed by critics, give an historical reference to her views on language. In these sections, and in the concluding prosae, Boethius challenges Cicero's view of the civilizing function of oratory. He rewrites the Ciceronian fable of the state of nature found at *De Inventione*'s opening, and he questions the Roman's conviction that writing can be a force of social change and a source of knowledge about the past. At its close, Book Two returns to the problems of virtuous and vacuous writing and of speech and silence developed in Book One. By the opening of Book Three, Philosophy has prepared the prisoner to engage fully in dialogue by displaying the strengths and weaknesses of their method.

The book begins by commenting on the silence of Book One. About to speak, Philosophy is silent, and as she collects her thought, her quiet modesty does more to gain the prisoner's attention than any device of classical forensics. "Philosophy was silent for a while; then, regaining my attention by her modest reserve, she said. . . ."[46] Her initial refusal to speak (the word *obticuit*) recalls Boethius' silent withdrawal from the noisy Senate in *Contra Eutychen* (his word *conticui*). Both characters meditate in quiet before voicing their knowledge or understanding. Just as Boethius had, in the tractate, abandoned the fruitless oratory of the forum, so Philosophy, for the moment, relinquishes her rhetorical skills. Philosophy also compares favorably against the prisoner in Book One. In his speech at prosa 4, he began by "collecting" his strength of mind ("collecto in vires animo," 1.pr.4.2). Philosophy performs a similar activity as she *collegit* or "collects" her own thoughts and, in effect, draws in the prisoner's attention to her reflective processes.[47] The similarities of phrasing compare Philosophy's calm with the prisoner's bluster and contrast the ineffective use of rhetoric with the effective use of silence. Her quiet, unlike his, comes close to the ideal of tranquillity which grants the mind insight into itself and others.

The book's initial concern with forms of expression colors Philosophy's opening remarks. In her first speech she sum-

---

[46] Green, trans., p. 21. "Post haec paulisper obticuit atque ubi attentionem meam modesta taciturnitate collegit sic exorsa est" (II.pr.1.1).

[47] See the remarks of Gruber, *Kommentar*, p. 163.

marizes the prisoner's relationship to fortune in terms of language. Different kinds of fortune, she claims, engendered different kinds of verbal responses. When the prisoner experienced good luck, he would "attack her [i.e., Fortuna] with firm language and chase her with arguments produced from our very sanctuary."[48] Bad fortune, though, has stripped the prisoner of his command of wisdom and eloquence. Philosophy implies that his inner, mental disturbance creates an outer, verbal incapacity. His present silence comes not from calm tranquillity, but from agitated speechlessness.[49]

When Philosophy appeals to the persuasive power of rhetoric, she again uses the imagery of the "way" to characterize its methodological and moral effectiveness.

> I shall use the sweet persuasiveness of rhetoric, which can only proceed along the right path if it does not swerve away from our teachings, and if it harmonizes with the Music native to our halls, whose songs are sometimes happy and sometimes sad.[50]

The path rhetoric follows is dictated first by the pragmatic course of their argument, and second by a higher set of ethical principles. As Philosophy noted at the close of i.m.7, and as Boethius himself emphasized in Book Two of *De topicis*, there are right and wrong ways to proceed. Philosophy warns of swerving away from the path of reason and rational discourse. Diversion presents a threat to the prisoner's education and his successful completion of the dialogue. When she asserts that their rhetoric must be in harmony with the "Music native to

---

[48] "Solebas enim praesentem quoque, blandientem quoque uirilibus incessere uerbis eamque de nostro adyto prolatis insectabare sententiis" (ii.pr.1.5). I use here the translation of the Loeb editors because it brings out the verbal nature of the prisoner's response to Fortuna.

[49] "Verum omnis subita mutatio rerum non sine quodam quasi fluctu contingit animorum; sic factum est ut tu quoque paulisper a tua tranquillitate descisceres" (ii.pr.1.6).

[50] The translation is mine. "Adsit igitur rhetoricae suadela dulcedinis, quae tum tantum recta calle procedit cum nostra instituta non deserit cumque hac musica laris nostri uernacula nunc leuiores nunc grauiores modos succinat" (ii.pr.1.8).

our halls," she introduces a metaphor basic to the *Consolation*. *Musica vernacula* is a form of expression intrinsic to the subject. Unlike the music and the Muses of the prisoner's opening lament, it will be both comforting and meaningful. Like *De Trinitate*'s spark of intelligence, this native music comes from within. It somehow belongs to us and resides in us. Philosophy's repeated use of the possessive (*nostra instituta*; *nostri laris*) emphasizes the sense of place and belonging which is central to the prisoner's cure. At the opening of Book One he had forgotten who and where he was. Philosophy could not show him the way to the spiritual *patria* without first setting him in his own house.

Her attempt to bring the prisoner home begins by goading him into speech. She achieves her purpose by impersonating another character, Fortuna, for if the prisoner will not respond to Philosophy's voice, perhaps he will respond to another. In his first words since the aborted dialogue of Book One, the prisoner appears to recognize the sham of Fortuna's rhetoric. After her long speech, Philosophy steps out of her imaginary role and back into the prisoner's forensic world. If Fortuna defended herself in this way, she states, "you would be unable to answer her."[51] She now offers him a chance to speak: "dabimus dicendi locum." The *locus* is an opportunity, but it is also a place or topic. The word signals a technical vocabulary at work, and enables the prisoner to reply in what appear to be his own terms. The arguments of Fortuna, he states, have a "honeyed sweetness," and her words please the listener only as long as Fortuna speaks. With her silence, his grief returns.[52] While Philosophy's music held an inner sweetness, Fortuna's is sugar-coated. The prisoner's word (*dulcedinis*) echoes lexically and grammatically Philosophy's earlier term used to de-

[51] Green, trans., p. 25. "His igitur si pro se tecum Fortuna loqueretur, quid profecto contra hisceres non haberes" (II.pr.3.1).

[52] "Speciosa quidem ista sunt, inquam, oblitaque rhetoricae ac musicae melle dulcedinis tum tantum cum audiuntur oblectant, sed miseris malorum altior sensus est; itaque cum haec auribus insonare desierint insitus animum maeror praegrauat" (II.pr.3.2).

scribe her own rhetoric (*dulcedinis*). Boethius has one speaker repeat the words of another to demonstrate verbal ambiguity. The meaning of this word is bound by context and intention. The prisoner's recognition of the two kinds of sweetness is his first real insight of the *Consolation*. When he speaks, then, he initiates a process of discovery; yet he has little to say throughout the book, save for an occasional assent which in fact belies his own misunderstanding.[53] Philosophy herself recognizes that even these limited attempts at engagement signal the prisoner's new abilities, and her prose arguments, fortified with "stronger medicines" (ii.pr.5.1), may dispense with the dialogue format.

Rather than exploring Philosophy's arguments in detail, I think the reader may come to terms with Book Two's explorations of language by taking a cue from the opening of the book: Philosophy's own announcement of music and rhetoric pressed into the service of philosophical poetry. The middle poems of Book Two have appeared to most readers as straightforwardly simple restatements of the prose passages, with little of the appeal that distinguishes the great Timaean hymn, the poems on Orpheus or Hercules, or the complex epistemological verses of Book Five.[54] Yet metra 2-6 do reinforce the pervasive earthly quality of the arguments on fortune. Moreover, they challenge the principles of written literary history and the ideals of a civilizing rhetoric which Boethius inherited from Cicero. These poems use exquisite

---

[53] He speaks only at ii.pr.4.1-2 (to which Philosophy replies that he has misjudged his condition), and at ii.pr.7.1 (to which Philosophy answers that public service offers little lasting reward).

[54] See W. Wetherbee, *Platonism and Poetry in the Twelfth Century* (Princeton: Princeton Univ. Press, 1972), pp. 74-82. His remarks on the poetry of the opening books underlie much of my argument: ". . . the poetry, in which cosmological imagery is prominent, and the development of the moral argument in the *prosae* are not wholly congruent. The *metra* of the opening books stress the harmonious aspects of cosmic life, and convey the sense of an all-embracing *amor*, but are acutely sensitive also to disruptive forces, and seem at times to hint that man is somehow incapable of participating in the harmony of the universe" (p. 77).

naturalism as an allegorical matrix for the larger theme of mutability.

Metrum 3 reaffirms seasonal change, and it offers, in effect, an alternative view of nature to that expressed in i.m.6. In the earlier poem, the *ordo* of change was central: the apparently chaotic change of seasons is nonetheless planned and governed by God. In ii.m.3, it is the unalterable fact of change itself, and the violent contrast between earthly beauty and seasonal destruction, which are the poem's subject. The place of action is the earth and not the cosmos, as Philosophy reminds the reader that nothing born can last.[55] Metrum 4 describes the limits of human ingenuity. The wind and the sea not only challenge the stability of natural creations; they work against human creations as well. The poem asks for limits to human ambition: to walk among the rocks rather than the mountains.[56] Metrum 5 pictures a golden pre-technological age in which man had neither altered the course of nature nor impinged on the development of other, human societies.[57] Metrum 6 portrays the ineffectiveness of man's achievements faced with one man's rage.[58] All of these poems explore the precarious balance between natural forces and the human structures built to contain them. Read literally, they are about history and technology; read symbolically, they recreate a history of civilization whose ascents and descents parallel the prisoner's individual journey up and down fortune's wheel. As a chronicle of human civilization, the poems move from the most general to the most specific. First, man builds a house as a shelter against the elements (m.4). Then he lives in a golden age, before cultivation, dyeing, winemaking, navigation, trade, war, and colonization (m.5). Now, great cities rise and fall, and the specific allusion to Nero comes to represent a civilization gone mad.[59] The poems also explore var-

[55] ii.m.3.5-8.
[56] ii.m.4.1-8.
[57] ii.m.5.1-5.
[58] ii.m.6.1-7; 14-15.
[59] On Nero and his literary afterlife, see Gruber, *Kommentar*, p. 210.

ious modes of literary history: from pastoral, georgic, and lyric, the sequence leaves fiction behind to write the chronicle of an age.

If the poems are read as a sequence of historical narratives, one element remains conspicuous by its absence. Boethius is responding to the essentially Ciceronian view of the civilizing nature of oratory, and the uniting power of language; what is missing is any mention of the discovery of speech. To Cicero, man's primary achievement was language; reasoned eloquence set him apart from the beasts and formed men into communities. Only with prosa 7 does Philosophy come to terms with speech and writing as devices of civilization and history. While her discussion is ostensibly about fame, it is in fact concerned with the mutability of language and the futility of written records. Her remarks hearken back to the problems of Book One and the tractates, and they alert the reader to the *Consolation*'s reflexive concern with forms of expression.

The prisoner opens II.pr.7 by apologizing for his apparent pursuit of fame. His weak rejoinder contrasts with the rhetorical afflatus of his earlier defense in Book One, and the force of his latest remarks rests on a notion of unappreciated altruism.

> You know that ambition for material things has not mastered me; but I have desired the opportunity for public service so that my virtue should not grow old and weak through lack of use.[60]

---

[60] Green, trans., p. 37. "Scis, inquam, ipsa minimum nobis ambitionem mortalium rerum fuisse dominatam; sed materiam gerendis rebus optauimus quo ne uirtus tacita consenesceret" (II.pr.7.1). Boethius' language is somewhat confusing here. *Tacita* in the passage can function both as an adverb and as an adjective, and render the phrase both "virtue that keeps silent" (and thus grows old), and at the same time, "virtue that grows old silently." Here and elsewhere, I am indebted for the fine points of Boethius' Latin to the attentions of Prof. J. J. O'Donnell, and to his generosity in letting me see the manuscript of his forthcoming student's edition and commentary on the *Consolation* (Bryn Mawr Latin Texts, 1984).

Even in this modest excuse, the prisoner betrays a rhetorician's fear of silence. Whatever virtues he may have possessed found their expression in the Senate. His failure as a public man can be seen as a failure to move the public. When he therefore voices his fear that his powers might dissipate through or as a result of silence, he expresses a limited, earthly concern with speechlessness. The higher, meditative quiet of Augustine or the tractates, or even of Philosophy herself, is absent from his mind. He thus reveals his own entrapment in a limiting, human form of expression, while at the same time publicly arguing for his dismissal of worldly ambition.

In her following arguments, Philosophy gives a broader relevance to the prisoner's condition. Glory cannot be immortal, she argues, for it is bound by reputation, and reputation is bound simply by words. Language and culture present barriers to the world-wide spread of human fame.

> Then, too, this small inhabited area is occupied by many nations which differ in language, customs, and philosophy of life. Do you suppose that the fame of individual men, or even of cities, can reach nations so remote and different, nations with which there is very little contact?[61]

Philosophy goes on to report that, in the time of Cicero, the fame of the republic had not extended beyond the Caucasus, and mention of the Roman signals the context for Boethius' arguments.[62] Cicero's claims that eloquence wisely used brings people together, fosters social mores, and establishes political unity stand behind Philosophy's rebuttal of human fame. The fable of man in the state of nature which opens *De Inventione* posits a world in which men lived as savages until

---

[61] Green, trans., p. 37. "Adde quod hoc ipsum breuis habitaculi saeptum plures incolunt nationes lingua, moribus, totius uitae ratione distantes, ad quas tum difficultate itinerum tum loquendi diuersitate tum commercii insolentia non modo fama hominum singulorum sed ne urbium quidem peruenire queat" (II.pr.7.7).

[62] "Aetate denique M. Tullii, sicut ipse quodam loco significat, nondum Caucasum montem Romanae rei publicae fama transcenderat et erat tunc adulta Parthis etiam ceterisque id locorum gentibus formidolosa" (II.pr.7.8).

a great and wise man brought them together into an audience for his rhetoric, and in turn, into a community of civic life.[63] Philosophy points out that language does not bring men together, except in very small groups. Rather, it separates them into mutually incomprehending neighbors. Her phrasing for the diversity of language (*loquendi diversitate*) also echoes Augustine, who had written in the *City of God*: "linguarum diversitas hominem alienat ab homine."[64] Language alienates man from man, and written records, as Philosophy will argue, serve only to alienate man from his past.

While the prisoner had offered to preserve his case for future readers (I.pr.4), Philosophy asserts, "Many men who were famous during their lifetime are now forgotten because no one wrote about them. But even written records are of limited value since the long passage of time veils them and their authors in obscurity."[65] Written records, like speech itself, have a limited spatial and temporal effect. The inscribed word cannot preserve a name for all eternity, she argues, and the prisoner's earlier claims now appear not only wrongheaded, but vain. "When you think about future fame, you imagine that you assure yourselves a kind of immortality. But, if you consider the infinite extent of eternity, what satisfaction can you have about the power of your name to endure?"[66] Philosophy's suspicion of the power of the written word again recalls Cicero's view of writing as a social force, and of the written record as a source of knowledge about the past. At the opening of *De Inventione* Cicero reports how he began "to search in the records of literature for events which oc-

[63] *De Inventione*, 1.2-4.

[64] *City of God*, XIX.7, quoted in Gruber, *Kommentar*, p. 215.

[65] Green, trans., p. 38. "Sed quam multos clarissimos suis temporibus uiros scriptorum inops deleuit obliuio! Quamquam quid ipsa scripta proficiant, quae cum suis auctoribus premit longior atque obscura uetustas?" (II.7.13.)

[66] Green, trans., p. 38. "Vos uero immortalitatem uobis propagare uidemini cum futuri famam temporis cogitatis. Quod si ad aeternitatis infinita spatia pertractes, quid habes quod de nominis tui diuturnitate laeteris?" (II.pr.7.14-15.)

curred before the period which our generation can remember."[67] Historical writing served as a repository of public memory; it substituted for the oral mnemonics of an earlier era. Throughout his later dialogues, Cicero repeated a concern for the power of the written word. It recorded historical acts, as in *De Inventione*. In *De finibus* writing preserved Greek and Latin masterpieces for contemporary edification and imitation.[68] In the *Tusculan Disputations* Plato's philosophical dialogues were themselves written documents. They preserved the structure of Socratic inquiry, and provided the models for Cicero's own essays in the form.[69]

But it would appear to Philosophy that letters are not a blessing but a curse. They do not preserve the truth for the future, but merely ossify the past in obscurity. In the course of her polemic, Philosophy retells a famous story about philosophical silence to illustrate the limits of the prisoner's understanding and, more importantly, the difficulties she herself will confront in trying to put thoughts into words. When the bogus philosopher of the story—after quietly enduring his challenger's insults—replies, "Now do you think I am a philosopher?" his taunter answers, "I would have thought so, if you had kept silent."[70] This ideal philosophical silence is a commonplace of Ancient thought, given a new resonance in

---

[67] *De Inventione*, I.i.1: ". . . cum autem res ab nostra memoria propter vetustatem remotas ex litterarum monumentis repetere instituo, multas urbes constitutas, plurima bella restincta, firmissimas societates, sanctissmas amicitias intellego cum animi ratione tum facilius eloquentia comparatas."

[68] *De finibus*, I.iii.10: "Quando enim nobis, vel dicam aut oratoribus bonis aut poetis, postea quidem quam fuit quem imitarentur, ullus orationis vel copiosae vel elegantis ornatus defuit?"

[69] *Tusc. Disp.*, v.iv.11: ". . . cuius multiplex ratio disputandi rerumque varietas et ingenii magnitudo, Platonis memoria et litteris consecrata, plura genera effecit dissentientium philosophorum, e quibus nos id potissimum consecuti sumus, quo Socratem usum aribitrabamur. . . ."

[70] Green, trans., p. 39. " 'Iam tandem,' inquit, 'intellegis me esse philosophum?' Tum ille nimium mordaciter: 'Intellexeram,' inquit, 'si tacuisses' " (II.pr.7.20). For the background to this anecdote, see Gruber, *Kommentar*, p. 219.

Boethius' larger context of speaking and writing. The story serves to highlight the prisoner's early reliance on faulty rhetoric directed at a foolish audience. As Philosophy reminds him: "You . . . know how to act justly only when you have the support of popular opinion and empty rumor."[71] For now, the alternative to vulgar chatter is philosophical silence. As Boethius illustrated in the preface to *Contra Eutychen*, the philosopher must remove himself physically and verbally from the crowd.

This imagery reinforces the commonly noticed visions of exile and loneliness throughout the *Consolation*.[72] It gives a new immediacy, and a new accessibility, to the complex Platonic idea of the soul trapped in the body and of the Neoplatonic notion of earthly life as a kind of banishment.[73] Furthermore, these images give a stark loneliness to Philosophy's history of the world in the poetry of Book Two. The apparently civilizing discovery of building sets man in embattled isolation from Nature. Even the vision of the golden age is a vision of alienation: "Nondum maris alta secabat / nec mercibus undique lectis / noua litora uiderat hospes" (II.m.5.13-15). Men were content with their own shores and did not seek to become strangers in new lands. In her prose arguments, Philosophy reinforces the linguistic imagery with which she expresses human isolation. Languages separate man from his neighbors and distance him from his ancestors. Speech, rather than making him part of a community, makes him an exile in his own world and from his own past. In

[71] Green, trans., p. 78, and further, "you are not satisfied with the assurance of conscience and virtue but seek your reward in the hollow praise of other men." The whole section reads: "Vos autem nisi ad populares auras inanesque rumores recte facere nescitis et relicta conscientiae uirtutisque praestantia de alienis praemia sermunculis postulatis" (II.pr.7.19).

[72] See, for example, Schmidt-Kohl, pp. 26-28, on the soul as stranger on earth and the philosophical background to the idea.

[73] See the sources cited in Schmidt-Kohl, pp. 26-28, and the discussions in P. Courcelle, "L'âme en cage," in K. Flasch, ed., *Parusia* (Frankfurt-am-Main: Minerva, 1965), pp. 103-116; and Michael Murrin, *The Allegorical Epic* (Chicago: Univ. of Chicago Press, 1980), pp. 31-32, and notes, pp. 214-215.

metrum 7 Philosophy takes up these themes and restates the transitory quality of human language along with the mutability of writing.

> Where now are the bones of faithful Fabricius? What has become of Brutus and stern Cato? Their slight surviving fame entrusts their empty names to some few books. But, although we know these fair words, we cannot know the dead. Then lie there, quite unknown, for fame will not keep fresh your memory.[74]

Unlike Cicero, who would find companionship in Antique writers, Philosophy can only ask, "Do we really know the dead?" It is this characteristic of language to make something limited, or transitory, which hinders Philosophy's exposition of her doctrine.

In her final prose statement of Book Two Philosophy questions the very vehicle of their dialogue. She expresses some trepidation at using a purely philosophical language, a language which makes no concessions to common opinion or to apparent credibility. How can the prisoner understand her thoughts when words constrain her arguments? "But perhaps you do not understand what I mean."[75] She attempts to convey to him the wonderful paradox of the benefits of bad fortune, and she fears that, argued straightforwardly, her idea will fall beyond the prisoner's grasp: "What I am about to say is so strange that I scarcely know how to make my meaning clear."[76] At issue here is the inability of *verba* to contain

[74] Green, trans., pp. 39-40. "Vbi nunc fidelis ossa Fabricii manent, / quid Brutus aut rigidus Cato? / Signat superstes fama tenuis pauculis / inane nomen litteris. / Sed quod decora nouimus uocabula / num scire consumptos datur? / Iacetis ergo prorsus ignorabiles / nec fama notos efficit" (II.m.7.15-22).

[75] Green, trans., p. 40. "Nondum forte quid loquar intellegis" (II.pr.8.2). In *De topicis differentiis*, Boethius considers philosophical discourse as concerned with necessary, but not readily believable truths (see Stump, trans., pp. 40-1; PL, 64: 1181B-C). See also Boethius' definition of a philosopher: "Philosophus vero ac demonstrator de sola tantum veritate pertractat, atque sint probabilia sive non sint, nihil refert, dummodo sint necessaria" (PL, 64: 1182A; see Stump, trans., p. 41).

[76] Green, trans., p. 40. "mirum est quod dicere gestio, eoque sententiam uerbis explicare uix queo" (II.pr.8.2).

sententia, and of rational argument (*explicatio*) to express marvels. Up to now she has avoided the problem by relying on "milder medicines"—namely, rhetoric and poetry—whose purpose was to soothe rather than to convince. But at this point she creates in the prisoner the expectation of understanding, and stimulates his reason and his voice.

By the opening of Book Three, still in silence, the prisoner finds a voice which can successfully initiate dialogue. The sweetness of Philosophy's last poem leaves him in expectant, attentive silence. For the first time in the *Consolation* it is the prisoner who willingly breaks a silence without waiting for Philosophy's goad. His opening exclamation, "O," set off from the rest of the sentence by an intrusive *inquam*, calls attention to the prisoner's vocal ability. He utters at first not a word but a non-verbal exclamation of joy. The long *O* of Philosophy's concluding verses, "O felix hominum genus" (II.m.8.28) must still ring in his ears as he echoes sound for sound.

But, for all his eagerness, the prisoner fails to make an open commitment to participating in the dialogue. He wishes only to be a listener, even though this silence will be more virtuous than that of the previous books. Philosophy herself notices this new quiet ("I knew it when I saw you so engrossed, silent, and attentive"),[77] and she makes an attempt to describe familiar matters as a kind of propaedeutic to more difficult issues. She will try to point out in words—*designare verbis*—"something you know much more about."[78] Her phrasing recalls her earlier inability to *verbis explicare*; but now she will deal not in marvels but in commonplaces, not with the goals of their inquiry but rather with its method. By explaining how they will proceed, Philosophy shows how the dialogue will move through human issues towards divine ones. Her

[77] Green, trans., p. 42, modified by me. "Sensi, inquit, cum uerba nostra tacitus attentusque rapiebas . . ." (III.pr.1.3).

[78] Green, trans., p. 42. "Faciam, inquit illa, tui causa libenter; sed quae tibi causa notior est, eam prius designare uerbis atque informare conabor . . ." (III.pr.1.7).

remarks embody that sense of the *gradus* found at the *Consolation*'s beginning and in Boethius' writing on the topics: a moral and methodological rectitude which guides the *via rationis*.

From this point onward, the prisoner's silence is no longer the speechlessness of the opening. When he fails to answer Philosophy's question, or accedes to her authority, he appears simply as an incompetent student or a faltering dialectician rather than as a man stripped of language. Finally, when his own presence disappears from the dialogue altogether at the end of Book Five, he will move closer to the higher form of philosophical silence which demands no company save the self and God. The *Consolation*'s beginning, however, marks only the initial search for a voice. The prisoner's character is less a physical presence than a verbal one, and to change his character Philosophy must direct his speech. By using the images and metaphors of writing and speaking developed in his technical and theological works, Boethius gives the *Consolation*'s beginning a firm place in the development of his literary career. By responding to Augustine's notions of a rhetoric of silence and to Cicero's views of oratory, he gives his work a place in the history of ideas. In their meditations on the written word, Cicero and the Saint provide the vocabulary for Boethius' own reflections on language and silence in society, and their texts will stand as landmarks against which to measure the prisoner's progress in Book Three.

CHAPTER III

LANGUAGE AND LOSS IN
BOOK THREE

The third book of the *Consolation* is perhaps the most philosophically rewarding and the most methodologically subtle
of all the dialogue's sections. Containing the great Timean
hymn (m.9), the long discourse on earthly goods (pr.3-9), the
intricate Platonic arguments of prosa 12, and the enigmatic
poem on Orpheus (m.12), the book challenges the prisoner's
expressive and interpretive abilities. It is little wonder that the
book has stimulated more criticism than any other part of the
Consolation. Most readers have found in it the heart of Boethius' Platonic thought and imagery.[1] Structurally, the book
has traditionally been seen as dividing itself, and in turn the
work as a whole, in two. While the first section (prosae 1-9)
appears to continue the Aristotelian dialectic of Books One
and Two, the second section (metrum 9 to the end) points
towards an explicitly Platonic epistemology.[2] This Platonism
may inform the concluding poem on Orpheus, as the hell-
descent it portrays carries with it a mass of Platonic and Neoplatonic allegorical implications.[3] The function of the metra

[1] See Karl Büchner, "Bemerkungen zum dritten Buch der Consolatio Philosophiae des Boethius," *Historisches Jahrbuch* 62-69 (1949), 33; Winthrop
Wetherbee, *Platonism and Poetry*, p. 76. More general approaches to the
Book's Platonism include F. Klingner, *De Boetii Consolatione Philosophiae*,
pp. 23-84; Courcelle, *Late Latin Writers*, pp. 295-318.

[2] See Gruber, *Kommentar*, p. 272; Courcelle, *La Cons. Phil.*, p. 161.

[3] To Klingner, the poem on Orpheus restates the allegory of the cave in
the *Republic* (p. 75). Courcelle considers Klingner's essay exaggerated in its
view of the Platonism of the Book as a whole, and this is but one example
he cites (*La Cons. Phil.*, p. 161).

themselves has also been understood as changing in the course
of the book. From what one critic has called "a larger dialogue
between rational argumentation and poetry," the poetry after
"O qui perpetua" seems "relegated to the role of a moralizing
chorus."[4]

My reading of Book Three qualifies and takes issue with
these earlier approaches. The opening prosae develop the relationship between dialectical and philosophical forms of argument explored in earlier books. The speakers come to talk
more and more about the structure of their dialogue itself.
Their discussion becomes self-reflexive, in that it is fundamentally concerned with elucidating its own method. It also
becomes self-referring, in that key terms presume the reader's
familiarity with their use elsewhere in Boethius' writings. I
will explore these qualities by finding the sources for the
Consolation's language in the technical vocabulary of the logical writings. Boethius' remarks on the relationship of probable logic to philosophical demonstration highlight one aspect
of Philosophy's conversation with the prisoner. While she
relies on proofs, he is content with opinions; while she addresses his mind, he responds through his senses. This tension
motivates the text's dramatic progress, and Boethius' constant
Platonizing of the dialectical terminology gives the discussion
an added dimension.

If the *Consolation*'s opening books represent the search for
a voice through which the prisoner may learn to argue, then
Book Three may be said to portray the search for a place
towards which he must direct his energies. That place has
been interpreted as the soul's home in the heavens, the *patria*
towards which the mind returns after death. The prisoner's
position thus places him in a state of loss or unfulfillment.
He lacks the awareness of his future spiritual goal and a present
intellectual direction. Philosophy's purpose in Book Three
will involve directing his mind (metaphorically described as
looking upwards) and developing his reason (methodologi-

---

[4] Wetherbee, *Platonism and Poetry*, p. 78.

cally depicted as learning how to argue). Images of loss, be they of purpose, direction, or meaning, permeate the book, from Philosophy's opening arguments on happiness, to the final poem on Orpheus' loss of Eurydice. As Philosophy herself puts it, the prisoner is menaced by psychological disturbances which create in him a feeling of emptiness or absence. Human desire, she argues, is motivated through an inner need to fill that absence with a spiritual beatitude. The longing for fulfillment or knowledge leaves man dependent on such earthly substitutes as wealth, fame, power, or sensory pleasure. These "external" ways to happiness are but by-paths on the path to the true good. Fulfillment will be gained, she argues, through self-sufficiency: through strength of mind and growth of spirit.

To this end, Book Three explores images of alienation and of the undeniable otherness which sets the self apart from the multitude. If the movement of the opening books was methodological, then in Book Three it is epistemological. The prisoner must come to know and to comprehend that process of knowing. In this sense, the book develops a vocabulary of wonder, both in the prose and the poetry. While Philosophy's arguments are calculated to eliminate admiration and foster comprehension, her poetry, especially the Timean hymn, is designed to inspire awe. Her poems turn nature into myth, for they figure forth the physical or psychological processes in literary narratives. Her poetry also contributes to the intellectual progress of the dialogue, embodying through its rhetoric and imagery the underlying order of rational inquiry.

Book Three is also the most obviously rhetorical of the *Consolation*'s sections, for in it Boethius uses structures of form and imagery to call attention to his thematic concern with technique. It offers a counterpoint to the "rhetoric of silence" explored in the Augustinianism of the tractates, and it presents a more rigorous system of argument than the forensics of Book One. Close examination of the formal structures of metra 2, 9, and 12 reveals how Philosophy presents herself not only as a model disputant, but as a model poet and musician. Through these devices, her poetry directs the prisoner's mind away from his earthly cares and towards the inspired meditation of the kind Boethius experienced in the *Contra Eutychen*. By filling the prisoner with a sense of wonder, she restores his emotional stability and points towards spiritual enlightenment.

I

After her initial commitment to describe in words the subjects familiar to the prisoner, Philosophy begins her extended analysis of human happiness in prosa 2. Like Boethius' own meditative process described in *Contra Eutychen*, Philosophy prepares for her speech by directing her vision and her voice away from external distractions and towards her own thoughts.[5] As in the tractate, the process of introspection appears in visual terms. Boethius was concerned with watching Symmachus, and with seeking to discover in his expression a source for his opinions.[6] Similarly, throughout the *Consolation*, the prisoner pays careful attention to Philosophy's countenance, from her opening look which fills him with awe (I.I.I) and her blazing eyes, to the gravity of her appearance at the opening of Book Four (IV.I.I).[7] The movement of turning away from or towards something becomes the central image of Boethian meditation (as when he turns away from the mob in *Contra Eutychen*), and it informs Philosophy's own

[5] "Tum defixo paululum uisu et uelut in augustam suae mentis sedem recepta sic coepit" (III.pr.2.I).

[6] ". . . ne si aegerrime quidem cuperem, uultum nutumque eius aspicere poteram ex quo mihi aliqua eius darentur signa iudicii" (*Contra Eutychen*, p. 74).

[7] I.I.I: ". . . astitisse mihi supra uerticem uisa est mulier reuerendi admodum uultus, oculis ardentibus et ultra communem hominum ualentiam perspicacibus, colore uiuido atque inexhausti uigoris. . . ." I.I.7: "Quae ubi poeticas Musas uidit nostro assistentes toro fletibusque meis uerba dictantes, commota paulisper ac toruis inflammata luminibus." IV.I.I: "Haec cum Philosophia dignitate uultus et oris grauitate seruata leniter suauiterque cecinisset. . . ."

injunction at the opening of Book Three for the prisoner to turn his eyes towards blessedness.[8] Moreover, Philosophy's appearance contrasts with the fallen look of the prisoner at the dialogue's beginning.[9] Just as she had sought to see into the prisoner's mind ("tuae mentis sedem requiro," I.pr.5.6), now Boethius echoes her own words in describing her thoughtful countenance (". . . suae mentis sedem recepta," III.pr.2.1). Her inward preparation for rational argument also recalls the prisoner's misguided attempt to shape his own arguments before his oratorical outburst at I.pr.4.[10]

In this manner, Boethius uses one of the *Consolation*'s prevalent metaphors to characterize Philosophy's intellectual virtue. From a purely technical standpoint, however, Philosophy's initial moves also correspond to the mental activity prescribed for a debater in Aristotle's *Topica*. Aristotle had outlined a three-step process for formulating and expressing an argument. First, the questioner must select the basis of the approach; second, he must frame and arrange his points in his own mind; finally, he must proceed to verbalize his argument to his partner.[11] Philosophy's preparation describes her as a textbook disputant, where the order of the argument corresponds to the ordering of thoughts. Her behavior also conforms to Aristotle's suggested habits of philosophical inquiry. While both dialecticians and philosophers, he wrote, start from the same tripartite system of inquiry, the philosopher may prefer to begin questioning with familiar axioms, and his initial argumentative moves may seem to progress

---

[8] "sed quae tibi causa notior est, eam prius designare uerbis atque informare conabor, ut ea perspecta cum in contrariam partem flexeris oculos uerae specimen beatitudinis possis agnoscere" (III.pr.1.7).

[9] I.pr.1.13.

[10] "Tum ego collecto in uires animo" (I.pr.4.2).

[11] In Boethius' Latin, the opening of *Topica*, viii reads: "Post haec autem de ordine, et quomodo oportet interrogare, dicendum. Oportet autem primum quidem interrogare eum qui debet locum invenire unde argumentandum, secundo autem interrogationes formare et ordinare singula ad se, relinquum vero et tertium dicere iam ea ad alterum." From L. Minio-Paluello, ed., *Aristoteles Latinus, V, Topica* (Leiden: Brill, 1969), p. 156 (153b3-7).

little from the given starting point.[12] When Philosophy decides, therefore, to present in words things better known to the prisoner, she commits herself to a method of inquiry consonant with the Aristotelian rules for reasoned investigation. It is from this commitment to begin with familiar subjects that, as Aristotle claimed, syllogistic reasoning grows (in the Boethian translation, "ex his enim disciplinales syllogismi," Minio-Paluello, p. 156).

It is significant that Philosophy speaks metaphorically in her opening remarks, and that her images are securely grounded in the vocabulary of direction developed in Boethius' logical writings. In the *In Topica Ciceronis* Boethius credited Cicero with preserving Aristotle's method for finding arguments directly and without error.[13] His own *De topicis differentiis* had developed the image of argument as a way through error into a controlling ethos of study.[14] When Philosophy comes to characterize the human and cosmic order, she draws upon a dialectical vocabulary to make her concepts understandable to the prisoner. Her repetitions reinforce the sense of direction which returns the mind to its proper home.

[12] The text, again in Boethius' Latin, reads: "Ergo donec inveniat locum similiter philosophi et dialectici consideratio, iam vero haec ordinare et interrogare proprium dialectici; ad alterum enim quod huiusmodi est; philosopho autem et quaerenti per se nichil pertinet, si vera quidem sint et nota per quae syllogismus, non ponat autem ea qui respondet eo quod propinqua sint eorum quae ex principio et praevideat quod accidere est; sed fortasse et festinabit quoniam maxime notae et propinquae sunt maximae propositiones" (Minio-Paluello, p. 156; *Topica*, 155b7-16).

[13] PL, 64: 1043A: ". . . ut sine ullo errore ad argumentorum inventionem via quadam et recto filo atque artificio veniretur," commenting on this passage in Cicero: "quam cum tibi exposuissem, disciplinam inveniendorum argumentorum, ut sine ullo errore ad ea ratione et via perveniremus, ab Aristotele inventam illis libris contineri" (Cicero, *Topica*, 2).

[14] See, for example, his remarks at the end of Book I, that the study of the topics points debaters to the path of truth ("viam quodammodo veritatis illustrat"), and that such study promised the paths of discovery ("inveniendi vias") (PL, 64: 1182C-D). See, too, the opening remarks at Book II of *De topicis* concerning the proper order and *gradus* of study.

Mortal men laboriously pursue many different interests along many different paths, but all strive to reach the same goal of happiness. . . . And, as I said, all men try by various paths to attain this state of happiness; for there is naturally implanted in the minds of men the desire for the true good, even though foolish error draws them toward false goods.[15]

In the course of her speech, Philosophy speaks more and more figuratively, developing her metaphors and similes into codes of behavior. She employs the imagery of vision to place before his eyes the range of human happiness.[16] In a simile which recalls the picture of the wandering ignorant or the fickleness of fortune, she explains how the mind no longer knows the good, "like the drunken man who cannot find his way home."[17] The symbolic drunkenness of the mind lost in sensory error contrasts with Philosophy's earlier claims for the sobriety of prudent caution.[18] Boethius has built these figures from the language of dialectic, and he equates propriety of speech and thought with propriety of action. The strong moral sense of error is also figuratively transformed into a kind of incompleteness. The prisoner lacks a sense of home (a *domus* or *patria*), and his spiritual error creates a psychological condition of insufficiency or emptiness.[19]

[15] Green, trans., p. 43, slightly modified by me. "Omnis mortalium cura quam multiplicium studiorum labor exercet *diuerso* quidem *calle procedit*, sed ad unum tamen beatitudinis finem nititur *peruenire*. . . . Hunc, uti diximus, *diuerso tramite* mortales omnes conantur adipisci; est enim mentibus hominum ueri boni naturaliter inserta cupiditas, sed ad falsa deuius *error* abducit" (III.pr.2.2,4, emphases added).

[16] "Habes igitur ante oculos propositam fere formam felicitatis humanae" (III.pr.2.12).

[17] ". . . quorum animus etsi caligante memoria tamen bonum suum repetit, sed uelut ebrius domum quo tramite reuertatur ignorat" (III.pr.2.13). Compare, I.pr.3.12: "Quorum quidem tametsi est numerosus exercitus spernendus tamen est, quoniam nullo duce regitur sed errore tantum temere ac passim lymphante raptatur."

[18] "itaque illam uideas uentosam fluentem suique semper ignaram, hanc sobriam succinctamque et ipsius aduersitatis exercitatione prudentem" (II.pr.8.4).

[19] Throughout the *Consolation*, *patria* refers to the spiritual home—the place

To this end, Philosophy, in her next prosa, questions the prisoner about his emotional condition. To his realization that at no time could he recall being free of worry, she asserts: "And wasn't it because you wanted something you did not have, or had something you did not want?" ("Nonne quia uel aberat quod abesse non uelles uel aderat quod adesse noluisses?")[20] Her questioning establishes a tension between wanting and having, reinforced by the rhetorical pattern of her speech. She arranges her words chiastically, with parallel sequences: *aderat / adesse* answers *aberat / abesse*. At the heart of the prisoner's misery is a deep void, expressed as a lack of direction and fulfillment. To Philosophy, the action of desire becomes a longing to fill that emptiness: "So you desired the presence of the one, and the absence of the other?"[21] As her argument develops, she delineates the relationship between the outer show of language, cheapened by time, and inner virtue. In characterizing the prisoner's condition of desire, she shows how such external qualities as language, wealth, power, and glory serve only to alienate man from man: to render him parasitic on the world rather than sufficient in himself. Fame, as she argued in Book Two, does not eliminate desire, it intensifies it. The fear of loss motivates worldly achievement, as the man enamored of earthly goods obsessively tries to guard them against theft. This activity, compounded by an equally compulsive appetite for personal ownership, creates insatiable need.[22]

In formulating Philosophy's arguments, Boethius draws on his own view of the individual's relationship to the mob ex-

---

in the heavens towards which the soul aspires—whereas *domus* refers to the physical house in which a man lives on earth. Yet, *domus* also signals, figuratively, the spiritual home, as in III.pr.2.13, and in IV.m.1.9-10, describing the soul's upward passage: "donec in astriferas surgat domos / Phoeboque coniungat uias."

[20] Green, trans., p. 47. III.pr.3.7.

[21] Here, I favor the literalism of the Loeb translators, p. 241. "Illius igitur praesentiam, huius absentiam desiderabas?" (III.pr.3.8.)

[22] ". . . auaritiae nihil satis est" (III.pr.3.19).

pressed in *Contra Eutychen* and adumbrated in the asides in his commentaries. His repeated use of the word *aliena* reinforces the split between the self and the other. Throughout the *Consolation* the word describes those external goods which, by directing man towards others, alienate him from himself.[23] The language of the mob also appears in these terms. Like rumor and popularity, the common speech of men is vapid and meaningless, rendering man passively subject to a corrupting force.[24] In Book Three Philosophy shows how public reputation and nobility depend on the perception of others.[25] Like fame, nobility brings man into the confusion of other men,[26] and the fame of others cannot redound to oneself.[27] Together, these images restate the fundamental emptiness of fame and the vacuity of power.[28]

Into this structure of imagery, Philosophy introduces the word *extrinsecus* to characterize spiritual and rational insufficiency. With its source in Cicero's and Boethius' dialectical writings, the word signals a discipline where belief takes precedence over truth. Because dialectic aims to convince, rather than demonstrate, it can employ *extrinseca argumenta* which depend on the authority of others for their credibility to the

[23] For the frequency with which forms of *aliena* appear in the text, see L. Cooper, *Concordance of Boethius*, pp. 17-18. See, e.g., this remark: "Quid inanibus gaudiis raperis, quid externa bona pro tuis amplexaris? Numquam tua faciet esse fortuna quae a te natura rerum fecit aliena" (II.pr.5.14). Compare, III.pr.9.5: "nam si quid est quod in ulla re imbecillioris ualentiae sit, in hac praesidio necesse est egeat alieno."

[24] "Vos autem nisi ad populares auras inanesque rumores recte facere nescitis et relicta conscientiae uirtutisque praestantia de alienis praemia sermunculis postulatis" (II.pr.7.19).

[25] "Plures enim magnum saepe nomen falsis uulgi opinionibus abstulerunt" (III.pr.6.2).

[26] "Quae si ad claritudinem refertur, aliena est" (III.pr.6.7).

[27] "quare splendidum te, si tuam non habes, aliena claritudo non efficit" (III.pr.6.8).

[28] See, too, this passage: "Iam uero quam sit inane, quam futtile nobilitatis nomen, quis non uideat?" (III.pr.6.7.) On the emptiness of titles, see II.m.7.17-18, and III.pr.4.15.

listener.[29] In *De topicis differentiis* Boethius classes arguments from judgment under the heading of *extrinsecus*, and he clarifies their difference from philosophical demonstration.

> There remains the Topic which he [i.e., Cicero] said is taken from without (*extrinsecus assumi*). This depends on judgment and authority and is only readily believable, containing nothing necessary.[30]

In the dialectical writings, *extrinsecus* is a term used to characterize an argument which derives its strength from outside opinion. In other writings, it is used metaphorically, to describe accidental qualities (as in *De Trinitate*)[31] or, in the *Consolation* itself, to refer to the power of God or the power of reasoning. God's grace is not received from outside, but is unique to and part of his nature.[32] Unlike the transitory, extrinsic things of this world—which depend on perception for their value—God needs no outside assistance in governing the Universe.[33] He remains the uniquely self-sufficient being of the cosmos.[34] Towards the end of Book Three, the prisoner

[29] Cicero, *Topica*, 24: "Quae autem assumuntur extrinsecus, ea maxime ex auctoritate ducuntur."

[30] Stump, trans., p. 70. PL, 64: 1199C: "Restat is locus quem extrinsecus dixit assumi, hic judicio nititur et auctoritate, et totus probabilis est, nihil continens necessarium."

[31] See *De Trinitate*, v, p. 26: "Quae quoniam sublato deperit servo, constat non eam per se domino accidere sed per servorum quodam modo extrinsecus accessum." See, too, the earlier phrasing, "Quod aliae quidem quasi rem monstrant aliae vero quasi circumstantias rei; quodque illa quae ita praedicantur, ut esse aliquid rem ostendant, illa vero ut non esse, sed potius extrinsecus aliquid quodam modo affigant" (p. 24).

[32] At III.pr.10.12-13 Philosophy states: "Ne hunc rerum omnium patrem illud summum bonum quo plenus esse perhibetur uel extrinsecus accepisse uel ita naturaliter habere praesumas quasi habentis dei habitaeque beatitudinis diuersam cogites esse substantiam. Nam si extrinsecus acceptum putes, praestantius id quod dederit ab eo quod acceperit existimare possis."

[33] See, e.g., III.pr.3.14: "Egebit igitur, inquit, extrinsecus petito praesidio quo suam pecuniam quisque tueatur."

[34] "Et ad mundum igitur, inquit, regendum nullis extrinsecus amminiculis indigebit; alioquin si quo egeat, plenam sufficientiam non habebit" (III.pr.12.11).

begins to recognize the structure of philosophical arguments in these terms, and he commends his partner: "And you proved all this without outside assumptions (*nullis extrinsecus sumptis*) and used only internal proofs which draw their force from one another."[35] Central to his praise is his characterization of Philosophy as a philosopher; he virtually echoes his own earlier definition of *De topicis differentiis*, and reveals that, by the conclusion of Book Three, he has learned something of method, if not of doctrine. The imagery here is not designed to suggest, as some have claimed, that the prisoner praises Philosophy for arguing without need of outside, *Christian* arguments. It is specifically couched in the language of the logical writings, and it contributes to the larger structure of imagery which to this point has focused on interiority, propriety, and self-sufficiency.[36]

II

Before the prisoner can recognize Philosophy's method for what it is, and long before he can attempt to imitate it, he must engage his teacher's arguments and learn to respond rationally. He has said nothing from the middle of prosa 3 to the beginning of prosa 9. When he begins to speak again, it is through a rhetoric of simple assents which reveal his apparent impatience with Philosophy's method and his lack of commitment to the proper order of inquiry. The concluding prosae of Book Three create the context for reflection and interpretation, as they continually take stock of the dialogue's progress. These prosae also develop the imagery of wonder

[35] Green, trans., p. 73. "Atque haec nullis extrinsecus sumptis, sed ex altero altero fidem trahente insitis domesticisque probationibus explicabas" (III.pr.12.35).

[36] The impression of logical completeness is intimately linked to the imagery of belonging which Philosophy used in describing the proper uses of rhetoric and music. The right method, like the right music, must be native: "domestic" at III.pr.12.35; "vernacular" at II.pr.1.8. See, too, the phrasing at v.pr.4.13, where Philosophy restates the goals of her method in the same terms Boethius anticipates in Book Three (see the discussion of this section in Chapter 5).

which Philosophy had earlier used to describe the inability to express divine wisdom in human terms. For verbal discussion to progress, she must eliminate the sense of wonder in the prisoner, a wonder which had kept him in silent awe of Philosophy's implied truths. In the *Contra Eutychen* Boethius had marvelled at the truth revealed through private meditation ("unde mihi maxime subiit admirari . . . ," p. 74). This emotional response resulted from the figurative opening of the door to knowledge, or from the experience of truth unmediated by public discourse. In the *Consolation*, however, where public discussion is but a propaedeutic to the revelation of enigmatic truth, arguments must proceed without amazement on the part of either disputant. Just as Philosophy had suppressed her own impending wonderment in order to proceed at the end of Book Two, so the prisoner must replace his sense of wonder with a sense of purpose.

Prosa 9 opens with Philosophy's explicit statement of procedure: "Up to this point, I have shown clearly enough the nature of false happiness, and, if you have understood it, I can now go on to speak of true happiness."[37] In the Latin, the phrasing emphasizes the proper sequence of inquiry: ". . . ordo est deinceps quae sit uera monstrare" (III.pr.9.1). This prosa will explore the various ways of understanding, and it repeatedly expresses the action of knowing as a process of seeing. The metaphorical structures have moved from telling (from Philosophy's earlier desire to *explicare*) to showing. Philosophy now attempts to *monstrare*, and the prisoner responds that he sees, albeit imperfectly, the purpose of her arguments. "I see," he begins, and then qualifies his statement with an image which recalls, by contrast, the metaphors of the tractates: "I think I glimpse them [i.e., Philosophy's reasons] as it were through a narrow crack, but I should prefer to learn of them more plainly from you."[38] At one level, the prisoner prefers to have Philosophy do his intellectual work

[37] Green, trans., p. 56. III.pr.9.1.

[38] Here, I prefer the literalism of the Loeb translation, p. 262. "Atqui uideo. . . . Tenui quidem ueluti rimula mihi uideor intueri, sed ex te apertius cognoscere malim" (III.pr.9.2-3).

for him. His desire to learn "more openly" (*apertius*) is a request to listen rather than to argue. At another level, the prisoner's statement illustrates the preliminary nature of dialogue, and it reveals the limitations of verbal explanation. In his request for a more open method of understanding, the prisoner hearkens back to the imagery of the tractates, where philosophical knowledge was wrapped in new and enigmatic terms, but also where truth itself could come revealed as through an open door. At the heart of the prisoner's imagery is a basic impatience with the slow moving method of question and response, and at the same time an awareness of the need for progressing through the steps of argument. He is not yet ready to see the truth openly, and his vocabulary here recalls the rhetoric of understanding reserved for the theological investigations of the tractates or the close of Augustine's *Confessions*.[39]

The prisoner's impatience extends to his evaluation of his own abilities. By the end of prosa 9 he has agreed with much of what Philosophy has said, and he itches to inform her of the scope of his understanding. For the first time in the *Consolation*, the prisoner reformulates her arguments, and he registers his attention to their outer structure and their inner substance.

> But this is clear even to a blind man, and you revealed it a little while ago when you tried to explain the causes of false happiness. . . . And to show that I have understood you, I acknowledge that whatever can truly provide any one of these must be true and perfect happiness, since all are one and the same.[40]

[39] Compare *De Trinitate*, preface, p. 4 (on the commitment to "veil in new words" philosophical ideas). In Augustine, see *De Doctrina Christiana*, II.7-8, where he notes that what is discovered through figures is often more pleasurable than that which is understood with ease (for discussion see Mazzeo, "St. Augustine's Rhetoric of Silence," p. 188). On the concepts of obscurity and ambiguity as expressed in sensory metaphors, and in terms of light and darkness, see Augustine, *De Dialectica*, ed. J. Pinborg, trans. B. D. Jackson, p. 104.

[40] Green, trans., pp. 58-59. "Atqui haec, inquam, uel caeco perspicua est

The prisoner's vocabulary revives the imagery he and Philosophy have developed to this point. Clarity appears in terms of sense perception, and even though the seeing is metaphorical, the prisoner's use of the blind man as his foil reinforces the notion of logical demonstration as a form of showing rather than explaining. He uses Philosophy's word *monstrare* here, and his term for explanation (*aperire*) echoes his own earlier request for philosophical revelation. The prisoner is also deeply concerned that Philosophy come to know something of his own interior state. He has understood her inwardly (*interius*), and he seems to exult in his discovery of a truth *sine ambiguitate*. He offers an attempt at pure philosophizing without the double edge of dialectic, and an attempt to move beyond that discourse in which, as Augustine noted, every word is ambiguous.[41]

While Philosophy is proud of her pupil, she qualifies her praise. She makes clear that the prisoner still labors under opinion: that, while he may grasp the form of her argument, he is still incapable of complete understanding. "Your observation is a happy one," she states, "if you add just one thing."[42] She focuses on an epistemological movement subtly different from the prisoner's, and the vocabulary shifts are important. While he attempted to *cognoscere*, she will show him how to *agnoscere*. I think the difference in these terms represents a difference between cognition and acknowledgment, or between the inner contentment of knowing and the outer expression of that knowledge through verbal activity.

---

eamque tu paulo ante monstrasti dum falsae causas aperire conaris. . . . Atque ut me interius animaduertisse *congnoscas*, quae unum horum, quoniam idem cuncta sunt, ueraciter praestare potest, hanc esse plenam beatitudinem sine ambiguitate *cognosco*" (III.pr.9.25, 27, emphases mine). On the word *aperire* as a term for the openness of Scripture and the open-endedness of the *Confessions*' conclusion, see *Conf.*, XIII.xxxviii, and the discussion in G. Mazzotta, *Dante: Poet of the Desert*, pp. 225-226 and n. 38.

[41] "Itaque rectissime a dialecticis dictum est ambiguum esse omne verbum" (*De Dial.*, p. 106).

[42] "O te, alumne, hac opinione felicem, si quidem hoc, inquit, adieceris" (III.pr.9.28).

Again, Boethius distinguishes between things understood passively, as through listening or revelation, and things learned actively, as through public argument.[43] This activity, however, will for the moment be postponed, as Philosophy offers in the Timaean hymn a poetic counterpoint to her prose argument. If her prose passages are calculated to eliminate wonder and foster verbal discussion, her poetry is designed to inspire awe and instill a reverent silence. As expressed in the visual metaphors of the Book, "O qui perpetua" directs the prisoner to look up to his heavenly goal, to see (*defigere, cernere*) not with the eyes but with the mind. In its use of the central figures of the *Consolation*'s thought, the Timaean hymn recapitulates the movement of the dialogue, and it imbues the terms taken from dialectic with a new philosophical and cosmological significance.

The poem's indebtedness to the *Timaeus* and its commentaries is so apparently obvious, and so frequently stressed by critics, that few of its readers have cared to notice how the poem functions within the dialogue itself. Generations of the *Consolation*'s readers have found in "O qui perpetua" a set piece of Boethian Platonism; next to Fortune's wheel, this is perhaps the most famous of all sections of the work.[44] By restating the fundamental images developed by the disputants, the poem comments on the terms in which Philosophy and the prisoner characterize their method and their music. One example of this restatement appears at the poem's opening. God acts without external causes, and forms within himself an image of the good impressed on all creation. "No external

[43] See the following exchange: "Essene aliquid in his mortalibus caducisque rebus putas quod huius modi statum possit affere? —Minime, inquam, puto idque a te, nihil ut amplius desideretur, ostensum est. —Haec igitur uel imagines ueri boni uel imperfecta quaedam bona dare mortalibus uidentur, uerum autem atque perfectum bonum conferre non possunt. —Assentior, inquam. —Quoniam igitur *agnouisti* quae uera illa sit, quae autem beatitudinem mentiantur, nunc superest ut unde ueram hanc petere possis *agnoscas*" (III.pr.9.29-31, emphases mine).

[44] See Courcelle, *Cons. Phil.*, 163-184, and Winthrop Wetherbee, *Platonism and Poetry*, p. 76.

causes impelled You to make this work from chaotic matter."[45] This phrasing recalls the language of extrinsic arguments developed by Boethius and explored, in its moral dimension, throughout the *Consolation*. It also looks forward to the description of God as sufficient in himself,[46] and it will give to the conversation later in Book Three—where the prisoner praises Philosophy's arguments as containing *nullis extrinsecus sumptis*—a certain philosophical resonance. The poem's initial effect depends on recognizing its uniquely Boethian vocabulary. The hymn takes Philosophy at her word by developing her earlier ideas of musical and cosmic order. It enacts this recapitulation by transforming earlier mythological motifs into an abstract Platonic cosmology. In two earlier poems, II.m.8 and III.m.2, Phoebus had been a figure for celestial harmony. The regularity of sunrise and sunset in these poems confirmed one's expectation of and faith in the essential rightness of the system.

| . . . that Phoebus in his golden chariot brings in the shining day, that the night, led by Hesperus, is ruled by Phoebe, . . . (II.m.8.) | Phoebus sets at night beneath the Hesperian waves, but returning again along his secret path he drives his chariot to the place where it always rises. (III.m.2)[47] |

In these metra the chariot symbolizes the process of travel and return. Phoebus and Hesperus appear as mythological

---

[45] Green, trans. p. 60. "quem non externae pepulerunt fingere causae / materiae fluitantis opus" (III.m.9.4-5).

[46] See III.pr.10.12-13.

[47] Green, trans., pp. 41, 46. The passages in Latin, read:

> quod Phoebus roseum diem
> curru prouehit aureo,
> ut quas duxerit Hesperos
> Phoebe noctibus imperet.
> (II.m.8.5-8)
> Cadit Hesperias Phoebus in undas,
> sed secreto tramite rursus
> currum solitos vertit ad ortus.
> (III.m.2.31-3)

representatives of day and night and of light and dark. In "O qui perpetua," however, the picture of Phoebus in his chariot becomes an image of the human soul's passage from heaven to earth and back to heaven. While the ideas expressed in the poem have their origins in Plato and Proclus, within the structure of the *Consolation* these lines resonate with earlier poetic treatments of the same image.

> In like manner You create souls and lesser living forms and, adapting them to their high flight in swift chariots, You scatter them through the earth and sky. And when they have turned again toward You, by your gracious law, You call them back like leaping flames.[48]

The Phoebus narratives which described features of living in the world prefigure the condition of living in the cosmos. The human sight of the sun returning in its rosy dawn becomes the divine vision of the soul returning in its celestial fire. By Platonizing the story of Phoebus, Boethius creates a new philosophical context in which to re-read the earlier passages. His structure of imagery unifies the poetic sequences in the early books. In this framework, the Timaean hymn reads less as an isolatable expression of Neoplatonic thought and more as an integral part of the *Consolation*'s progress.

The image of returning expressed in the lines above complements the theories of harmony which find thematic and structural expression both in the hymn itself and in Philosophy's earlier poem, "Quantas rerum flectat habenas" (III.m.2).[49] This metrum foreshadows the metaphorical and

---

[48] Green, trans., pp. 60-61.

> Tu causis animas paribus uitasque minores
> prouehis et leuibus sublimes curribus aptans
> in caelum terramque seris, quas lege benigna
> ad te conuersas reduci facis igne reuerti.
>   (III.m.9.18-21)

[49] For the imagery of binding and stringing, and the musical theory underlying the poem's execution, see Gruber, *Kommentar*, pp. 281-282, and Chamberlain, "Philosophy of Music in the *Consolatio*," p. 88.

structural patterns of the hymn, and points toward a theory
of poetic composition embedded in the poetry. In III.m.2,
Philosophy restates her moral and methodological aims. The
opening lines reformulate her earlier injunction against the
vicious muses of the prisoner's opening song, and she presents
him with an example of music at its best.

> Now I will show you in graceful song, accompanied by pliant
> strings, how mightily Nature guides the reins of all things; how
> she providently governs the immense world by her laws; how
> she controls all things, binding them in unbreakable bonds.[50]

The instrumental music she offers in this poem fosters wisdom
and virtue, and the imagery of its opening lines associates the
strings on which she plays with the bonds which unite all
elements of the universe.[51] Concord is both instrumental and
cosmic, and even the formal structure of her verse mimes the
metaphorical structure of her subject. The Latin is intricately
woven in its syntax; internal and end rhymes complement the
patterns of assonance; the first sentence, six lines long, suspends its agent *cantu* ("in song") until the very last word.
Philosophy's elaborate display of technique exemplifies the
poet as orderer and creator. Throughout this poem Philosophy uses structural devices to imitate her subject. In her description of the caged bird, she employs a self-conscious formal pattern to give new expression to the old Platonic idea,

---

[50] Green, trans., p. 45.

> Quantas rerum flectat habenas
> natura potens, quibus immensum
> legibus orbem prouida seruet
> stringatque ligans inresoluto
> singula nexu, placet arguto
> fidibus lentis promere cantu.
>   (III.m.2.1-6)

[51] On the history of the imagery of binding, and its possible sources in
Stoic cosmology, see M. Lapidge, "A Stoic Metaphor in Late Latin Poetry:
The Binding of the Cosmos," *Latomus* 39 (1980), 817-837.

dubbed by Courcelle, of "l'âme en cage."[52] The bird shut in her cavernous cage suggests the Platonic image of the soul imprisoned in the body.[53] In the final two lines of this description, anaphora marks the bird's vocal longing with a metrical pattern: "Siluas tantum maesta requirit, / siluas dulci uoce susurrat" (III.m.2.25-26). The poem's end brings the reader structurally and thematically back to its beginning. The sense of returning home in the last lines combines with the idea of order expressed in the first sentence. The ordered course is "that which connects the beginning to the end" (*quod fini iunxerit ortum*, 37). While this moral statement comments on the poem's structure as a whole, the text's final lines give a unifying conclusion through a pattern of repetition:

> currum solitos vertit ad *or*tus.
> Repetunt proprios quaeque recursus
> redituque suo singula gaudent
> nec manet ulli traditus *or*do
> nisi quod fini iunxerit *or*tum
> stabilemque sui fecerit *or*bem.[54]

Through the repeated *or*- syllable, the ideas embodied in the poem's vocabulary are reified through sound, as well as sense.[55]

The Timaean hymn appears as a complex restatement of the problems posed by this earlier poem, for it uses rhetoric and musical imagery to express its philosophical content. The expression of Timaean world harmony and the imagery of binding the elements develop the poetic and mythological material of the earlier poem into a statement of divine cos-

---

[52] P. Courcelle, "L'âme en Cage," in K. Flasch, ed., *Parusia* (Frankfurt-am-Main: Minerva, 1965), pp. 103-116; the poem's lines are discussed on p. 115 and n. 40.

[53] See Gruber's summary of the scholarship, *Kommentar*, p. 245.

[54] III.m.2.33-38. The sense of the passage is rendered by Green: "Thus all things seek again their proper courses, and rejoice when they return to them. The only stable order in things is that which connects the beginning to the end and keeps itself on a steady course" (p. 46).

[55] See Gruber, *Kommentar*, p. 246.

mology. The phrasing of "O qui perpetua" has been seen, in one critic's words, as offering "man a pattern of love and order by which to guide his own life."[56] But these patterns also suggest imaginative structures: habits of mind which find their voice in virtuous metrics. Philosophy's language points to a poetry subject to the divine *ordo*, yet also governed by the speaker's own power. The self-reflexive qualities which the poem attributes to God are embodied in the verbal patterns of the text. As the mind of God turns inward from the world created in its own likeness, and as the soul turns inward to comprehend itself, so the text creates a system of self-reference through rhetorical echoes. As in III.m.2, the order of reason becomes the order of poetry.

"O qui perpetua" contains in its opening sentence a series of repetitions which establish the reflective patterning. It opens with what Gruber calls, "der Relativstil der Prädikation . . . mit dem anaphorischen *qui . . . qui . . . quem.*"[57] It then works through a rhetorical system of interlacement to reinforce God's impression of his own mind on the outer shape of creation.[58] Using a limited vocabulary charged with meaning, the poem mirrors itself metrically and sonically, as creation mirrors creator. The entire text is punctuated by rhetorical parallels which mark the progress of the argument. Through antistrophe, Boethius repeats line endings (*cuncta moueri*, 3; *cuncta superno*, 6; *cuncta mouentem*, 13). Through anaphora, he restates the form of address in an almost litan-

---

56 Chamberlain, "Philosophy of Music," p. 90.

57 Gruber, *Kommentar*, p. 277.

58   quem non externae pepulerunt fingere causae
     materiae fluitantis opus uerum insita summi
     forma boni liuore carens, tu cunta superno
     ducis ab exemplo, *pulchrum pulcherrimus* ipse
     mundum mente gerens similique in imagine *formans*
     perfectasque iubens *perfectum* absoluere partes.
     (III.m.9.4-9, emphases added to illustrate repetitions.)

Notice also the patterns of alliteration and assonance: *pul- pul- / per- per- par- / m*undum *m*ente.

izing way (*Tu numeris*, 10; *Tu triplicis*, 13; *Tu causis*, 18). The appearance of words for earth and sky sets up a chiastic pattern of echo and return.

> terrarum caelique sator . . . (2)
> . . . deducant pondera terras. (12)
> . . . conuertit imagine caelum. (17)
> in caelum terramque seris, . . . (20)

The concluding repetitions, "Da, pater, . . . / Da fontem . . . , da luce" (21-22), and, "tu namque serenum, / tu requies . . ." (26-27), bring the poem to an emphatic climax, directing the reader's mind away from the forms of God's work to divinity itself. The poem's final vision thus fulfills the prisoner's "eager longing" for the way to happiness.[59]

The poetry thus differs from the prose in that it shows rather than argues. It is designed to instill wonder not simply by stating God's power but by presenting the poet's skills. The elaborate rhetorical patterns in poems such as III.m.2 and III.m.9 are an integral part of Philosophy's purpose; rather than the vacuous displays of the prisoner's early poetry, these technical flourishes enact the themes of the metra. They show Philosophy as a master of poetic diction, as well as of dialectical and philosophical argument, and her return to these systems of rational inquiry may come as something of an anticlimax to the prisoner and reader. In prosa 10 she returns to structures of reason from patterns of wonder. Even though the prisoner has seen (*uidisti*) the form of the good, he must use logical inquiry to understand its earthly counterpart. Now, Philosophy's commitment is to demonstrate (*demonstrare*) her truths.[60] As in her earlier decision to "designare verbis," or to "explicare," her terminology signals a rational rather than a transcendental process. By directing the prisoner back to a system of questioning (her word *inquirendum*,

[59] See his earlier remark: "Id quidem, inquam, iam dudum uehementer exspecto" (III.pr.9.31).

[60] ". . . nunc demonstrandum reor quonam haec felicitatis perfectio constituta sit" (III.pr.10.1).

III.pr.10.2) she restates the dialectical contract made in Book One.[61] But, as before, the prisoner is unable to follow her arguments precisely and to fulfill his role in the discussion. Whereas his earlier failures revealed themselves either through silence or incomprehension, his problems at the close of Book Three are masked by a misguided self-confidence and an impatient readiness to agree with anything Philosophy says.

III

As the dialogue continues through prosae 10-12, the prisoner responds to Philosophy's arguments with a bold, confident series of assents. His ready responses voice a concern with the formal correctness of reasoning rather than an intuitive awareness of higher truths. Behind his assents lies the voice of Fabius from the early *In Isagogen*, and, as I will suggest, it has a strong analogue with the figure of Adeodatus from Augustine's *De Magistro*. At times, the prisoner's words read like a schoolboy's vain attempt to impress the master with his command of terminology and the intensity of his attention. "That is firmly and truly established," he avers on one occasion.[62] Soon after, he answers, "I agree. Your argument cannot be contradicted."[63] To another argument, he chimes, "Rectissime" (III.pr.10.16), and he asserts the impregnability of Philosophy's line of reasoning as proof of her claims: "I found your earlier arguments unassailable, and I see that this conclusion follows from them."[64] In his desire to hear, rather than talk, the prisoner prefers the silent passivity of the pupil

[61] "In quo illud primum arbitror inquirendum . . ." (III.pr.10.2). Compare, I.pr.6.1, "Primum igitur. . . ."

[62] Green, trans., p. 61. "Firmissime, inquam, uerissimeque conclusum est" (III.pr.10.6).

[63] Green, trans., p. 62. "Accipio, inquam, nec est quod contra dici ullo modo queat" (III.pr.10.10).

[64] Green, trans., p. 63. "Nec propositis, inquam, prioribus refragari queo et illis hoc inlatum consequens esse perspicio" (III.pr.10.17). See, also, his later remark: "Nihil, inquam, nec reapse uerius nec ratiocinatione firmius nec deo dignius concludi potest" (III.pr.10.21).

to the activity of the debater. He asks Philosophy to clarify
her arguments through specific examples; he longs to hear
her conclusion; he is waiting for the rest of her proofs.

> I wish you would explain this point by recalling what is in-
> volved.[65]
> I understand the problem now and am eager to have your
> answer.[66]
> There is no doubt about that, but you have not yet given me
> the solution.[67]

The prisoner opens prosa 11 continuing his rhetoric of assent,[68] and Philosophy now responds to his desire to know
God by conceding to his brand of reasoning. Answering his
earlier request for her to explain (*patefacere*, III.pr.10.29), she
announces: "I will show you (*patefaciam*) this with certainty."[69] As if to interject a bit of modesty, however, she
qualifies her assertion and seems almost to request the prisoner
to let the conclusions stand ("maneant modo quae paulo ante
conclusa sunt," III.pr.11.4).[70] But the prisoner will have none
of these qualifications; her remarks *will* stand ("Manebunt,"
III.pr.11.4). His confidence in Philosophy's reasoning betrays
that lack of doubt which has permeated the tone of his responses ("ne dubitari" is his favorite expression of agreement).[71] Arguments still appeal to his all-too-human judgment

[65] This and the following two quotations are from Green, trans., p. 64.
"Vellem, inquam, id ipsarum rerum commemoratione patefaceres"
(III.10.29).

[66] "Intellego, inquam, quid inuestigandum proponas, sed quid constituas
audire desidero" (III.pr.10.32).

[67] "Id quidem, inquam, dubium non est, sed id quod restat exspecto"
(III.pr.10.35).

[68] "Assentior, inquam" (III.pr.11.1).

[69] Green, trans., p. 66. "Atqui hoc uerissima, inquit, ratione patefaciam"
(III.pr.11.4).

[70] *manent* here is subjunctive hortatory, but polite. J. J. O'Donnell is my
source for this grammatical observation and its consequences for the tone of
the dialogue (see note to III.pr.11.4, in the Bryn Mawr Commentary).

[71] III.pr.9.7: "At hoc, inquam, ne dubitari quidem potest." III.pr.11.6: "Demonstratum, inquam, nec dubitari ullo modo potest."

and opinion. They are acceptable not because they are true, but because they are incapable of being challenged, doubted, or denied.[72] The prisoner expresses positive assent in negative terms, and his phrasing reveals a habit of mind which relies on structures of belief rather than on proof. His diction reflects the fundamental subjectivity behind the ways in which he sees the world and follows Philosophy's arguments. His commendations of her rational coherence depend only on his *perception* of that coherence, as a language of seeming (e.g., in his term *videtur*) predominates. In short, for Philosophy, things are; for the prisoner, they seem to be.[73]

By prosa 12, however, the dialogue begins to break down, and Philosophy must exhort the prisoner to maintain his side of the discussion. As before, the prisoner notices the manner and method of her speech at the expense of its meaning. In one case in particular, he is so taken with the beauty of her reasoning that Philosophy must stop the discussion altogether and reaffirm their contract. Both disputants develop an imagery of sweetness and delight which leads up to that moment of breakdown. Philosophy begins by noting that the highest good disposes all things sweetly.[74] The prisoner responds:

> I am delighted not only by your powerful argument and its conclusion, but even more by the words you have used.[75]

Most readers of this exchange have considered the prisoner's apparent delight to derive from the Book of Wisdom.[76] For-

---

[72] III.pr.11.9: "Negare, inquam, nequeo." III.pr.11.35: "Confiteor, inquam, nunc me indubitato cernere quae dudum incerta uidebantur." III.pr.11.39: "Nihil, inquam, uerius excogitari potest."

[73] E.g., III.pr.9.6: "Sic uidetur." III.11.7: "Ita, inquam, uidetur." IV.pr.2.13: "Sic uidetur." IV.pr.4.16: "Sic, inquam, uidetur."

[74] "Est igitur summum, inquit, bonum quod regit cuncta fortiter suauiterque disponit" (III.pr.12.22).

[75] Green, trans., p. 72. "Quam, inquam, me non modo ea quae conclusa est summa rationum, uerum multo magis haec ipsa quibus uteris uerba delectant . . ." (III.pr.12.23).

[76] See Gruber's summary of the scholarship, beginning with Rand's original observation (*Kommentar*, p. 311). In the Vulgate, the passage in question

tescue considered this moment the most certain of all possible Biblical allusions in the *Consolation*, and many have argued that the prisoner's pleasure is the joy of recognizing the word of God.[77] Whether Boethius puts the words of Wisdom into Philosophy's mouth, or whether this vocabulary was received second-hand through Augustine, Philo Judaeus, or others, is less important than the effect of the diction within the dialogue itself.[78] Boethius presents this rational sweetness as an alternative to the dubious sweetness of Fortuna's rhetoric in Book Two. The prisoner himself had warned against the "specious sweetness" of her arguments, honeyed with music and rhetoric (II.pr.3.2). His words were also designed to echo Philosophy's praise of right rhetoric, whose sweet persuasiveness was only effective if it kept to the path of reason (II.pr.1.8). Now, in Book Three, the prisoner recognizes almost intuitively the elegance of reason and the kindly strength which, as Philosophy tells him, sets desire in its rightful place. The imagery has its counterpoint in the violent pictures of the tortured prisoner, the warring Giants, and the clash of arguments which Philosophy proposes. Taken together, these impressions of conflict and beauty figuratively restate the original system of question and answer which motivated the dialogue, and point towards the rewards of verbal struggle:

> You have read in the fables of the poets how giants made war on heaven; but this benign power overthrew them as they deserved. But now let us set our arguments against each other and perhaps from their opposition some special truth will emerge.[79]

---

reads: "attingit [Sapientia] . . . fortitier et disponit omnia suaviter." Courcelle expresses his own skepticism of the Biblical allusion, *La Cons. Phil.*, p. 340. Chadwick, *Boethius*, attempts a synthesis of the arguments for and against, assessing the possible Biblical citations as ambiguous and certainly not inconsistent with the philosophy being espoused. But he does consider this citation, "as good as certain" (pp. 238-239).

[77] See, for example, Wetherbee, *Platonism and Poetry*, p. 78, n. 12; C. S. Lewis, *The Discarded Image* (Cambridge: Cambridge Univ. Press, 1964), p. 79; Chadwick, *Boethius*, pp. 238-239.

[78] See Gruber, *Kommentar*, p. 311.

[79] Green, trans., p. 72. "Accepisti, inquit, in fabulis lacessentes caelum

Unlike Boethius in the *De Trinitate* preface, where the writer's spark of reason was fired by solitary meditation, Philosophy applies the same, essentially Platonic, image to characterize public discussion. She establishes a complex metaphorical environment in which to reflect upon the dialogue's formal progress. In addition, she explicitly reminds the prisoner of his experiences as a reader, and her characterization here will have great importance for the interpretive demands which her poem on Orpheus will make on him.

In this context of imagery, allusion, and metaphor, it is significant that the prisoner responds to Philosophy also in a figurative way. He complains that she is playing games with him, losing him in an inextricable verbal labyrinth. His restatement of her procedure summarizes many of the central figures of thought developed in the *Consolation* thus far: the imagery of the way; the notion of philosophical wonder; the explicit use of mythological allusion in the mention of the labyrinth.

> You are playing with me by weaving a labyrinthine argument from which I cannot escape. You seem to begin where you ended and to end where you began. Are you perhaps making a marvelous circle of the divine simplicity?[80]

Philosophy must convince him that it is no game (*minime ludimus*, III.pr.12.36), but a process grounded in a formal method and directed towards a vital truth. But her explanation sustains the metaphorical coloring of their discussion, as Boethius lets diction do the work of reason. The prisoner and Philosophy exchange the metaphors of inner and outer which they developed earlier. He praises her arguments for developing proofs not from outside but from within.[81] Philosophy

---

Gigantas; sed illos quoque, uti condignum fuit, benigna fortitudo disposuit. Sed uisne rationes ipsas inuicem collidamus? Forsitan ex huius modi conflictatione pulchra quaedam ueritatis scintilla dissiliat" (III.pr.12.24-25).

[80] Green, trans., p. 72. "Ludisne, inquam, me inextricabilem labyrinthum rationibus texens, quae nunc quidem qua egrediaris introeas, nunc uero quo introieris egrediare, an mirabilem quendam diuinae simplicitatis orbem complicas?" (III.pr.12.30.)

[81] III.12.35. For the Latin, see n. 35.

takes up his imagery, giving his argument precision and concentrating on its emotional effect.

> You ought not be surprised that I have sought no outside proofs, but have used only those within the scope of our subject, since you have learned, on Plato's authority, that the language we use ought to be related to the subject of our discourse.[82]

As she adopts the prisoner's explication of her method, Philosophy places it in a stated Platonic context. The intrinsic/extrinsic dichotomy now has an epistemological purpose, and she builds her theory of knowledge out of the language of topical argument and the figurative expression of wonder. While her thought is clearly Platonic, and her Greek Presocratic, her diction is uniquely Boethian. The relationship between *res* and *verba* is calculated to confirm the prisoner's own intuitions. She invokes the authority of Plato and Parmenedes if only to make her truths believable to the prisoner. If it is the opinions of the wise he needs—as any dialectician would—then Philosophy is ready to provide them.[83] Moreover, the prisoner should not wonder ("nihil est quod ammirere") at these truths, but accept them as sanctioned by their authors.

A similar problem arises in *De Magistro*, where Augustine

---

[82] Green, trans. p. 73. "Quodsi rationes quoque non extra petitas sed intra rei quam tractabamus ambitum collocatas agitauimus, nihil est quod ammirere, cum Platone sanciente didiceris cognatos de quibus loquuntur rebus oportere esse sermones" (III.pr.12.38).

[83] For the dialectician as relying on outside authorities, in contrast to the philosopher, see *De topicis differentiis*, PL, 64: 1199C-D, Stump, trans. p. 70; *In Topica Ciceronis*, PL, 64: 1166D-1167D. Both of these discussions focus on extrinsic arguments which depend on judgment and authority ("hic judicio nititur et auctoritate," in the words of *De topicis differentiis*; "testimonia" in the terms of the *In Topica Ciceronis*). Thus, in this passage, Philosophy advocates a self-sufficient method of demonstration, while at the same time conceding to the prisoner's need for authoritative sources. A similar ploy introduced the Timaean hymn (III.pr.9.32), and was picked up by the prisoner at III.pr.12.1 ("Platoni, inquam, uehementer assentior"). For the history of the notion that "authority is the weakest source of proof," see M. D. Chenu, *Nature, Man, and Society*, p. 77, and note too Cicero's remarks in *De Natura Deorum*, I.v.10.

must make clear to Adeodatus that the playful or taunting appearance of his questions is a systematic prelude to a more difficult form of investigation. In this dialogue, however, the figurative diction lacks the poetic resonance which it has for Boethius, and yet it offers an analogue to the *Consolation*'s thematic treatment of formal structure. Midway through the discussion (*De Mag.*, VIII.21) Augustine recognizes the seeming formlessness of his line of questioning and the obscurity of his train of thought.

> But it is difficult at this point to say just where I am striving to lead you by so many circumlocutions. For it may seem that we are quibbling (*ludere nos*) and so diverting the mind from earnest matters with naive questions, or that we are seeking after some mean advantage.[84]

Both the prisoner and Adeodatus confront a loss of rational and verbal direction. While it may seem that they are playing a game, Augustine shows his son the importance of their goal and the validity of their method: "But I want you to believe that I wish neither to have occupied myself with quibbles in this discussion, although we cannot afford to play if the matter is not viewed naively; nor to have labored for petty or unimportant ends."[85] He entreats Adeodatus to follow their course, as argument becomes a *praeludo*, and not a *ludus*, which exercises the mind and develops the reason.[86] When their dialogue begins again Adeodatus seems stunned to find Augus-

---

[84] Trans. G. Leckie, *Concerning the Teacher*, p. 30. "Sed quonam tantis ambagibus tecum peruenire moliar, difficile dictu est hoc loco. Tu enim fortasse aut ludere nos et a seriis rebus auocare animum quasi quibusdam puerilibus quaestiunculis arbitraris aut paruam uel mediocrem aliquam utilitatem requirere . . ." (*De. Mag.*, VIII.21.4-9).

[85] Trans. G. Leckie, p. 30, modified by me. "Ego autem credas uelim neque me uilia ludicra hoc instituisse sermone, quamuis fortasse ludamus, idque ipsum tamen non puerili sensu aestimandum sit, neque parua bona uel mediocria cogitare" (*De Mag.*, VIII.21.11-14).

[86] "Dabis igitur ueniam, si praeludo tecum non ludendi gratia, sed exercendi uires et mentis aciem, quibus regionis illius, ubi beata uita est, calorem ac lucem non modo sustinere, uerum et amare possiums" (VIII.21.19-22).

tine asking him "whether man is a man." He takes *homo* to be the signified object, rather than the word, and in his confusion Adeodatus protests, "Nunc uero an ludas nescio" (VIII.22.29). Augustine has prepared for this moment, developing the language of game and providing the vocabulary in which his son can express his confusion.

By pausing in the dialogue to explain its purpose, Augustine raises the discussion of method to a statement of theme. He builds the reader's awareness of how discussion directs reason rather than perfects it. The imagery of the "way" and of the *ludus* in Boethius and Augustine, then, achieves three effects. First, it makes the formal constraints of dialogue a suitable subject matter. By taking the time to justify their method or defend their techniques, the speakers create an environment in which no outside excuses are necessary. They close off the world of the dialogue by making it uniquely self-referring. Second, these pauses create in the listener (either Adeodatus or the prisoner) certain expectations. They bring to the fore the hidden desire which motivates the soul, and they turn that desire into an interest in the process of discovery itself. Finally, the moments when dialogue collapses reveal the limits of human understanding and expression. While the prisoner seems lost in a tangle of language, Adeodatus is perplexed by the reference of a single word. Both these examples posit the relationship between the student's failure at formal argument and his relative success at adopting his teacher's phrasing.[87] Where Boethius differs sharply from the Saint is in his use of a highly figurative language to recall the diction of poetry and to create, in the speaker, the sense of wonder associated with the transcendent poetry of Book Three. By denying the prisoner the opportunity to marvel, Philosophy distinguishes between the emotional effects of poetry and prose. She points him, instead, to a hermeneutic principle based on reflection and literally presented as a process of looking back. Augustine is seldom so concerned with reviewing in the *De Magistro*.

---

[87] See the discussion of *De Magistro* in Chapter I.

He pauses to restate the formal constraints of the discussion, but his argument, and Adeodatus' remarks at the dialogue's end, stress a linear progress.[88]

For Boethius, however, literary interpretation follows the same reflective patterns as the structure of the *Consolation* itself. The prisoner is constantly called upon to look back over the progress of his life and his discussion with Philosophy.[89] As I have already shown, passages of the *Consolation*'s poetry will recast earlier images from the text, and the prisoner and Philosophy will frequently echo each other to establish a unity of diction and a continual sense of repetition as the governing principle of the *Consolation*'s composition. In the final poem of Book Three, Orpheus becomes a figure for the prisoner himself, for not only does his journey recapitulate the prisoner's early condition, but the very effect of the poem is designed to make the prisoner learn from the narrative. The following analysis of metrum 12 explores the ways in which Boethius rewrites earlier moments of the *Consolation*'s text into this new mythological context. Like the Timaean hymn, the poem on Orpheus reviews the progress of the dialogue by drawing upon the diction, imagery, and narratives developed earlier in the work. Like the hymn as well, the poem is a "reading" of an outside text: here, not of Plato but of Seneca. Boethius recasts scenes from Seneca's *Hercules Furens* to measure the prisoner's progress and Philosophy's authority. The principle of rewriting which operated within the *Consolation* itself now operates on an outside text as well. Philosophy presents a poem to be read and interpreted; for its ultimate effect, however, Boethius relies on his reader's recognition of the Senecan "super-text" to his metrum, as we measure the prisoner, Philosophy, and the author of the *Consolation* him-

---

[88] "Verumtamen huic orationi tuae, qua perpetua usus es, ob hoc habeo maxime gratiam, quod omnia, quae contradicere paratus eram, praeoccupauit atque dissoluit . . ." (XIV.46.40-42).

[89] E.g., "Si priora, inquit, concessa *respicias*, ne illud quidem longius aberit quin recorderis quod te dudum nescire confessus es" (III.pr.12.2, emphases mine).

self as readers and rewriters of the tragic mythology which stand behind their words. In its presentation of musical ideas, its self-conscious metrical structuring, and its concluding moral, the poem takes as one of its subjects the formal problems of literary execution. By encapsulating the central hermeneutic movements of the *Consolation*, the text also comments on the process of loss and recovery characteristic of the prisoner's spiritual development.[90]

IV

The parallels are clear between Orpheus and the prisoner at the *Consolation*'s beginning. Both are oppressed by grief and are subject to those Muses who stifle reason and engender passion. In this and the opening metrum, the speakers contrast former happiness with present grief. The prisoner bemoaned his lost literary abilities (1.m.1.1-2), and Philosophy shows how Orpheus' grief also impedes the exercise of his poetic power.

[90] The literature on the poem is vast; like the Timaean hymn, it has been subjected to a variety of medieval and modern readings. According to Courcelle (*La Cons. Phil.*, pp. 19-20), both Martianus Capella and Fulgentius would have provided models of moral allegories extracted from mythological narratives. Guillaume of Conches' view of Orpheus has been summarized by Wetherbee as an allegory of "the wise and eloquent man who seeks, having learned the emptiness of temporal life, to fix his desire on higher things" (*Platonism and Poetry*, p. 96). For medieval literary transformations of this poem and other mythological narratives in the *Consolation*, see Richard Dwyer, *Boethian Fictions* (Cambridge, Mass.: Medieval Academy of America, 1976). Alice Miskimin finds its sources in ancient allegoresis, and sees it as depicting the struggle between the rational and irrational in the poet (*The Renaissance Chaucer* [New Haven: Yale Univ. Press, 1975], pp. 151-153). John Block Friedman sees Boethius as "the first Latin writer to develop an ethical allegory from the story of Orpheus and Eurydice in the underworld." Friedman considers the poem an allegory of earthly and spiritual desire—of man "dragged back by [the] inability to reject *temporalia*" (*Orpheus in the Middle Ages* [Cambridge, Mass: Harvard Univ. Press, 1970], p. 95). For the history and historiography of the Orpheus myth, see Friedman's study and the bibliography cited in Gruber, *Kommentar*, p. 315.

> Long ago the Thracian poet mourned for his dead wife. With
> his sorrowful music (*flebilibus modis*) he made the woodland
> dance and the rivers stand still.[91]

Through *flebilibus modis* Orpheus' songs, while they reorder
nature and calm the beasts, fail to soothe the singer. The
prisoner wrote tearful verses (*flebilis modos*, I.m.I.2), having
taken dictation from the Muses. For both Orpheus and the
prisoner, extreme grief comes to represent the loss of power
and of poetry. Vocal imagery permeates both poems. Written
in silence, it shows how his lament goes unheard: "Death . . .
turns a deaf ear to the wretched."[92] Death is a process of literal
calling (*vocata*, I.m.I.14), as the poem details the prisoner's
emotional and creative responses through specific sensory
imagery.

In the poem on Orpheus repeated patterns of musical and
vocal imagery also express artistic and psychological tensions
by marking the movement of his song and the progress of
his descent. Verbal parallels highlight the formal nature of the
text and draw attention to the technical devices used to punctuate emotion.

> captus carmine ianitor (III.m.12.30)
> emptam carmine coniugem (43)

At the poem's opening, structural parallels again reinforce
psychological problems. Orpheus' infelicity appears twice at
the poem's opening:

> Felix, qui potuit boni (1)
> felix, qui potuit grauis (3)

In his opening carmen, however, the prisoner tried to objec-
tify his unhappiness by placing the blame on friends
(I.m.I.21). Both poems offer images of *felicitas* turned into
suffering, as their speakers move from a language of music

[91] Green, trans., p. 73. "Quondam funera coniugis / uates Threicius gemens / postquam flebilibus modis / siluas currere mobiles, / amnes stare
coegerat" (III.m.12.5-9).

[92] "Eheu, quam surda miseros auertitur aure" (I.m.I.15).

to a language of sensation. While Philosophy's poem stresses
Orpheus' lost clarity of vision, the prisoner's poem concentrates on the opacity through which he discerns the world.
The fog which obscures true vision oppresses the prisoner;
his life is ruled by the clouded, cheating face of Fortune (19);
his eyes will not close in death (16). For Orpheus, who could
once behold the fountain of goodness, his gaze has turned to
Hell and he is lost. Echoes mark the narrative movement:

> fas sit lumina flectere (46)
> uictus lumina flexerit (56).

In one brief line, Orpheus sees, loses, and kills his love, and
with her dies his truth: "uidit, perdidit, occidit" (51).

Metrum 12 restates in mythological terms the literary and
psychological condition of the prisoner. It also develops the
philosophical diction expressed in the *Consolation*'s poetry,
and the Timaean hymn provides one foil for its opening image. In her final prayer, Philosophy had petitioned the mind
to raise itself towards God, to wander by the fountain of the
good (III.m.9.22-24).[93] Orpheus, however, cannot look upon
the *fons boni*, nor can he lift his vision to the light. He must
face downward to darkness, for while Philosophy points desire towards Heaven, his passion leads him to Hell. The divine
serenitas and *tranquillitas*, granted to the blessed in the Timaean
hymn and effected in the speaker by prayer, are denied an
Orpheus unsoothed by his own music. The phrasing which
describes his *fervor* recalls the picture of the prisoner struck
dumb by Philosophy's poetry at the opening of Book III, and
this recollection highlights the relationship between music and
emotion present throughout the *Consolation*. Parallels in the
Latin pointedly bring this out.

[93]   "Da, pater, augustam menti conscendere sedem,
da fontem lustrare boni, da luce reperta
in te conspicuos animi defigere uisus."
                                     (III.m.9.22-24)

cum flagrantior intima
feruor pectoris ureret
nec qui cuncta subegerant
mulcerent dominum modi,

(III.m.12.14-17)

Iam cantum illa finiuerat, cum me
audiendi auidum stupentemque
arrectis adhuc auribus carminis
mulcedo defixerat.

(III.pr.1.1)[94]

Central to these passages is the effect of music on the listener, and his ability to attend to the possibilities of meaning in song. Implicit also in these two passages is the difference between human and beastly reactions to music. True music addresses the soul directly and brings it into harmony with the heavenly concord. It is a limited music which affects only the passions and which charms the beasts without calming Orpheus' mind. The differences, then, between the prisoner at the opening of Book Three and Orpheus at its close depend for their effectiveness on a pattern of rewriting which give a unity to the reading of the *Consolation*.

Such patterns of rewriting operate on the cosmological metra of Book Two, as well. The poem on Orpheus draws on the naturalism and mythology of the earlier metra to make figurative statements about man's place in the world. While Orpheus could once tame the beasts of the wood with his song, to retrieve his wife he must subdue the inhabitants of Hell. He had reshaped the natural order to his own will; the fearful are tamed, and the eternal torments of the damned stop for one brief moment. These images of music altering the natural and supernatural order stand as a climactic inversion of the thematic movement of the *Consolation*'s poetry. The stable concord Philosophy praised in II.m.8 had kept the sea within its bounds and the land within its borders. The love which joined the married had bound the world—but now that bond is broken as Orpheus faces the *funera coniugis*. The sequence of naturalistic poems in Book Two, depicting the

---

[94] Green's translations read: "But as the sorrow within his breast burned more fiercely, that music which calmed all nature could not console its maker" (III.m.12, p. 73). "When her song was finished, its sweetness left me wondering and alert, eager to hear more" (III.pr.1., p. 42).

stability of a rural golden age and the trauma of an urban Roman past, established a controlling tension between order and chaos at the level of human civilization. The ideas of order developed in the poetry are instinctively perverted in the picture of Orpheus the poet. His abilities to transform the observed world into his own image comment on the creative power of the *vates*. As one critic has noticed, "the poem gives eloquent expression to the very impulse it is intended to curb," for it confounds the natural harmony of Philosophy's world view.[95] In its illogic, the story presents a pervasive disharmony, from the breaking of the bonds of marriage, through Orpheus' fervor, and finally to the mad pursuit of the dead. The poem suspends the workings of necessity to admit the power of passion, if only to negate that power in the end.

In the image of Orpheus turning back, Philosophy incorporates the poem's interpretive key. Not only is her moral *not* to turn back towards earthly goods, but in it lies the complementary movement of looking back to review the prisoner's life. Her admonition presents the prisoner, and the reader, with a method of interpretation as well as a guide to behavior.

> This fable applies (*respicit*) to all of you who seek to raise your minds to sovereign day.[96]

The word *respicit* here embodies one of the central metaphors of the *Consolation*. It signifies the human contemplation of heaven or the enlightened contempt of the world. To *respicere* is literally to *re-spicere*, to "review" or "see again," and it signals the full exercise of rational abilities and the desire to review and interpret past events as guides for present behav-

---

[95] Wetherbee, *Platonism and Poetry*, p. 78.

[96]   "Vos haec fabula respicit
            quicumque in superum diem
            mentem ducere quaeritis."
                         (III.m.12.52–54)

ior.[97] When Philosophy notes that her fable itself *respicit* she means two things. First, she implies that the narrative looks back over the prisoner's progress to this moment. The poem itself points backwards to the worldly concupiscence which enslaved him, and forward to the higher day towards which he must direct his mind. Second, Philosophy enjoins the prisoner to interpret her fable. She prods him into activity, showing how the story retells his life and how he must act upon it. The poem is explicitly a *fabula*, and like the *fabulae* which had earlier illustrated the proper order of being (III.pr.12.24), it is designed to be read and interpreted. Like the fables of the Giants which the prisoner had read, the poem on Orpheus will become a text against which he can measure both the order of the world and the reordering of his own psyche. In turn, just as the Giants attempted to rule Heaven, so Orpheus made his bid to sway Hell. In their own ways, these fabled characters challenged the benign strength which controls earth and sky and which points the prisoner on his moral path.

Philosophy has to this point been directing the prisoner's interpretive abilities. She explicitly refers to his earlier acts of reading, and her monitory moral is as much a guide for the prisoner as it is for the reader outside the *Consolation*'s fiction. The ways in which the poem on Orpheus rewrites earlier portions of the *Consolation*'s prose and verse, moreover, signal a process of rereading and revision: the reader is, in effect, encouraged to return to earlier portions in the text to notice, not simple repetition, but subtle shifts in tone and emphasis. Through these structural devices, Boethius measures the

---

[97] Uses of the term earlier in the *Consolation* include Philosophy's lifting of her head to pass beyond human sight (I.pr.1.2); Philosophy's injunction to direct the prisoner's sight from earth to the stars (III.pr.8.8); her request for the prisoner to reflect upon their argument and his new-found knowledge (III.pr.12.2). Later in the work, Philosophy reserves the word for the enlightened. The *vulgi* cannot look up from their base lives, nor can they see with understanding (IV.pr.4.29-30). By Book Five, reason itself *respicit*, comprehending in one movement the imaginable and sensible qualities of the world (V.pr.4.34).

progress of his prisoner; he also enables the reader to measure himself against the work's persona. These injunctions towards the end of Book Three also return the reader to the figure of the prisoner as a reader and writer expressed in the opening metrum. Read in the larger context of Boethius' self-styled literary career, and his development of a reading persona throughout his earlier works, these injunctions sustain the fictional construct at the heart of the Boethian corpus.

With these issues in mind, I now turn to what has long been recognized as the clearest source for the poem on Orpheus, Seneca's *Hercules Furens*, to show how Boethius rewrites not only his own text but that of another.[98] The undeniable presence of Seneca's text behind Boethius' reveals, at another level, the activity of the prisoner as a reader, and it also gives a new facet to Philosophy's abilities as a writer of philosophical poetry. Orpheus appears in Seneca's play in an exemplary moral chorus anticipating Hercules' arrival on stage. Boethius adapts verbatim about one-third of Seneca's material (*Herc. Fur.*, 570-595), and his editing and expansions chronicle a reader's response to the meaning of Seneca's scene for the *Consolation*'s prisoner.[99]

Because the poem on Orpheus so consciously directs its purpose and phrasing to the earlier stages in the prisoner's development, Boethius naturally redirects the focus of Seneca's lines away from public grief and towards private loss. From the opening of his poem, Boethius makes Orpheus' own pain the subject of his verse, while Seneca continuously shifts the acts of grieving and weeping to other characters. In Boethius, it is the Thracian poet who mourns, while in Seneca it is the chorus of Thracian brides. Seneca stresses the power of Orpheus' music to tame the beasts, alter heaven, and soothe

[98] For a review of scholarship and a reassessment of Seneca's plays in the *Consolation*, see the Appendix to this study. For other revisions of Senecan scenes within the work, see my discussions of IV.m.7 and I.m.5.

[99] The text of *Hercules Furens* used here is from the Loeb edition. Parallel texts of III.m.12 and the chorus from the play, as well as other scenes from the play relevant to the poem, are printed in the Appendix.

Hell. Boethius, however, concentrates on the ways in which Orpheus' music fails to soothe himself. His use of the word *dominus* to characterize Orpheus himself counterpoints the phrasing *dominos umbrarum* in both his own and Seneca's text. His usage reinforces a focus on the condition of Orpheus' mind, and directs the reader's attention to the inner workings of his character's psyche. Seneca continually points to the outer effects of Orpheus' music on an audience. In *Hercules Furens* it is the gods of Hades who weep; in the *Consolation* it is Orpheus himself. Whereas Seneca's Orpheus is admonished not to *respicere* and lose his wife, it is the prisoner whom Philosophy advises to look back, as the poem itself refers and reviews (*respicit*) his own life. Moreover, while Seneca's Orpheus is warned not to turn until he reaches daylight, it is Philosophy's metrum which directs the prisoner to seek the "higher day." Boethius' penultimate lines echo Seneca's introductory verses to the Orpheus chorus, and he thus contrasts the upper world towards which his hero strives with the higher daylight granted the mind in heaven.

To turn Seneca's Orpheus into a figure for the prisoner, Boethius' revisions have concerned tone and focus. He also redirects the doctrinal emphases of the play's chorus by altering the relationship of love and law in the legend. Both poems present Pluto's judgment as law, but while Seneca's *lex* is violated only by true love's hatred of delay, Boethius points directly at love's denial of all laws save its own (*HF*, 582-598; *Cons. Phil.*, III.m.12.40-48). Boethius' description of the conquest of Pluto appears as a nearly verbatim quotation from the Chorus:

Tandem, "Vincimur" arbiter
umbrarum miserans ait
      (III.m.12.40-41)
	tandem mortis ait "vincimur"
	  arbiter
	
	           (*HF*, 582)

In transforming the motives of Hell's court, Boethius shifts the notion of judgment and authority away from individually empowered beings and towards a higher, abstract law. Within the structure of Seneca's play, Pluto's system of judgment—

and his status as an *arbiter mortis*—complements the picture of
arbitrary doom envisioned by Theseus, and it counterpoints
the visions of divine and human judgment presented in Juno's
spiteful prologue and Hercules' final indecision.[100] In *Hercules
Furens* Orpheus participates in Seneca's system of judgment
and retribution. His confrontation with Pluto's *lex* challenges
ruling authority, and, in one sense, the story illustrates the
dynamics of legal decision-making. Orpheus' rejection of Plutonian decree will, in Seneca's play, prefigure Hercules' mad
attempts to challenge the gods and his own family. The meaning of the Orpheus myth for Seneca is thus a fundamentally
public one. It expresses a relationship between individual will
and institutional constraint, and it poses a deeply social question about the nature of human, and divine, institutional behavior and man's personal conformity to public judgment.
The public nature of this theme, too, complements Seneca's
focus in the choral poem on the effects of Orpheus' music on
others rather than on himself. In the context of the entire
chorus, Orpheus represents a vision of misdirected Stoic *virtus*, and the equation between infernal and human legal systems appears immediately before Orpheus' story in the chorus' address to Hercules (*HF*, 558-558).

Boethius rejects Seneca's reading of the myth. In the *Con-*

---

[100] Juno taunts Hercules (*HF*, 1-122), and her anger focuses on the reversal
of cosmic order brought on by Hercules' conquest of Hell: "foedus umbrarum
perit" (49). Her phrasing is similar to Philosophy's at the end of the poem:
Hercules brings back the spoils of Hell to the upper world (*ad superos*, 48);
she mocks his Atlan achievement ("quaerit ad superos viam" 74). Hercules'
own final speech (1321-1341) focuses on his exile after losing wife, family,
and sanity: "ubique notus perdidi exilio locum" (1331). He requests return
to Hell, to a final judgment on his own guilt, yet at the same time passes
judgment on himself. Earlier in the play, Theseus had outlined the system
of Plutonian judgment with a tone of formal dispassion. He describes the
tripartite legal system in great detail (931-947), and he catalogues the punishments of Ixion, Sisyphus, Tantalus, and Tityus (750-756). His lines here
may provide one source for Boethius' lines on the torments of Hell, for this
description is absent from the Chorus which is the poem's major source. For
texts, see Appendix.

solation Orpheus obeys a *maior lex* given neither by gods nor men but by love. Instead of seeking a moral that strength conquers as forcefully as music (*HF*, 590-591), Boethius points towards the true power behind Orpheus' gift. Rather than using his *moralitas* to foreshadow future events, Boethius directs his poem at the prisoner's past life. This structural change in the purpose of the myth resonates with the *Consolation*'s pervasive attempts to point away from human laws to divine injunctions. The progress of the prisoner himself had worked through a rejection of the human legal system which condemned him to death. His long tirade at I.pr.4 lamented that the result of his innocence had been not reward but punishment, and his speech at I.m.5 had placed this inequity in a larger, cosmic framework. The arbitrary judgments of the court appear to Boethius not as versions of either divine or Plutonian rule, but as the inexplicable manifestations of a human illogic ruled by Fortune. Unlike the prisoner's earlier lament, though, Philosophy's poem replaces the Senecan system of judgment with a pattern of divinely given order. Gone are the trappings of the law-court and jury. Gone, too, are the laments that natural and human order operate to different ends.[101] If, as she claimed in II.m.8, the love which rules the stars may also rule men's hearts, then the unity she proposes shifts the whole system of judgment and retribution away from institutions to an eternal unity. The search for that unity is enacted through the mind's struggle, and at the same time makes it a deeply personal problem for the prisoner. Seneca's Hell remains a prison and a courtroom, and his Orpheus enters only as another plaintiff. Boethius' Hell becomes a state of mind, and in order to avoid the weakness of Orpheus, his prisoner must reject the display of legalism and instead seek that knowledge granted the mind alone. For Seneca, finally, the "upper world" and "bright day" which stand to welcome Orpheus are but the details of this life. For Phi-

---

[101] See I.m.5, and my later discussion of the poem and its source in Seneca's *Hyppolitus*.

losophy, however, the "higher day" is lit not by the sun and stars but by the light of reason and the glow of heaven.

Book Three may be said to end in the way it began, with Philosophy commenting explicitly on the intent and method behind her dialogue with the prisoner. Her arguments in prose and her statements in poetry re-state phrases developed elsewhere in Boethius' writing, and her diction alerts the reader to sources in earlier literary and philosophical texts. Boethius creates unified structures of allusion in the Book: to his earlier remarks in the *Consolation*; to his definitions and idioms of the logical writings; to the persona of the tractates and commentaries. In sustaining the figure of a reader and a writer, Boethius provides a guide for the *Consolation*'s audience: they may measure themselves against the prisoner's progress and include themselves in Philosophy's final injunction; but they may also measure the prisoner against the corpus of Boethius' earlier works. These patterns of self-reference are also articulated in the dialogue's moments of pause and breakdown. By stopping to reflect on technique, the disputants make method their theme; they take as their subject the creation of the dialogue inscribed within the *Consolation*'s text. In the poetry, rhetorical forms create structures of imagery which unify the metra into narrative sequences. Moreover, the prose dialogue itself frequently moves through figurative diction and allusive metaphor. Through these patterns of literary allusion and imagery, the *Consolation*'s progress can be charted in ways which complement the straightforward and apparently linear movement of the dialogue's logic.

Book Three has an integrity of movement which reenacts the themes of returning, reviewing, and recapitulating in its very structure. A deep feeling of loss permeates the book, and it is only at its end that the prisoner witnesses the possibility of recovering a stability of mind and a strength of purpose. Book Three is also a book of transformations, as its poetry turns mythological narrative and Senecan tragedy into an almost religious cosmology, and as its prose turns the language of Aristotelian dialectic into a suitable medium for philosophic inquiry. The book gradually moves from literal explanations of method to figurative expressions of truth. While Philosophy begins with an attempt to explain her purpose in words, her final poem points towards a form of self-knowledge accessible only through individual meditation on literary symbols. The prisoner himself has been transported from a physical reliance on the impressions of his eyes and ears to a spiritual awareness granted the mind. He has moved from the limits of dialectic to an inkling of philosophic method, and his growth as a speaker and as a reader will inform the purpose of Book Four.

CHAPTER IV

READINGS AND REWRITINGS IN
BOOK FOUR

By the beginning of Book Four the prisoner has grown from a writer of complaint to a reader of moral fable. From his first, insecure autobiographical statements of Book One, he has moved towards a confident reading of mythological poetry. At one level, the prisoner develops literary abilities and a gradual awareness of the moral implications of poetry. From the whores of the theater he has turned to Philosophy's Muses; from taking dictation, he is capable of finding inspiration. At another level, his responses point to a change in the focus and subject matter of the metra themselves. While the early poems drew on the details of Boethius' life and the palpable experience of history and nature, Philosophy's later poems drew on abstract structures of belief and myth. The Timaean hymn and the poem on Orpheus point the prisoner away from a literal interpretation of himself to a philosophical understanding of his condition. These shifts in literary purpose signal a change in the biographical nature of the *Consolation*. The prose and poetry of Book Four take on a new spiritual direction, and Boethius highlights this change in purpose by rewriting earlier scenes from the text into these new contexts. The work continues to depend for its effect on the reader's ability to recognize echoes and responses to earlier material. In turn, Philosophy's instruction also depends on the prisoner's ability to recall earlier moments of dialogue and poetry, and to measure his new development against his former state.

There is thus a double process to the *Consolation*'s development at this point. The text operates both on its fictional prisoner and on its outside audience. Philosophy's poems, for instance, are designed to have spiritual and emotional effects on the prisoner: they illustrate philosophical truths, but they also offer respite from the rigors of argument. The prisoner is asked to interpret her poetry rightly, and his responses offer some guidance for the *Consolation*'s reader. The prose passages delineate the prisoner's growth as a philosopher: they narrate his mastery of a method. Boethius' work therefore tells of the education of the prisoner, while it offers an education to the reader.[1] To explain this process, I will treat the prisoner's growth in Book Four as moving through two parallel processes. First, I will illustrate how the prose passages recast earlier portions of the *Consolation* to bear witness to his newfound philosophical skills and his beginning mastery of Philosophy's argumentative techniques. As the prisoner's skills mature, the dialogue itself gradually moves to philosophical monologue. This is a much different process than the exhortative lectures Philosophy gave at the work's opening, and the prisoner's growing silence towards the end of Book Four is markedly different from his silence in Book One. In this and the next chapter, I show that his silence becomes that of a reader: that he begins to treat Philosophy as an *auctor* as her words take on the status of a text to be read rather than discussed. Second, and parallel with this development, is the allegorical representation of the prisoner's progress through mythological poetry. Boethius establishes an interpretive context in which to read the voyages of Ulysses and the labors of Hercules as versions of the prisoner's own struggle to mas-

---

[1] This double process has been explored most extensively for medieval texts by Dante scholars. See, for example, Gabriel Josipovici, *The World and the Book* (London: Macmillan, 1971), pp. 45-69, esp. p. 59; G. Mazzotta, *Dante: Poet of the Desert*, esp. pp. 141-145 (on writing as a process of return from exile), pp. 151, 157 (on reading as an act of self-disclosure and ambiguity as a goad to interpretation), p. 233 (on the art of reading as a quest), and the bibliography cited on pp. 228-229.

ter his mind. Orpheus in Hell, Ulysses on Circe's island, and Hercules in heaven present a coherent movement upwards, and these poems offer mythological landmarks against which the prisoner can measure his own progress.

In discussing the mythological poems I will spend a fair amount of time dealing with the source material for Boethius' lines. This process is designed to show how Boethius rewrites earlier texts into new contexts, making them refer uniquely to the prisoner's personal and spiritual growth. The structures of literary allusion presented in the poems write the auto-biography of a reader's life: he learns to see himself through the texts he has read, whether they are the narratives of Homeric epic, Roman verse, or Senecan tragedy. Boethius' fictions become self-consciously literary, and this quality reflects on Lady Philosophy as well. She becomes a "writer" of *fabulae* and *exempla*, of literary texts designed to be interpreted. Her status as an *auctor* devolves, then, not simply to her author-itative presence or her intellectual skills, but to her perceived literary abilities as well. Two fundamental acts of reading and rewriting therefore structure the fourth book: first, the activ-ity of the prisoner and reader reviewing the earlier arguments and poetry of the *Consolation* itself; second, the shared activity of reworking literary source material taken from outside the text and making it relevant to the prisoner's experience. Book Four becomes a book of rewritings, as Boethius adapts texts written by himself and others to chronicle the education of his prisoner and his audience.

I

From the opening of Book Four there is a change in the prisoner. He takes the verbal initiative, interrupting Philos-ophy before she can continue. Posing the question of just reward for good and evil, he reveals an inkling of her method; yet, as Philosophy's answer shows, he is still far from truth. The first prosa of the book pinpoints these developments by recalling the verbal structures and images explored earlier in the *Consolation*. The book's opening clause synthesizes earlier visions of Philosophy into what is by now an iconic portrait. Her dignity and gravity of countenance recall her initial appearance in Book One. Her sweet singing points back to the opening of Book Three, where the "sweetness of her song" held the prisoner stupefied. The word *suauiter* at IV.pr.1.1 also returns the reader to the reference to that highest good which, Philosophy had argued, "sweetly disposes" all things (". . . suauiterque disponit," III.pr.12.22). More pointedly, the opening of Book Four rewrites the previous Book's beginning. Book Three opened with the prisoner in silence, and the long break between Philosophy's last words and the prisoner's first was recreated by the period and the new sentence introducing his words, " 'O,' inquam, 'summum lassorum . . .' " (III.pr.1.2). But in Book Four the prisoner's impatience infects the syntax of the prose, as the first sentence rushes on, with clause piled on top of clause. The prisoner's words, prefaced by a single "et," begin, " 'O,' inquam, 'ueri praeuia liminis . . .' " (IV.pr.1.2). His initial O, again set off by an intrusive *inquam*, highlights the excitement of his reason. Instead of commenting on the emotional effect of Philosophy's sweet songs, as he had in the opening of Book Three, now the prisoner suggests a group of analytical issues. Instead of noticing such superficial features as the pleasures of her verse ("canendi . . . iucunditate," III.pr.1.2), he remarks on method. Comparing the Books' opening sentences illuminates how far the prisoner has come, and how much further still he has to go.

III.pr.1	IV.pr.1
O, I said, you are the perfect comforter for weak spirits. I feel greatly refreshed by the strength of your ideas and the sweetness of your music.[2]	O, I said, guide to true light, all that you have so far told me is divine in itself and perfectly convincing by virtue of your argument.[3]

[2] Green, trans., p. 42. "O, inquam, summum lassorum solamen animorum, quam tu me uel sententiarum pondere uel canendi etiam iucunditate refouisti" (III.pr.1.2).

[3] Green, trans., p. 75, slightly modified. "O, inquam, ueri praeuia luminis,

Book Three's beginning remarked on both the weight of Philosophy's arguments and the delights of her songs, but Book Four opens with a statement about argument alone. To the prisoner, the power of her reasoning stems from its absolute truth and its coherent presentation. His praise reveals his linking of divine purpose and his continuing awareness of verbal method. His phrasing revives the central metaphor of the "way" (here, *praeuia*) and elevates Philosophy to an ideal, Ciceronian presence. She embodies the union of *ratio* and *oratio*, not, however, in the service of public life, but in the pursuit of hidden truth. Book Four opens on this reflective note, bringing together words and images developed earlier in the *Consolation* into an explicit statement of method's relationship to matter.

Philosophy's response (IV.pr.1.6-9) summarizes, among other things, the metaphorical transformation of *domus* to *patria*: from an earthly house to a spiritual home. This vocabulary has been developing from the *Consolation*'s opening, as Philosophy tried to remind the prisoner of his soul's "native country" (I.pr.5.3). In Book Three she compared the soul trapped in the body to a drunk man lost on the way home (III.pr.2.13). There, she had made explicit the force of her figurative language. Now, in Book Four her statement of a moral and methodological goal gives the metaphors of the "way" and of the homeland a new vitality. She begins with an analogy between God's creation and the well-kept house of a great man.[4] She then directs the prisoner's attention to the premises of her argument and reinforces their demonstrative purpose.[5] Contrary to the prisoner's focus on wonder (his word *ammirari*), she reminds him of what she has just

---

quae usque adhuc tua fudit oratio cum sui speculatione diuina tum tuis rationibus inuicta patuerunt . . ." (IV.pr.1.2).

[4] "Et esset, inquit, infiniti stuporis omnibusque horribilius monstris si, uti tu aestimas, in tanti uelut patris familias dispositissima domo uilia uasa colerentur, pretiosa sordescerent" (IV.pr.1.6).

[5] "nam si ea quae paulo ante conclusa sunt inconuulsa seruantur . . ." (IV.pr.1.7).

shown him (her word is *monstrante*).[6] Repeating her earlier promise, she will show the prisoner home. Here the *via* is less methodological than moral, and the *domus* becomes the soul's residence rather than the body's. Finally, in a sentence which echoes the Timaean hymn, Philosophy offers to raise the prisoner's mind to that true *patria* in the heavens:

> And I shall give wings to your mind which can carry you aloft, so that, without further anxiety, you may return safely to your own country under my direction, along my path, and by my means.[7]

She has transformed the hymn's controlling imagery: her direction to the prisoner, to return his mind to the divine seat, replaces the hymn's swift chariot with her own carriage.[8] Her words *dux* and *semita* echo those of the hymn's final line ("principium, uector, dux, semita, terminus idem," III.m.9.28), and her concluding rhetorical flourish, with its anaphora on the personal pronoun, heightens the drama of her speech as the final stretto of the hymn amplified its power. But the subjects of the poem and the prose are fundamentally different. In "O qui perpetua," the subject was always God, expressed through the repeated second person address which directed the vision to Him alone (*Tu namque, tu requies, tu cernere*). In Book Four Philosophy moves to first-person declaration. In this way she makes herself not only the guide along the way, but, in effect, the intercessor between the

---

[6] The prisoner had said: "Quae fieri in regno scientis omnia, potentis omnia, sed bona tantummodo uolentis dei nemo satis potest nec *ammirari* nec conqueri" (IV.pr.1.5, emphasis mine). Philosophy responds: "Et quoniam uerae formam beatitudinis me dudum monstrante uidisti, quo etiam sita sit agnouisti, decursis omnibus quae praemittere necessarium puto uiam tibi quae te domum reuehat ostendam" (IV.pr.1.8)

[7] Green, trans., p. 76. "Pennas etiam tuae menti quibus se in altum tollere possit adfigam, ut perturbatione depulsa sospes in patriam meo ductu, mea semita, meis etiam uehiculis reuertaris" (IV.pr.1.9).

[8] Compare Philosophy's phrasing, "uehiculis reuertaris," with III.m.9.19-21: "prouehis et leuibus sublimes curribus aptans / in caelum terramque seris, quas lege benigna / ad te conuersas reduci facis igne reuerti."

prisoner and divinity. Morally, in "O qui perpetua," it is God's way the prisoner follows; practically, in the first prose of Book Four, it is Philosophy's way.

Her introductory remarks at prosa 1 also restate her own commentary on the hymn. She had made clear that the prisoner's comprehension of her poem involved an equation of seeing and understanding. The mind's inner vision presented at the hymn's close pointed towards a process of demonstration through seeing. Immediately after the hymn, she noted that the prisoner had seen the form of the good, and that their present purpose was to show (*demonstrare*) its place. Similarly, in Book Four, Philosophy reminds the prisoner that she has shown (*monstrante*) the form of blessedness, that he has seen it, and has recognized its place.

These verbal echoes from one book to another are not simply designed to teach through repetition, nor are they bald reminders to the prisoner and reader of the progress of the argument. They serve to create a coherent structure of imagery for the *Consolation*, a figurative diction through which both poetic effect and philosophical argument can be described and discussed. Philosophy's specific wording points the prisoner repeatedly back into his own mind. It forces him to reflect on his cognitive processes, just as their public dialogue involved his reflection on his verbal abilities. Combined with her emphases on returning home, this language sustains one of the *Consolation*'s basic movements: a progressive turning inward, a movement from external things (the Muses, worldly goods, extrinsic arguments, sensations) to internal qualities (virtue, self-consistent arguments, the *musica vernacula*). In this manner, the dialogue becomes explicitly concerned with its own terms and structure. It tries to articulate its method, while attempting to direct the prisoner and reader to reflect upon their own rational abilities.

The structure of echo and repetition continues through Book Four, and metrum 1 specifically addresses problems in the previous poem on Orpheus. Taken together, these poems posit the two alternatives to human existence: either the

downcast mourning of Orpheus' loss, or the uplifting cele-
bration of Philosophy's discovery. The opening lines of the
metra compare Orpheus' lost ability to reassure his spirit and
raise his sight with the prisoner's new-found aspiration to
seek the soul's true home and look down upon the earth.[9]
While the prisoner's soul has swift wings, Orpheus' body has
only heavy fetters. In contrast to Orpheus' lethargy, the prisoner's mind is granted a new liveliness. If Orpheus' condition
was meant to characterize the early stages of the prisoner's
development, then the opening poem of Book Four symbolically restates the new enthusiasm with which he reopened
the dialogue. The language of perception dominates both
poems. Orpheus had looked back to lose his wife, and, while
the metrum itself reviewed the prisoner's life (through the
word *respicit*), iv.m.1 begs him to look down (*despicit*) and
reject the earth. The verbal similarities of one answer the
other, as looking back in longing becomes looking down in
discarding.

The contrast between the terms *respicit* and *despicit* pinpoints
the prisoner's own movement away from earth and towards
heaven. Further parallels reinforce the moral and geographical
direction of his ascent. To regain his wife, Orpheus enters
the households of Hell ("infernas domos," iii.m.12.19), while
the spirit in Book Four ascends to the homes of the stars
("astriferas domos," iv.m.1.9). While Orpheus confronts the
lord of the shades ("umbrarum dominus," iii.m.12.28) and
the judge of the dead ("arbiter umbrarum," iii.m.12.40-41),
the spirit greets the lord of kings ("regum dominus,"
iv.m.1.19) and the master of all things ("rerum arbiter,"
iv.m.1.22). Orpheus' journey to the house of the dead is
guided by a misdirected sense of loss, and it progresses
through a series of sensory and spiritual deceptions until he
is left standing alone at the edge of night. The spirit in Book

---

[9] Compare iii.m.12.1-4 with the opening of iv.m.1: "Sunt etenim pennae
uolucres mihi / quae celsa conscendant poli; / quas sibi cum uelox mens induit
/ terras perosa despicit, / aeris immensi superat globum" (1-5).

Four seeks its natural home, and if it too is left at the edge of earth's night ("terrarum noctem," IV.m.1.27-28), it is to seek the company of God. Eurydice's death projects Orpheus into an afterlife turned upside down, whose *domus* and *dominus* are neither the spiritual fatherland nor its father. The progressive disharmonies created by his poem are restored in the stable rule affirmed in IV.m.1.

The conclusion to the metrum establishes a sense of return, as the penultimate lines rework the familiar imagery of the *via* and the *gradus* into a spiritual schema:

> If the road (*via*) which you have forgotten, but now search for, brings you here, you will cry out: "This I remember, this is my own country, here I was born and here I shall hold my step (*hinc sistam gradum*)."[10]

The *gradus* along which the prisoner's moral and methodological development was directed ends with the soul's return to heaven. The Platonic doctrine of reminiscence informs a vocabulary of recognition, where the imagery of sight and the language of thought combine. The spirit's glance is voluntary, but it is an act of will far different from Orpheus' desperate turn of the head. If it pleases you to look, Philosophy advises, then you will see only exiles.[11] The spirit's act of seeing here involves more than perception: it necessitates a true discernment, a recognition of both his condition and that of others. Like the poem on Orpheus, this metrum involves the prisoner's abilities in interpretation and understanding. Orpheus could not comprehend the nature of his loss; his sight was simple and in its simplicity, deadly: "uidit, perdidit, occidit." It was to the prisoner's insight that Philosophy directed the poem, and the admonition to reflect on its meaning should give the prisoner a new understanding of his state.

---

[10] Green, trans., p. 76, slightly modified. "Huc te si reducem referat uia / quam nunc requiris immemor, / 'Haec,' dices, 'memini, patria est mihi, / hinc ortus, hic sistam gradum' " (IV.m.1.23-26).

[11] "Quodsi terrarum placeat tibi / noctem relictam uisere, / quos miseri toruos populi timent / cernes tyrannos exsules" (IV.m.1.27-30).

Similarly, at the conclusion of iv.m.i., the spirit will sense itself at home, returned not to the alien underworld but to the recognizable homeland. The very rhetoric of these final words, with the repeated pointing demonstratives, *huc, haec, hinc, hic,* both grammatically and physically localizes the spirit's place. The rhetorical strategy reinforces the prisoner's sense of a homecoming, in contrast to the exiles whom he sees trapped in the essential otherness of earth.

Boethius is now, very early in Book Four, demonstrating his new insights—insights, if not into truth, at least into method. Philosophy's first metrum spoke directly to the prisoner's opening impatience, and he sustains his excitement well into prosa 2. He shouts ecstatically, and begs not to be held back in his pursuit of knowledge.[12] After these outbursts, Philosophy's calm and deliberate methodological preliminaries slow the pace of the dialogue, and they redirect the reader's attention away from the emotional response to dispassionate argument. She announces the goal of the prosa, and her commitment to confirming her arguments from two sides recalls the Ciceronian commitment to argument *in utramque partem.*[13] Once again, Philosophy asserts her authority as a model disputant, and Boethius recognizes that her proofs are both in-

---

[12] "Papae, inquam, ut magna promittis! Nec dubito quin possis efficere, tu modo quem excitaueris ne moreris" (iv.pr.2.1).

[13] She claims, "Sed uti nostrae sententiae fides abundantior sit, alterutro calle procedam nunc hinc nunc inde proposita confirmans" (iv.pr.2.4). For the possible backgrounds in Ciceronian argumentative theory, see the discussion in Chapter I, and see in particular, Cicero, *De finibus,* v.iv.10 (on the Peripatetic development of argument *in utramque partem*), and *De Fato,* i. 1 ("Quod autem in aliis libris feci, . . . ut in utramque partem perpetua explicaretur oratio, quo facilius id a quoque probaretur quod cuique maxime probabile videretur . . ."). Solmsen's paraphrase of Aristotle, *Topica* 163b, "by looking at a question from both sides we sharpen our eyes for truth" (in Owen, ed., p. 54), is also relevant here. Boethius' Latin version of the Aristotelian passage reads: "Ad omnem autem positionem, et quoniam sic et quoniam non sic, argumentum considerandum, et invenienti solutionem statim quaerendum; sic enim simul accidet et ad interrogandum et ad respondendum exerceri. Et si ad nullum alium habemus, ad ipsos" (*Top.,* 163b1-5; Minio-Paluello, ed., *A-L, Topica,* p. 177).

ternally coherent and objectively true. To her remarks on the relationship of good and evil, he responds: "To doubt that would be to disregard the nature of things and the force of the argument."[14] Clearly, he has enough confidence by now to argue from an understanding of the nature of the world as well as the nature of philosophical reasoning.[15] The prisoner is beginning to express himself like a philosopher, and to Philosophy's next sequence of arguments he again recognizes the coherence of necessary truths. "And I see clearly the consequence of your line of reasoning. For it follows that the good are powerful and the wicked are impotent."[16] His concern with necessity, with sequential reasoning, and with the proper order of argument suggests now that his facility in method has given him insight into truth. Philosophy notices his new fluency by remarking how "you run ahead" (*praecurris*, IV.pr.2.25). He can follow her arguments and even anticipate her conclusions, using the language of philosophical proof.

Boethius' statements not only mark him as a philosopher, they reveal him as a man. His *erecta natura*—his upright, human nature—comes out as the prisoner leaves behind the downcast look of an Orpheus.[17] Philosophy commends his mastery of method in moral terms. She combines her roles

[14] Green, trans., p. 78. "Quisquis, inquam, dubitat nec rerum naturam nec consequentiam potest considerare rationum" (IV.pr.2.16).

[15] For an analogous view of a system of reasoning, see Cicero, *De finibus*, IV.xix.55. Cicero is arguing against the blind rigor of Stoic logic. After reviewing a series of fallacious syllogistic lines of argument, Cicero states: "Sensus enim cuiusque et natura rerum atque ipsa veritas clamabat quodam modo non posse adduci ut inter eas res quas Zeno exaequaret nihil interesset." In the idiom of modern philosophy, one might say that the prisoner praises Philosophy's arguments as true by coherence and correspondence: i.e., that they follow logically from one another and that they verify facts about the world.

[16] Green, trans., p. 79. "nam etiam quod est consequens patet. Ex his enim quae concesserim bonos quidem potentes, malos uero esse necesse est imbecilles" (IV.pr.2.24).

[17] Philosophy states: "Recte, inquit, praecurris idque, uit medici sperare solent, indicium est erectae iam resistentisque naturae" (IV.pr.2.25).

as doctor and teacher: the doctor recognizes in his eagerness a healthy nature; the teacher sees in his readiness a greater intelligence. Philosophy prepares to abandon the slow techniques of dialectic for the more advanced patterns of philosophy. Rather than offering to "clash together" their arguments—as her exhortation at III.pr.12 sought—she alone will heap them together ("crebras coaceruabo rationes," IV.pr.2.26). She opens the door to monologue, and the remainder of prosa 2 is little more than a sequence of rhetorical questions Philosophy poses to herself. Prosa 3 is an unbroken lecture, too, and it is clear that her argument has reached a new level of sophistication and insight. In short, the prisoner's education in method has prepared him for a corresponding lesson in humanity. His physical nature now corresponds to the moral condition outlined in IV.m.1. Central to these prose exchanges are the prisoner's achievements of a new spiritual status, not through actions but through words. Boethius shows how learning a method of argument is in itself a moral activity; in the mastery of the technique lies the awareness of truth.

As the dialogue revives in Book Four, the focus turns again to distinguishing between elite knowledge and common opinion. Philosophy and the prisoner will pause frequently to remark on an argument's inaccessibility to the multitude. While these problems are discussed, Philosophy will continue to take a more authoritative role in the discussion: she concedes less and less to the prisoner's hesitation, and the prisoner himself becomes more ambitious in his attempts to engage philosophically with his partner. At prosa 4 he takes up the verbal initiative. To his wish that the wicked not have the power to destroy good, Philosophy cautions that the answer will be shown "at the proper time."[18] She returns the prisoner to the importance of the right order of argument, and she reassumes her earlier role as a master of *dispositio*. In turn, the prisoner willingly returns to the rhetoric of assent to marvel

---

[18] Green, trans. p. 84. ". . . uti conuenienti monstrabitur loco" (IV.pr.4.2).

at his teacher's skill. To her first set of arguments, he reacts: "That is a wonderful conclusion, but I recognize that it follows from that which I have already conceded to be true."[19] Philosophy's response synthesizes the techniques of inquiry and the metaphors of understanding which she had developed over three and a half books. Structurally, her speech functions in the manner of her opening outline of method at I.pr.6 and her exhortations at III.pr.12. Her advice now, however, is not designed either to initiate or sustain the prisoner's speech; rather, its goals are the refinement of technique. Returning to the idiom of Aristotelian topics theory, she outlines two proper responses if one finds a conclusion hard to concede: either show that the argument's premises are false or that the premises in sequence do not give a necessary conclusion. Furthermore, she states that her following point may seem no less wonderful, but that it too follows necessarily from her premises.[20]

[19] Green, trans., p. 85, slightly modified. "Mira quidem, inquam, et concessu difficilis inlatio, sed his eam quae prius concessa sunt nimium conuenire cognosco" (IV.pr.4.10).

[20] "Recte, inquit, aestimas, sed qui conclusioni accedere durum putat aequum est uel falsum aliquid praecessisse demonstret uel collocationem propositionum non esse efficacem necessariae conclusionis ostendat; alioquin concessis praecedentibus nihil prorsus est quod de inlatione causetur. Nam hoc quoque quod dicam non minus mirum uideatur, sed ex his quae sumpta sunt aeque est necessarium" (IV.pr.4.11-12). Of the many possible sources for Philosophy's advice, the most relevant is perhaps the discussion beginning in Aristotle's *Topica*, 161b19, on the five ways in which an argument is open to criticism. Among them, Aristotle claims that an argument may be criticized when the conclusion reached is untenable because the premises on which the conclusion is based are either false or not generally believable; and when the reasoning itself based on the premises is not appropriate to the thesis. In Boethius' Latin, these passages read: "Per se autem orationis quinque sunt increpationes, prima quidem quando ex interrogatis non concluditur neque quod propositum est neque omnino nichil cum sint vel falsa vel improbabilia, aut omnia aut plura, in quibus est conclusio, et neque ablatis quibusdam neque additis neque his quidem ablatis illis vero additis fit conclusio. Secunda autem si ad positionem non fiat syllogismus et ex talibus et sic ut dictum est prius" (*Top.*, 161b19-25; Minio-Paluello ed., *A-L*, *Topica*, p. 172). For the sense of these problems as commonplace issues by the time of Cicero, see

Philosophy's remarks return the dialogue to the strictures of topics theory. They restate the fundamental problem of truths which are necessary but not readily believable to the common man. The problem, so central to Boethius' *De topicis differentiis*, motivates much of the rest of the *Consolation*'s discussion.[21] It expresses a tension between the understanding of the common man based on judgment and opinion, and the knowledge of the philosopher based on reason and argument. The prisoner himself delineates the issue later in prosa 4:

> When I consider your arguments, I find that nothing could be more true. But, if we consider the ordinary judgment of men, who is likely to find these ideas credible, or who will even listen to them?[22]

To ordinary human judgment, Philosophy's argument would seem unbelievable, and she explains in terms of the *Consolation*'s basic imagery that such listeners "cannot raise eyes accustomed to darkness to the light of clear truth" (Green, trans., p. 86). Philosophy's arguments become limited to the kind of elite audience Boethius himself had addressed in the theological tractates. By exploiting the vocabulary of topics theory, she removes the discussion from the world of experience to the arena of intellection; she makes their conversation hinge on technical terms. No longer do historical examples suffice, as in the earlier books. The autobiographical stance,

---

the remarks at *De finibus*, IV.xix.55, that the *dialectici* teach that if the conclusion which follows from a proposition is false, then the proposition itself is false. Gruber (*Kommentar*, p. 343) feels that Philosophy's diction in this passage is Ciceronian, and he focuses on the terminology of *conclusio* and *collocatio* to point to sources in the *Hortensius*, *De Oratore*, and other texts.

[21] See *De topicis differentiis* on the distinction between readily believable arguments and necessary arguments (Stump, trans., p. 39, PL, 64: 1180C-D; Stump, trans., pp. 40-41, PL, 64: 1181B-C). See, too, Boethius' definition of a philosopher as one who concerns himself with necessary arguments which may or may not be readily believable to the listener (Stump, trans., p. 41, PL, 64: 1182A).

[22] Green, trans., p. 86. "Cum tuas, inquam, rationes considero, nihil dici uerius puto; at si ad hominum iudicia reuertar, quis ille est cui haec non credenda modo sed saltem audienda uideantur" (IV.pr.4.26).

too, is long gone. Even Philosophy's apparent barb at the judicial system of the day (IV.pr.4.38-40) quickly loses its contemporary reference behind the metaphors of healing and the mythology of reward and punishment familiar from the poetry. The context of the discussion will from now on be much more rarefied, and the prisoner can no longer rely on his experience to engage in dialogue. The pauses in the discussions now take on a new purpose: they seem to prepare the reader for a new kind of discourse. By rejecting human opinion, the *Consolation* moves towards the techniques of pure philosophy as defined in *De topicis*. Structurally, the dialogue itself will change to monologue. Save for the introductory questions at IV.pr.6 and V.pr.1, and the brief exchange at IV.pr.7, the rest of the work is a series of lectures. Book Five, too, save for the prisoner's final prosimetrical reflections (V.pr.3.,m.3), reads as an unbroken treatise. By IV.pr.6 a fundamental reordering of the dialogue's purpose and method is underway, and Boethius' claim for a "new beginning" will point the reader away from the methods of dialectic towards the techniques of pure philosophizing.

Parallel to the exposition of the prisoner's education is the allusive chronicle of his growth written in the poetry. Both movements take Orpheus as their starting point: for the early prosae, he is the backdrop against which to light the prisoner's aspirations; for the succeeding metra, he is the first in a series of mythological treatments of the prisoner's progress. In what follows, I will show how allegory works as well as argument in defining the prisoner's moral growth, and how Boethius sets out to educate his reader through these poems.

II

The poems on Ulysses and Hercules (IV.m.3.,m.7) have as their ultimate origin the myths of Homer and his successors, and Boethius would no doubt have received his Greek material through scholia and Late Antique commentaries. What interests him most in these poems, however, is not their absolute allegorical meanings, as inherited from the commentators, but rather the interpretive problems they pose for the prisoner. These are texts to be read and interpreted in the light of their literary heritage and in the context of the prisoner's experience. This section first outlines some of the major critical views of the myths before illustrating how Boethius turned away from the abstractly Platonic and Stoic schemata of interpretation to present the poems as culminations of images specific to the *Consolation*.

The work of Erich Kaiser and Felix Buffière has shown how Homer was very early on subjected to allegorical and symbolic readings.[23] The earliest of these attempts came in the sixth century B.C., as Greek readers tried to explain away the embarrassments of Homer's gods.[24] Readings which stressed moral, psychological, and physical allegories developed, reaching their fullest surviving expression in the works of Heracleitos and Porphyry.[25] Kaiser has suggested in par-

[23] See Erich Kaiser, "Odyssee-Szenen als Topoi," *Museum Helveticum* 21 (1964), 109-136, 197-224; F. Buffière, *Les Mythes d'Homère et la Pensée Grecque* (Paris: Belles Lettres, 1956). See also Hugo Rahner, *Griechische Mythen in Christlicher Deutung* (Zurich: Rhein Verlag, 1957), esp. pp. 414-486 ("Odysseus am Mastbaum"). For a summary of the early allegorists which stresses their influence on later Latin poetry, see Michael Murrin, *The Allegorical Epic*, pp. 3-25. On the criticism of Homer with special reference to Ulysses, see W. B. Stanford, *The Ulysses Theme* (Ann Arbor: Univ. of Michigan Press, 1968), pp. 118-127, 146-158.

[24] See Stanford, pp. 94-95, on Hesiod's condemnation of Homer's treatment of the gods. Buffière, pp. 81-84, stresses the early allegorists attempt to make physical processes out of the gods' actions. For the origins of the sixth century techniques, see M. Detienne, *Homère, Hésiode, et Pythagore* (Brussels: Collection Latomus, 1962), pp. 62-69.

[25] For the early physical allegorists, see Buffière, pp. 85-132; for moral allegory, especially Stoic readings of Ulysses, see pp. 365-391; for psychological readings, see pp. 251-278. The allegories of Heracleitos are one of the major sources for Buffière's study. In addition to the texts cited and discussed in his work, see also his edition and translation, with commentary, *Héraclite: Allégories d'Homère* (Paris: Belles Lettres, 1962). For Porphyry and the traditions of Neoplatonic allegory, see *Les Mythes*, sections on the "Cave of the Nymphs," pp. 419-459. For critical discussion of the poetic uses of the allegories, see Murrin, pp. 3-11.

ticular that Boethius would have come to the Homeric legends with the presupposition that they would be reconciled with Platonic myths.[26] Both the structure of the *Odyssey* as a whole as well as individual scenes were explained as allegories of the soul's wandering journey home. What Kaiser labels "das Thema der Seelenwanderung" appears clearly articulated in writers such as Plotinus and Numenius as well, especially in the view of Ulysses as a figure for the soul's struggle with earthly temptation.[27] Plotinus compares Ulysses' journey with the "catharsis of the soul," and Numenius considered his voyages to figure forth "an image of the soul's troubled exile in the world of matter."[28] Kaiser's argument, however, is not only that the *Odyssey* itself received allegorical treatments, but that scenes such as those with the Sirens, Circe, and the Phaeacians became isolated and survived as *topoi* in later writers. These *topoi* had the status of mythological exempla, pressed into service by commentators and philosophers in the course of their arguments.[29]

Buffière, however, argues for a variety of complementary readings of the Homeric stories, readings derived from Platonic, Stoic, Cynic, and Christian philosophies.[30] In this way,

---

[26] Kaiser, "Odyssee-Szenen," p. 203 (on Boethius' use of the Circe episode), and pp. 205-206, in general.

[27] Kaiser, "Odyssee-Szenen," pp. 205-208. For a reading based on the Greek Christian traditions, see Rahner, pp. 430-444 ("Die Seefahrt des Lebens").

[28] The references to Plotinus and Numenius, and the characterization of their allegories, are taken from David Thompson, "Dante's Ulysses and the Allegorical Journey," *Dante Studies* 85 (1967), pp. 35-58. For Plotinus, see *Enneads*, i.vi.8, and the remarks in E. Brehier, *The Philosophy of Plotinus*, trans. J. Thomas (Chicago: Univ. of Chicago Press, 1958), pp. 1, 14-51, 35. On Numenius, Thompson, p. 43 and n. 32, cites as his source, P. Courcelle, "Quelques symboles funéraires du néoplatonisme latin," *Revue des études anciennes*, 46 (1944), 90-91. For a discussion of Numenius' explications of the *Odyssey*, as transmitted through Porphyry and Proclus, see Murrin, pp. 31-33, and p. 215, n. 19.

[29] Kaiser, "Odyssee-Szenen," p. 110.

[30] For remarks on the syncretism of Buffière's method, and the encyclopaedic goals of the project, see *Les Mythes*, pp. 3-5.

the figure of Ulysses, for example, could stand for various incarnations of the human ideal, whether he embodies a Platonic version of the soul in exile or a Stoic model of *virtus* in action.[31] In addition, the *Iliad* and the *Odyssey* could be read in sequence together as "poèmes mystiques," where the Greeks and Trojans signify the spiritual and carnal properties of the soul, respectively.[32] Homer's two poems were seen as telling two halves of the same story, where the soul's relationship to heaven and earth is expressed in both. The tradition of allegorical commentary on the Homerica survived in the Late Antique commentaries on Virgil's *Aeneid*, a work which Macrobius argued combined both Iliadic and Odyssean narratives, and which Fulgentius read as an allegory of education.[33]

By the time of Boethius, the exploits of Ulysses and Hercules had been subjected to a variety of figural readings, and perhaps the clearest link between the two heroes can be found in the writings of the Stoics. The myths provided their thought with ideal narratives of *virtus*.[34] In one essay, Seneca

[31] See Buffière, *Les Mythes*, pp. 364-391 for discussions of Ulysses as a figure of intelligence; for Cynic readings of the Odyssean voyages; for Stoic readings of Ulysses as a figure of virtue and strength; for Ulysses as a figure of Platonic wisdom. Buffière quotes Heracleitos' summary of the general program of allegory: "Toute la course errante d'Ulysse, si l'on veut bien y regarder de près, n'est qu'une vaste allégorie. Ulysse est comme un instrument de toutes les vertus, qu' Homère s'est forgé, et dont il se sert pour enseigner la sagesse: car il déteste les vices qui rongent l'humanité" (*Les Mythes*, p. 378. Text of the translation, with the original Greek, in Buffière, ed. and trans., *Héraclite*, p. 75, ch. 70). For a review of the history and scholarship of the Ulysses tradition, see the studies of Stanford, Mazzotta (pp. 74-75), and Thompson. See too P. W. Damon, "Dante's Ulysses and the Mythic Tradition," in W. Matthews, ed., *Medieval Secular Literature* (Berkeley and Los Angeles: Univ. of California Press, 1965), pp. 25-45.

[32] Buffière, *Les Mythes*, pp. 410-418, esp. pp. 411-412.

[33] Macrobius, *Saturnalia*, v.2.6: "iam vero Aeneis ipsa nonne ab Homero sibi mutata est errorem primum ex Odyssea, deinde ex Iliade pugnas?" (ed. J. Willis [Leipzig: Teubner, 1963], p. 244). For Virgil as Homeric imitator in the opening lines of the *Aeneid*, see *Sat.*, v.2.5-11.

[34] See Buffière, *Les Mythes*, p. 376.

had associated Ulysses and Hercules as men who, after great struggles, achieved victory over earthly temptation.

> We Stoics have declared that these were wise men, because they were unconquered by struggles, were despisers of pleasure, and victors over all terrors.[35]

Hercules did not remain a figure of brute force; he came to symbolize the triumph of the spirit. Buffière cites Heracleitos to record this added symbolic value: Hercules is a spiritual figure, "initiated in celestial wisdom, who made philosophy, which had previously been plunged into a murky fog, shine with a lively burst."[36] Hercules' labors parallel Ulysses' voyages in that both reenact the various combats of the wise against the many forms of vice and temptation.

There are thus two important features of the mythological allegories which characterize Boethius' treatment. The first is the tendency to rewrite geographical journeys into moral struggles: voyages over land come to represent spiritual pilgrimages, and the physical home sought by the hero symbolizes the spiritual home sought by the soul. The second tendency was to select individual moments (Kaiser's *topoi*) from the epics and read them symbolically. The legend of Circe in particular developed an interpretive life of its own throughout the Middle Ages, quite independent of the continuing traditions of Homeric scholarship.[37] Such a critical environment enabled Boethius to use the legend of Circe alone in IV.m.3, both as a self-contained allegorical narrative and as

---

[35] "Hos enim Stoici nostri sapientes pronuntiaverunt, invictos laboribus et contemptores voluptatis et victores omnium terrorum," Seneca, *De Constantia Sapientis*, ii.1. Text cited in Buffière, *Les Mythes*, p. 376, n. 39. I quote the Latin and translation from the Loeb edition.

[36] *Les Mythes*, p. 376. I am translating the French version printed in Buffière, *Héraclite*, p. 39. ch. 33: "ce fut en sage, initié à la sagesse céleste, qui fit briller d'un vif éclat la philosophie, jusqu'alors plongée dans un épais brouillard."

[37] See Kaiser, "Odyssee-Szenen," pp. 200–208; Buffière, *Les Mythes*, pp. 379, 464. See also B. Paetz, *Kirke und Odysseus* (Berlin: De Gruyter, 1970), esp. pp. 25–28, 29–32.

a metonymy for the entire Odyssean experience. In contrast, however, Boethius takes the entire story of Hercules' labors for the subject of IV.m.7, and dovetails this narrative with individual allusions to the *Iliad* and the *Odyssey*. This poem therefore operates as a work of summary and review: it synthesizes a great body of mythological and historical material specifically within the structure of imagery developed for the *Consolation*. The reader's understanding of Boethius' purpose, and of the prisoner's development, in Book Four depends on reading the poems sequentially, finding in each repeated modes of journey, labor, and conquest. Read together, they recapitulate the moral education of the prisoner, and they reinforce the prose arguments which Philosophy develops in the course of the book.

The three poems on Orpheus, Ulysses, and Hercules express the prisoner's journey in the traditional geographical allegories. The poems depict the places of myth, yet also states of mind. As conditions of moral being, Orpheus' Hell, Circe's island, and Hercules' Heaven chart a path from loss to restitution, from night to day, and from bodily harm to spiritual health. The echoes and parallels between the three poems are complex and interlocking, and the following chart schematically presents their relationships. These parallels point towards the shared movements of conquest and gain in all three poems. Orpheus subdues Hell only to lose his love; Circe conquers men's bodies, only to wound their intact minds; Hercules fulfills physical labors and receives a reward in heaven. There is the urge to encyclopedize in the poems as well: Boethius lists the triumphs of Orpheus in Hell, the varieties of Circe's metamorphic wiles, and the canon of Hercules' labors. In each poem, too, lists of animals reify the individual hero's relationships to created nature.

While the poems may have their philosophical basis in the heritage of Platonic and Stoic allegory, their diction is firmly grounded in the poetic language of Roman verse and drama. In the Ulysses poem in particular, Boethius plays off of complex structures of allusion to reinforce the imaginative setting

CHART FOR MYTHOLOGICAL METRA

ORPHEUS (III. m. 12)	ULYSSES (IV. m. 3)	HERCULES (IV. m. 7)
Hell	*Earth*	*Heaven*
Orpheus' power over beasts through *carmine*	Circe's power of men as beasts: "tacta *carmine* pocula."	Hercules' power over beasts in his labors: lion, birds, dragon, dog, steeds, boar
hind, lion, hare, hound	lion, tiger, wolf, pig	
Power and conquest; subduing of Hell: *vincimur*	Power and conquest; loss of human *vigor*	Power and conquest; Hercules as *victor*
Loss: *perdidit*	Loss: *perditis*	Reward: *pretium*
Man looks down; ideal to lead the mind into upper day: "mentem ducere in superum diem quaeritis."	Man is dragged down (*detrahunt*): "nec nocentia corpori mentis uulnere saeuiunt."	Man is lifted up; apotheosis: "Ita nunc fortes ubi celsa magni ducit exempli uia."
Granting of will: Pluto's *donamus*		Granting of heaven: *sidera donat*

of its events.[38] The poem's force lies not merely with the simple fact of Ulysses' men changing into beasts. It is essential to the poem's meaning that they be identified with specific animals from specific lands, and, moreover, that their epithets be identified with individual poetic sources. One man becomes an African lion (*Marmaricus leo*, 11), and this phrase owes its origin to Seneca and Lucan.[39] Another becomes an

[38] Text of the poem printed in full in the Appendix.

[39] Cassandra's words at *Agamemnon*, 738-739 read: "uictor ferarum colla sublimis iacet / ignobili sub dente marmaricus leo." See *Hercules Oeteus*, 1057: "sedit Marmaricus leo." R. J. Tarrant (*Agamemnon*, ed., p. 310) notes that *Marmaricus* is an odd word in the *Agamemnon*'s context; that it does not appear, in this form, in Augustan poetry, but has its sources in Pliny, *Natural History*, XIII.127, and Lucan, *Pharsalia*, III.293 ("Marmaricas . . . cateruas"), VI.309 (". . . Marmaricus . . . harenas"). Gruber, *Kommentar*, cites only the Senecan allusions without comment (p. 340).

Indian tiger (*tigris Indica*, 15), a phrase borrowed from Juvenal.[40] The wolves howl not as real animals, but as Virgil's wolves ("formae magnorum ululare lupum," *Aeneid*, VII, 18).[41] When Mercury descends into this scene he comes not by name but by place: he is the Arcadian flyer, and his point of origin lies with a poetic rather than a purely geographical locus. Boethius draws his description from a variety of Latin sources, including Ovid, Statius, and Sidonius.[42] Even Circe and Ulysses, the main actors in this drama, appear nowhere by name. Instead, Boethius calls Circe by her traditional periphrasis, the daughter of the sun.[43] Ulysses is the Neritian leader, a phrase which localizes him as an Ithacan, and which too finds its source in Virgil and Ovid.[44]

The poem operates in a world of literary allusion and elaborate circumlocution. By refusing to name precisely any of his characters, Boethius focuses on their conditions or points of origin to highlight how Ulysses' men, changed to animals, return to a base earthly existence. The subjects of the poem hover unsteadily between where they have come from—Neritia, Arcadia, Troy—and where they are going: Ithaca, home, Heaven. Instead of sending them to their true home, however, Circe figuratively scatters them over a beastly earth, from Marmorica to India—to the ends of the known world.[45] Her

[40] Juvenal, *Satires*, XV.163-164: "Indica tigris agit rabida cum tigride pacem / perpetuam. . . ."

[41] Cited in Gruber, *Kommentar*, p. 340, note to IV.m.3.14.

[42] See the citations of Ovid and Statius in Gruber, p. 340.

[43] He calls her *solis semine* (IV.m.3.5). For the origins of the name, see Paetz, *Kirke*, pp. 11-12, who cites later Latin uses in Virgil, Ovid, Tibullus, Petronius, Servius, Fulgentius, and others (p. 12, nn. 9-16).

[44] See Gruber, p. 339, for citations to Ovid's *Tristia* and *Fasti*, as well as to *Aeneid*, III.271.

[45] E. R. Curtius, *European Literature and the Latin Middle Ages*, pp. 160-161, discusses the "India topos" as a way of metonymically encompassing the entire world: to be known in India signals great fame; to stretch from home to India signals great power. India and Thule become, in Boethius' earlier poem, III.m.5, the extremities of the world: "etenim licet Indica longe / tellus tua iura tremescat / et seruiat ultima Thyle, / tamen atras pellere curas / miserasque fugare querelas / non posse potentia non est" (5-10). Philoso-

island becomes a microcosm of the earth, and Boethius' poem becomes a synthesis of literary and mythological material. Its actions, for all their geographical specificity, happen only in the world of poetry.

This pervasive instability appears from the poem's opening lines. Ulysses' voyage reenacts the many symbolic journeys portrayed earlier in the *Consolation*. His wandering fleet recalls the first foreboding voyage to unknown lands expressed in Book Two.[46] Metrum 5 had depicted a golden age, before technology and travel fired human greed and led to war. One of the pervasive themes of the *Consolation*'s poetry has been the transformation of nature by man, and the poetry of Book Two, notably metra 2-4, had written a history of human technological civilization. The poem on Orpheus also presented the figure of man conquering nature; but this lyric differentiated between the conquest of earthly and infernal worlds and the hero's failure to overcome himself. The poem on Circe begins with the vision of Ulysses' men wandering aimlessly. Like earlier visions of man against nature, he is buffeted by winds. The southeast wind (Eurus) drives him to Circe's island, as the same wind had threatened the prudent man's home in Book Two.[47] Recalling the prisoner's opening lament for himself and his kind, the poem portrays a man rocked by fortune's seas.[48] The reader of the poem would be reminded, too, of Philosophy's initial injunction against Fortune: "If you hoist your sails in the wind, you will go where

---

phy's injunction in this poem may resonate ironically with Circe's powers in IV.m.3: while the man who claims to rule from India to Thule has no power if he cannot withstand sorrow, Circe scatters Ulysses' men figuratively from Africa to India, and her own *potentia* remains limited only to physical transformation.

[46] Compare II.m.5.13-15: "Nondum maris alta secabat / nec mercibus undique lectis / noua litora uiderat hospes."

[47] "Quisquis uolet perennem / cautus ponere sedem / stabilisque nec sonori / sterni flatibus Euri" (II.m.4.1-4).

[48] Compare I.m.5.44-45: "Operis tanti pars non uilis / homines quatimur fortunae salo."

the wind blows you, not where you choose to go."[49] The sense of instability which permeates the poem also signals itself through an individual word. In the second line the word *vaga* echoes earlier moments in the *Consolation* which describe a break in the natural flow of things: stars running off course, the sea encroaching on land, Vesuvius erupting, the prisoner wandering.[50] All these appearances of the word, in its various forms, depict a deep disorder in the structure of creation. God's hand always enters, in these earlier poems, to stay the sea or nudge the stars. In IV.m.3, however, that force becomes usurped by the archetypical false magician. As a figure of lust rather than love, Circe reigns over a mock creation. Her nature is to be sought, finally, not in the books of God but in the verses of men. The poem's opening announces a physical and ethical uncertainty, as Ulysses and his crew have lost both a geographical direction and a moral directive.

The dynamic of loss and recovery operates at the poem's end as well as its beginning. The loss of speech suffered by Ulysses' men points directly to Boethius' central concern with verbal control, and it defines the crewmen as inhuman in the special context of the prisoner's own search for articulate argument ("et nihil manet integrum / uoce, corpore perditis," IV.m.3.25-26). The sense of loss here, expressed in the word *perditis*, points back to Orpheus' loss of his own self-control and excellence ("quicquid praecipuum trahit / perdit, dum uidet inferos," III.m.12.57-58). Boethius explores the relationship of different kinds of power and impotence. On the one hand, he seems to focus on the crewmen's loss of human control; on the other hand, he stresses the limited power of Circe's potion. Her herbs are fundamentally powerless, for while they may control the limbs of men, they cannot change

---

[49] Green, trans., p. 22. "Si uentis uela committeres, non quo uoluntas peteret sed quo flatus impellerent promoueres" (II.pr.1.18).

[50] I.m.2.10: "et quaecumque uagos stella recursus"; I.m.4.7-8: "nec ruptis quotiens uagus caminis / torquet fumificos Vesaeuus ignes"; II.m.8.11-12: "ne terris liceat uagis / latos tendere terminos." For other uses see Cooper, *Concordance*, p. 443.

their hearts (IV.m.3.31-32). This same contrast between the control of the body and the heart motivated Orpheus' descent, for while he was able to tame beasts, he could not soothe his own heart.

It is this hybrid state which characterizes both the subjects of Boethius' poem and its own literary execution. Eschewing the unambiguous pain of an Orpheus or the rarefied glory of a Hercules, the poem leaves its men both unharmed and wounded at the same time. Whereas Orpheus' *fabula* concluded with a monitory moral, and Hercules' *exemplum* will end with a challenge, Ulysses' poem seems somehow incomplete. By struggling with definitions and with names, the metrum focuses on the unsure nature of Ulysses' wanderings and the hybrid nature of his hexed men. It takes us to a world of futility and impotence, and leaves us wondering about the fate of its heroes. It is a profoundly unsettling poem precisely because it offers no fixed center and no firm ending. Instead, it leaves the Homeric story unfinished: Ulysses never leaves Circe's island, and we never see his men restored.

The concluding poem of Book Four, like that of Book Three, effectively presents the prisoner's mental development in mythological terms. As in her poem on Orpheus, Philosophy offers an interpretable text, here an *exemplum* rather than a *fabula*, designed to affect the prisoner as a reader.[51] If Orpheus' story was monitory, the verses on Hercules are inspirational. The poem completes the cycle of mythological metra, as the prisoner passes from Hell, through an earthly beastliness, to Heaven. As a poem of summation and review,

---

[51] Philosophy's wording, "Ite nunc, fortes, ubi celsa magni / ducit exempli uia" (IV.m.7.32-33), could refer to Hercules himself as the example of virtue; or it could refer to the story of Hercules as the example. In my argument, I follow the distinction presented by W. Trimpi, "The Quality of Fiction," *Traditio* 30 (1974), p. 99, who distinguishes between a rhetorical *exemplum*, which is an "illustrative and hortatory" fable or story, and a philosophical *exemplar*, which is figure of behavior. Philosophy's word is clearly *exemplum*, and I take it as referring to the poem/fable itself, in a manner analogous to the ending of III.m.12.

metrum 7 also recapitulates the underlying Homeric journey from *Iliad* to *Odyssey*. Its opening lines on Agamemnon and Ulysses restate the fundamental theme of loss and restitution shared by all the mythological poems. Agamemnon must lose a daughter to gain a wind; Ulysses gains some compensation for his eaten men by blinding the Cyclops. Read together, these opening scenes link the two Homeric stories as moral narratives of the life of man.[52]

The verses on Agamemnon show family relationships violated and twisted to the hero's vengeful ends. As a brother, he turns fraternal duty into vengeance; as a father, he is left to sacrifice a child. What Gruber calls the "Rollenwechsel" from father to priest enacts the perversion of familial roles.[53] The Trojan war itself is also presented as a family matter: not only is the hero motivated as a brother, but the *thalamus* which has been violated is the marriage bed of Helen and Meneleaus. The origin of these lines, however, lies most directly not in the Homeric epic or Greek tragedy, but in Seneca's *Agamemnon*.[54] Verbal echoes to the play mark the sacrifice of Iphigenia, and in particular, it is Clytemnestra's speech at the play's opening which provides much of the tone and phrasing for Boethius' lines.[55] Clytemnestra's monologue (*Ag.*, 162-75) counterpoints Philosophy's version of the same events. Boethius preserves the language of rite and sacrifice, and the line "cruore ventos emimus" (*Ag.*, 170) points, in the words of the play's most recent editor, "to the monstrous inequity of the purchase" of a wind with a child's blood.[56] Agamemnon's

---

[52] Text of the poem printed in the Appendix alongside Senecan sources and parallels.

[53] *Kommentar*, p. 373, comparing the phrasing with its Senecan source.

[54] For full discussion of Senecan source material see the Appendix.

[55] Compare IV.m.7.1-7 with *Agamemnon*, 166, 170, 624. These parallels had been noticed as long ago as Peiper's edition of the *Consolation* (Leipzig: Teubner, 1871), p. 228-233, and are mentioned by Gruber, *Kommentar*, pp. 372-373. Scheible claims that, regardless of the Senecan parallels, the real "source" for Boethius' lines lies with Euripides' *Iphigenia at Aulis* (*Die Gedichte in der Consolatio Philosophiae*, p. 152).

[56] Tarrant, p. 207. For the text of Clytemnestra's speech, see Appendix.

sacrifice offers a negative version of the dynamic of reward, the positive side of which will be Hercules' story. The horrified voice of Clytemnestra, too, is essential to the scene's force in the play, and its tone offers a foil against which the reader can assess the calm narrative of Lady Philosophy. While the sacrifice of Iphigenia moves Clytemnestra to vengeance and to crime, it is designed to move the prisoner to peace, and from Agamemnon's horrible bargain, the poem turns to the personal emotionalism of Ulysses as another negative example for the prisoner.

The verses on Agamemnon show his last acts in Troy. The lines on Ulysses describe the first adventure on his journey. Taken together, they localize the Homeric action in a transitional period: a time of setting out, a time of sacrifices to get a voyage underway. The Ulysses of metrum 7 is not the figure of *virtus* and *sapientia* of the allegories, nor the wandering hero of his earlier appearance in the *Consolation*, but a man made captive to his tears. His blinding of Polyphemus cannot bring back the dead, but can only requite personal grief. He exemplifies the failed version of the wise man, who in Philosophy's earlier terms, "ought not regret his struggles with fortune."[57] His weeping, emphasized twice in the poem (IV.m.7.8, 12), bespeaks that loss of wisdom and reason which had beset the prisoner and Orpheus. His "labor" here, the blinding of the Cyclops, stands beside Agamemnon's deed as a false achievement in contrast to the moral reward which greets Hercules' success. Throughout these verses, a specific vocabulary renders these heroes' actions less than epic. Agamemnon buys back (*redimit*) a wind with blood. Ulysses is paid back (*respendit*) for his comrades' loss. The mercantile imagery, combined with the scenes of familial disharmony and weeping, deny an epic resonance to these scenes. They place them in the temple, the home, and the marketplace, and

---

[57] Green, trans., p. 99. "Quare, inquit, ita uir sapiens moleste ferre non debet quotiens in fortunae certamen adducitur . . ." (IV.pr.7.17).

make their actions so commonplace and earthly that the truly heroic achievements of Hercules stand out in sharper contrast.

Boethius shapes the Hercules myth and its literary sources to conform to the pattern of loss and recovery portrayed in the earlier metra and in the prisoner's own progress.[58] As part of a poem of summation and review, these lines culminate the development of two of the *Consolation*'s central metaphors, and they also synthesize a wealth of Senecan source material into a coherent rewriting of the Stoic hero. Hercules' labors link his actions to those of Orpheus and Ulysses. All three figures appear in varying relationships to beasts, but while Orpheus temporarily subdued them and Ulysses' men momentarily became them, Hercules conquers them. In all three poems Boethius specifies the animals, and in so doing he writes the life of his heroes through a catalogue of encounters. The verses on Hercules encyclopedize his mythic biography, and it is significant that Boethius does not explore the individual moral or allegorical meanings of each individual labor as his contemporary Fulgentius did. Rather he offers a canon of experience to be read and understood whole. The labors show Hercules' conquest over the entire scope of earthly hardships. Taken as a collection, the beasts and fiends embody the tribulations of earthly existence. They stretch from Africa to Asia, from Hell to Heaven, from youth to age. They encompass human experience in all its geographical and chronological variety.[59]

Philosophy's lines also synthesize the prisoner's explicitly described Herculean struggle of argument and reason through a series of labors. Throughout the *Consolation* the imagery of labor and struggle defines humanity, the prisoner, and Philosophy's achievement. Mankind's yearning for beatitude fig-

[58] For a review of the history of the Hercules myth, see G. Carl Galinsky, *The Herakles Theme* (Oxford: Blackwell, 1971). The link with Ulysses has already been suggested (Buffière, pp. 376-377).

[59] On the development of the canon of Hercules' labors and the allegorical readings they engendered, see Buffière, *Les Mythes*, p. 377. For earlier literary treatments of the labors, see Gruber, *Kommentar*, p. 374.

uratively appears as a labor.[60] Philosophy herself had characterized her own argumentative task as a labor,[61] and early in Book One she had offered herself up as a Herculean figure, sharing the burden, not of Atlas, but of the prisoner ("An . . . te, alumne, desererem nec sarcinam quam mei nominis inuidia *sustulisti* communicato tecum *labore* partirer?" I.pr.3.4, emphases added). In Book Four the prisoner becomes a type of Hercules when he confronts the Hydra-like difficulties of philosophical argument.[62] Immediately before metrum 7 itself, Philosophy had anticipated the moral of the concluding poem by defining virtue and the virtuous man's struggle to maintain the mean: "You are engaged in a bitter mental strife with every kind of fortune," she noted, and she offered a reward for such labor.[63] The encyclopedic nature of her exhortation against every kind of fortune looks forward to the canonical variety of Hercules' labors. Her notion of reward anticipates her poem's end, where Hercules receives Heaven for his struggle.

In addition to the imagery of labor, the poem also recalls the consistent imagery of enchainment which has been developing throughout the *Consolation*'s poetry. From the opening of the work through its first three books, the image of fettering characterizes the impediments to the prisoner's intellectual development. Philosophy first sees the prisoner with chains around his neck, and she comments that the man who is no master of himself subjects his life to contrary emotions

---

[60] "Omnis mortalium cura quam multiplicium studiorum labor exercet diuerso quidem calle procedit . . ." (III.pr.2.2).

[61] ". . . sed, ut arbitror, haud multum tibi haec in memoriam reuocare laborauerim" (II.pr.1.4).

[62] "Talis namque materia est ut una dubitatione succisa innumerabiles aliae uelut hydrae capita succrescant" (IV.pr.6.3).

[63] I prefer the literalism of the Loeb translation here (p. 378). "Proelium cum omni fortuna animis acre conseritis ne uos aut tristis opprimat aut iucunda corrumpat" (IV.pr.7.20). On the reward for labor: "Firmis medium uiribus occupate; quicquid aut infra subsistit aut ultra progreditur habet contemptum felicitatis, non habet praemium laboris" (IV.pr.7.21).

and "fastens the chain by which he will be drawn."[64] Fortune, too, leads her devotee by the neck, and Philosophy notes that vain men long to shake the yoke of mortality from themselves.[65] In her naturalistic poem at the beginning of Book Three, Philosophy depicted the Carthaginian lions who, while chained and tamed, may break free to kill their trainer.[66] The enchainment imagery develops throughout Book Three, as lust holds the high-spirited man by the neck,[67] and Orpheus himself remains unable to break the bonds of earth. When Hercules appears in IV.m.7, dragging Cerberus by the neck, he comes to embody the radical change from conquered to conquerer through one of the *Consolation*'s motivating images. His achievement is all the more stunning as it effectively enacts the prisoner's own release from the physical and spiritual chains which have bound him like an animal throughout his life. While Circe's transformed men prowled tame around the house, Hercules leads his conquered spoil for all to see. That his tamed Centaurs were once *superbe*, moreover, sustains the imagery of the proud man subject to the chains of fortune and the senses. Finally, when Hercules can bear up the world with unbended neck (IV.m.7.29-30), he signifies the dramatic change in the prisoner from a man whose heavy chains about his neck had forced him to look only at the dull earth.[68]

If the verses on Hercules return the reader to earlier moments in the *Consolation*, they also return Boethius to Seneca, as he combines in complex ways allusions to the *Agamemnon*

---

[64] Green, trans., p. 9. "at quisquis trepidus pauet uel optat, / quod non sit stabilis suique iuris, / abiecit clipeum locoque motus / nectit qua ualeat trahi catenam" (I.m.4.15-18). Compare I.m.2. 25-27: "et pressus grauibus colla catenis / decliuemque gerens pondere uultum / cogitur, heu, stolidam cernere terram."

[65] "Postremo aequo animo toleres oportet quicquid intra fortunae aream geritur cum semel iugo eius colla summiseris" (II.pr.1.16). Compare II.m.7.7-8: "Quid, o superbi, colla mortali iugo / frustra leuare gestiunt?"

[66] III.m.2.7-16.

[67] "nec uicta libidine colla / foedis summittat habenis" (III.m.5.3-4).

[68] I.m.2.23-27.

and *Hercules Furens* to set off his new heroic figure. As in the poem on Orpheus, Senecan drama filters mythological narrative down to Boethius; but, unlike the concluding poem of Book Three, that of Book Four takes not a single scene but a variety of scenes from several plays to illustrate the culmination of Boethius' use of the dramatist. The metrum places Hercules in the context of Homeric heroics similar to the *Agamemnon*, and to a certain extent it is in this play that the poem's unity may be found. The Chorus of Argive women is the major source for these lines, and while its verbal echoes are perhaps less striking than those of *Hercules Furens*, it is rather the overall structure and purpose of the Chorus which stand behind Boethius' verses.[69] First, Boethius retains the female voice of the Chorus. As in his use of Clytemnestra's speech in the lines on Agamemnon, this background serves to set off Philosophy as an ideal female divinity putting mythic history to higher purposes. Second, he establishes a relationship between Hercules and Troy which is implicit in Seneca's scene. In the play, Hercules' labors are designed to contrast the achievements of one famous Argive with another, Agamemnon himself.[70] The Chorus ends by comparing Hercules' conquests to the siege of Troy, and the final lines, "te duce concidit totidem diebus / Troia quot annis" (*Ag.*, 865-866), return the reader to the opening context of the myth in Boethius' poem ("Bella bis quinis operatus annis," iv.m.7.1). Third, and most important, is Boethius' handling of the canon of labors chronicled by the Chorus. Seven of the twelve labors are shared, and, significantly, both Boethius and Seneca omit the cleaning of the Augean stables. The play's most recent editor argues for a thematic importance to this omission, and his claims may also illuminate Boethius' text. Tarrant shows that the Chorus eliminates "any aspect of his myth which would diminish [Hercules'] glory," and the cleaning of the

[69] Tarrant had suggested that the Chorus (*Ag.*, 808-866) may have "inspired" Boethius' poem (*Agamemnon*, ed., p. 324, n. 6). For parallels to *Hercules Furens*, see further in this chapter and in the Appendix.

[70] See Tarrant, *Agamemnon*, p. 323.

stables is omitted because it would appear more like a trial than a triumph.[71] In both Seneca and Boethius, the labors, in fact, do not appear inflicted as punishments or tests, but read like self-imposed tasks whose reward is divinity. The hortatory tone of the Chorus anticipates Boethius' exemplum, as the Argive praise, "o puer subiture caelum" (*Ag.*, 828) and "tuus ille bis seno meruit labore" (*Ag.*, 812-813) anticipate the concluding reward in the *Consolation*: "ultimi caelum meruit laboris" (iv.m.7.31).

But there is a difference between the Argive and Boethian Hercules. His idealization in Seneca is, as Tarrant notes, one-sided.[72] There is no sense of motivation here, no drama to the achievement. The absence of Juno's goading, so immediate in *Hercules Furens*, makes Hercules' labors less forceful than they could be.[73] In short, the Argive Hercules is only part way to becoming the exemplum for the prisoner. To reinforce the power of the myth—and the Herculean achievement of the prisoner—Boethius superimposes a negative reading of the hero taken from *Hercules Furens*. In this play, the hero's pride and physical prowess are developed at the expense of his moral character. The verbal echoes to the drama are striking, and they show how Boethius rewrites the details of Seneca's portrait to fit his own goal. The first lines on Hercules firmly ground the poem in the *Hercules Furens*, and the phrase *spolium leoni* (iv.m.7.15) is a touchstone of Herculean pride in the play. In *Hercules Furens* the image of the *spolia* appears in the lines of nearly all the play's central characters as a reminder of Hercules' exploits and, structurally, as a way of punctuating the progress of his fall. Juno ruefully restates

[71] Comparing the discussion of labors in *Hercules Furens* as well as in the Euripedean plays (Tarrant, *Agamemnon*, p. 324).

[72] Tarrant questions the very place of the Hercules story in the play at this time (*Agamemnon*, pp. 323-324).

[73] See *Hercules Furens*, 1-122. In the following discussion of this play, I am indebted to the study of D. Henry and B. Walker, "The Futility of Action: A Study of Seneca's *Hercules Furens*," *Classical Philology* 60 (1965), 11-22.

Hercules' labors and the rewards of his conquest.[74] Amphytryon applies the image of the spoils of labor to the conquest of the dragon.[75] At the play's end, Hercules, returned to sanity, sees the loss of his spoils in tandem with the death of his family.[76] Boethius' phrasing resonates with the image of Seneca's proud hero, whose conquests led him only into loss. Boethius' line, "abstulit saeuo spolium leoni," (IV.m.7.15) ironically echoes Hercules' own futile question in *Hercules Furens*: "Cur latus laevum vacat / spolio leonis?" (*HF*, 1150-1151).

In a similar manner, the figure of Cerberus chained appears repeatedly in Seneca's play as an emblem of Herculean achievement, violating the *foedus umbrarum* and shocking the world. Juno associates the fettering of the dog with the binding of Pluto.[77] When the Chorus reviews the effects of Hercules' madness, they too remind the audience of Cerberus still chained in Hell.[78] Boethius' vision of Hercules leading the chained dog brings with it now the ambivalent history of Hercules' pride and madness. Like the lion's spoils, this image from Seneca offers a counterpoint to the new ideal of Hercules that Boethius constructs. These Senecan moments of conquest and reward contrast sharply with the final *pretium* Philosophy offers.

Boethius has synthesized the figures of Hercules and versions of his labors from two plays; he borrows positive features to set them against a negative background. These echoes

---

[74] *HF*, 50-52: "vidi ipsa, vidi nocte discussa inferum / et Dite domito spolia iactantem patri / fraterna."

[75] *HF*, 239-240: "post haec adortus nemoris opulenti domos / aurifera vigilis spolia serpentis tulit."

[76] *HF*, 1150-1151: "cur latus laevum vacat / spolio leonis?"

[77] *HF*, 52-63: "cur non vinctum et oppressum trahit / ipsum catenis paria sortitum Iovi / Ereboque capto potitur et retegit Styga? / parum est reverti; foedus umbrarum perit . . . / viso labantem Cerbero vidi diem / pavidumque Solem; me quoque invasit tremor, / et terna monstri colla devicti intuens / timui imperasse."

[78] *HF*, 1103-1107: "gemitus vastos / audiat aether, audiat atri / regina poli vastisque ferox / qui colla gerit vincta catenis / imo latitans Cerberus antro."

also help define the authority of Philosophy herself as the female voice guiding the prisoner. The clearest analogue to Philosophy's speech is Juno's opening monologue in *Hercules Furens*, a spiteful account of Hercules' conquests. Juno reviews his achievements only to belittle his struggle and taunt him into hubris.[79] She stresses the cosmic perversion and fundamental anarchy behind Hercules' accomplishments. He will invert the hierarchies of divine power and filial obligation.[80] By redirecting his goal from Hell to Heaven, Hercules will seek the ruin of the Universe. His final labor is, to Juno, a further inversion of the natural order. He takes up Atlas' rightful burden, and if his shoulders will elevate the world, his actions will denigrate Juno herself. Lady Philosophy, however, stresses the restorative power of Hercules' ultimate labor, and she emphasizes the new cosmic order which is his rightful reward (IV.m.7.27-35). What is a theft for Juno is a gift, according to Philosphy, and her own exhortation so strikingly recalls Seneca's lines that we must hear the vengeful goddess behind the philosopher.

IV.m.7.32-3	*Hercules Furens*, 89-90
Ite nunc, fortes, ubi celsa magni ducit exempli uia.	I nunc, superbe, caelitum sedes pete humana temne.

Behind these lines, too, may stand the lines of Seneca's Medea, who goaded Jason, "I, nunc, superbe, virginum thalamos pete, relinque matres" (*Medea*, 1007-1008), as well as the lines of the Chorus earlier in that play, who had praised Hercules himself: "Ite nunc, fortes, perarate pontum / fonte timendo" (*Medea*, 650-651).[81] These parallels show something of Phi-

---

[79] Concluding with *HF*, 68-74: "robore experto tumet, / et posse caelum viribus vinci suis / didicit ferendo; subdidit mundo caput / nec flexit umeros molis immensae labor / meliusque collo sedit Herculeo polus. / immota cervix sidera et caelum tulit / et me prementem. quaerit ad superos viam."

[80] *HF*, 65-66: "caelo timendum est, regna ne summa occupet / qui vicit ima - sceptra praeripiet patri."

[81] All modern commentators follow Peiper's original suggestion that the

losophy's rhetoric, as well as of Seneca's own literary technique. In all three of the analogues there is, as Clarence Mandell had pointed out, a certain irony in the "exhortation to do something which has proven disastrous."[82] The "I, nunc," idiom combined with the vocative address has its origins in Satire, and the bitter tone of the source material creates one more foil for Lady Philosophy's benign injunction.[83] As women, Juno, Medea, and Philosphy exhort their men to action; yet, if Juno fears a world upside down, and Medea predicts violence, Philosophy promises a righted universe. Juno's ire remains in the background, along with the passion of the other Senecan women, to set off the rational narrative of Philosophy. By shifting the female voice from vengeance to virtue, Boethius' reaffirms his teacher's authority. The unity of metrum 7 thus lies with its coherent rewriting of Senecan material, its relationship to the earlier poems of the *Consolation*, and its synthesis of the dialogue's patterns of im-

---

lines from *Medea* are the actual source for Boethius' lines. In this play, the Chorus retells a variety of myths to counterpoint Medea's desire for revenge on Jason. The Chorus offers a version of the Hercules story (*Med.*, 634-651), which concludes with the lines: "meruere cuncti / morte quod crimen tener expiavit / Herculi magno puer inrepertus, / raptus, heu, tutas puer inter undas. / ite nunc, fortes, perarate pontum / fonte timendo" (646-651). Added weight for Boethius' use of this passage is given three lines later, when describing a completely different myth, Seneca uses the phrase "Libycis harenis" (653), anticipating Boethius' use in IV.m.7.25 ("strauit Antaeum Libycis harenis"). My argument here is that Boethius constructed the details of his portrait of Hercules out of both negative and positive allusions found in Seneca's plays; that the vengeful female voices stand behind Philosophy's; and that he prefers to recast entire scenes or passages, rather than create a pastiche of unrelated bits and fragments from the plays. It might be worth mentioning in passing that the variety of possible Senecan sources for a line of Boethius, as adduced by Peiper, might tell us more about Seneca's favorite motifs rather than about Boethius' own habits of composition. For an attempt to make some sense out of the availability of Senecan texts in their entirety to Boethius, and in turn, the recognizability of his allusions to Late Antique readers, see the discussion in the Appendix.

[82] Clarence Mandell, *Our Seneca* (New Haven: Yale Univ. Press, 1947), p. 167.

[83] *Ibid.*

agery. In the preceding analysis, I have argued that Boethius
does not pick his sources at random, but rather chooses to
recast entire scenes, speeches, or traditions. Metrum 7 completes the patterns of moral growth figured by the mythological, geographical, and historical allusions presented in
the text. It is encyclopedic in scope, encompassing both *Iliad*
and *Odyssey*, the canon of Hercules' earthly labors, and the
cosmic movement from Hell, to Earth, to Heaven. It answers
the poem on Orpheus structurally as a concluding myth to a
book; mythographically, as the answer to Orpheus' pain and
Hell; and poetically, as the synthesis of Senecan source material already explored in the Orpheus poem. In turn, the
metrum validates Philosophy's final authority: both comparatively, as a benign female divinity measured against Senecan
harridans; and objectively, as an *auctor* of philosophical exempla.

Boethius' use of Senecan drama shows him as a reader and
rewriter of classical texts. Philosophy's injunctions offer an
education not only in the art of reading but in the techniques
of writing. The engagement with Philosophy's metra thus
illustrates a process of reading a variety of authors and authorities. The levels of myth, Homeric epic, tragedy, lyric,
and history which are present in the mythological poetry suggest that one set of meanings for the verse lies in the structure
of literary allusions they chronicle. Isolating these various
sources writes, in effect, a syllabus of literary study: a Late
Antique paedeia comparable to the system of intellectual *auctores* articulated in Boethius' commentaries and in the *Consolation*'s prose dialogue. It is this notion of *auctoritas*, both in
its literary and intellectual senses, that will form the heart of
Book Five's dynamic. In the later sections of the work, Philosophy's role shifts, and the role of *auctores* in her prose
passages takes on a new and more visible purpose. Philosophy
will add to her status as an author of poetry the position of
philosophical *auctor*. Her prose passages take on the character
of a philosophical treatise, and the dialogue soon shifts completely to monologue. The text of the work itself changes in

CHAPTER V

A NEW BEGINNING

The sequence of mythological poems from the close of Book Three to the close of Book Four had provided a framework for an allegorical reading of the prisoner's growth as well as an insight into Boethius' own experience of Greek and Latin literature and criticism. Parallel with this sequence was the narrative development of the prisoner's education as a philosopher which had been presented in the prosae. The prisoner and Philosophy redefined their roles along the lines of literary authority and methodological competence. These developments might suggest that by the close of Book Four Boethius has neatly concluded the central symbolic and methodological business of the *Consolation*, and that Book Five should stand as a relatively unproblematic piece of straight philosophy— "unproblematic" because its issues appear to lie not with the patterns of its structure but with the details of its doctrine. Most readers of Book Five have focused on Boethius' supposed debts to such philosophers as Ammonius, and the final sections of the *Consolation* have sparked a series of investigations into Late Antique epistemology.[1] But, as Courcelle

[1] The fullest arguments for Boethius' debt to Ammonius and his school are Courcelle's, *Cons. Phil.*, pp. 215-231; "Boèce et l'Ecole d'Alexandrie," *Mélanges de l'Ecole française de Rome* 52 (1935), 185-223; *Late Latin Writers*, pp. 304-318. For researches into the doctrine of the final books, see in particular, E. Gegenschatz, "Die Freiheit der Entscheidung in der 'consolatio philosophiae' des Boethius," *Museum Helveticum* 15 (1958), 110-129, and, "Die Gefährdung des Möglichen durch das Vorauswissen Gottes in der Sicht des Boethius," *Wiener Studien* 79 (1966), 517-530. See, too, Volker Schmidt-Kohl, *Die Neuplatonische Seelenlehre in der Consolatio Philosophiae des Boethius*.

implied, the final argumentative movement of the *Consolation* begins not with Book Five but with IV.pr.6, where Philosophy takes up a new strategy of argument and Boethius announces her plans as a new beginning.[2] Prosa 6 signals a basic reordering of the dialogue's purpose and method, and it is the goal of this chapter to explain the prisoner's gradual disappearance in Book Five and the fact that the work concludes without a final, complementary poem.

To this end, I will return to several of the themes and texts presented at the beginning of this study. The relationships to such authoritative figures as Symmachus and John the Deacon stand behind the prisoner's final relationship to Philosophy, and the concluding prosae of Book Four return to the dedicatory idioms of the tractates and the technical terminology of *De topicis differentiis*. The vision of Philosophy as an intellectual master and the disappearance of the prisoner also echo the patterns of Augustine's early dialogues. I began with a comparison of Boethian and Augustinian silence, and I return to the problem of silent reading to assess the *Consolation*'s close. Finally, the chapter shows how these earlier analogues help define the final arguments of Philosophy as a prose treatise designed to be read rather than discussed. *The Consolation of Philosophy* becomes at these moments most self-consciously a written tract, and Philosophy herself becomes an *auctor* on a par with those classical *auctores* she cites and discusses in Book Five.

I

The opening sentences of IV.pr.6 explicitly redefine the technical problems besetting the prisoner, and they point towards one of the *Consolation*'s implicit themes: the limits of human language itself. Throughout her argument, Philosophy will pause to reflect on the limitations of her method and on the problems of sustaining philosophical discourse through an

[2] Courcelle, *La Cons. Phil.*, p. 203.

inadequate medium. The prisoner opens the prosa by redefining Philosophy's office as that of explainer and revealer.
His choice of phrasing associates her principal functions as
both poet and philosopher, and he returns the reader to the
idiom of the theological tractates. In *De Trinitate* Boethius
had employed a language, he claimed, so private that it almost
heirophantically preserved his truth from the common reader:
"So I purposely use brevity and wrap up (*velo*) the ideas I
draw from the deep questioning of philosophy."[3] By enveloping the truth in "new words," his figures successfully preserve an elect audience in the face of public demands for interpretation. Similarly, the *Quomodo Substantiae* addressed the
problem of explanation. But here, writing to John the Deacon,
Boethius had shifted somewhat the relationship of reader and
writer, and the opening lines of the tractate distinctively outline the methodological issues faced by Philosophy and the
prisoner.

> You ask me to state and explain somewhat more clearly that
> obscure question in my *Hebdomads*. . . . You urge that this dem-
> onstration is necessary because the method of this kind of treatise
> is not clear to all.[4]

To John the Deacon, Boethius replied with the same arguments for privacy he had employed in *De Trinitate* and *Contra
Eutychen*. He will "think over the *Hebdomads* with myself, and
I keep my speculations in my own memory rather than share
them with [the frivolous]."[5] To preserve the truth as well as
his own intellectual integrity, Boethius again opts for brevity

---

[3] "Idciro stilum brevitate contraho et ex intimis sumpta philosophiae disciplinis novorum verborum significationibus velo . . ." (*De Trinitate*, p. 4).

[4] "Postulas, ut ex Hebdomadibus nostris eius quaestionis obscuritatem
. . . , digeram et paulo evidentius monstrem; idque eo dicis esse faciendum,
quod non sit omnibus notum iter huiusmodi scriptionum" (*Quomodo Sub.*,
p. 38).

[5] "Hebdomadas vero ego mihi ipse commentor potiusque ad memoriam
meam speculata conservo quam cuiquam participo quorum lascivia ac petulantia nihil a ioco risuque patitur esse seiunctum" (*Quomodo Sub.*, p. 38).

and for a discourse which preserves the *archana* of philosophical speculation.[6]

Book Four, prosa 6, of the *Consolation* takes these tropes and inverts them. Philosophy's purpose, the prisoner claims, is not to conceal but to reveal. Rather than expressing the desire to *volvere*, her office should be to *evolvere*. She will disclose the hidden cause of things by brushing away the mists that shield them from the uninitiated. The prisoner pleads for public disclosure, whereas Boethius had earlier used this imagery to assert the private nature of intellectual inquiry. In turn, while Boethius sought brevity in new words, the prisoner seeks a full explanation in familiar terms. Finally, the prisoner points back to the problems of wonder expressed in the preceding line of verse (IV.m.5.22), and he beseeches Philosophy to transform such wonder into reason.[7] The act of intuitive marvelling which had greeted Philosophy's cryptic poetry before will now be transformed into a discursive explanation. In response to this plea for explanation, Philosophy embarks on the longest bit of uninterrupted prose in the *Consolation*, and perhaps the most important feature of her speech is that it is so long.[8] It dramatically contrasts the brevity of the tractates, and it offers a practical example of the new office assigned to Philosophy. She answers the prisoner's question, not by reestablishing the dialogue—as she had, for instance, at III.pr.12—but by abandoning the form altogether. Her remarks *will* be long, she states, even while apologizing that "almost no discourse, however exhaustive, is sufficient" to explain her subject.[9] Philosophy reasserts her authority in two

---

[6] "Prohinc tu ne sis obscuritatibus brevitatis adversus, quae cum sint arcani fida custodia tum id habent commodi, quod eum his solis qui digni sunt conloquuntur" (*Quomodo Sub.*, p. 38).

[7] The entire opening speech reads: "Ita est, inquam; sed cum tui muneris sit latentium rerum causas euoluere uelatasque caligine explicare rationes, quaeso uti quae hinc decernas, quoniam hoc me miraculum maxime perturbat, edisseras" (IV.pr.6.1).

[8] Gruber calls it the longest sustained text in the entire work (*Kommentar*, p. 353).

[9] I prefer the literalism of the Loeb translators here, p. 355. The Latin

complementary ways. First, she makes herself the interpreter of a subject which nearly goes beyond words to explain; in recognizing the constraints both of her method and of their time together, she places herself as the only capable expositor of the subject. But, second, is the way she metaphorically associates her authority with that of the Creator, and the images she uses to describe her project, combined with Boethius' own announcement of a new beginning, present a scene of divinely inspired philosophical reasoning.

Philosophy's description of her argumentative copia bound by a controlling order points directly to the binding of the cosmos through Nature, God, or the concord of the spheres. She will "weave arguments for you bound to each other in due order," and her words recall the description of Nature at III.m.2, and of the corresponding powers of her poetry to bind up the natural order into an artistic whole.[10] In IV.pr.6, while she abandons music itself, her very comments will obey the laws of order and appear, figuratively, as under her controlling hand. Philosophy offers a link between natural creation and her own intellectual exposition—that is, between the order of things and the order of words—and Boethius' next line reinforces the link in initiating the *Consolation*'s new beginning: "Tunc uelut ab alio orsa principio ita disseruit" (IV.pr.6.7). Much has been made of this single line, and whether we take it as an announcement of an Aristotelian

---

reads: "Tum illa paulisper arridens: Ad rem me, inquit, omnium quaesitu maximam uocas, cui uix exhausti quicquam satis sit" (IV.pr.6.2).

[10] Again, the Loeb translation, p. 357. Green's translation, "while I put together the pattern of my argument" (p. 91), misses the metaphors of weaving and textuality inherent in the Latin. "Quodsi te musici carminis oblectamenta delectant, hanc oportet paulisper differas uoluptatem dum nexas sibi ordine contexo rationes" (IV.pr.6.6). Compare III.m.2.1-6: "Quantas rerum flectat habenas / natura potens, quibus immensum / legibus orbem prouida seruet / stringatque ligans inresoluto / singula nexu, placet arguto / fidibus lentis promere cantu." Compare, too, the description of Philosophy's entry: "Vestes erant tenuissimis filis subtili artificio indissolubili materia perfectae, quas, uti post eadem prodente cognoui, suis manibus ipsa *texuerat*" (I.pr.1.3, emphasis mine).

protreptikos, or the initiation of a theological argument, it does indicate both a shift in method and a change in Philosophy's image.[11] She focuses on the divine role in generation and control. Her opening words, "Omnium generatio rerum . . ." (IV.pr.6.7), and her emphasis on the *ordo* imposed by the divine mind, reinforce the metaphorical equation between Philosophy's skills in arranging her arguments and God's power in disposing his Creation. Her vocabulary, too, becomes pointedly theological: *generatio* is a word unique in the *Consolation* and is otherwise reserved for the tractates.[12] Her diction also recalls the Platonism of the Timaean hymn, as God's stability of mind echoes the *stabilitas* which guides the Creator in the poem.[13] Philosophy's further comparison of God to an *artifex,* again using a word unique in the *Consolation,* develops explicitly the Chalcidian vision of the Creator which stands behind III.m.9.[14] In short, Philosophy recasts some of the basic themes and images of the pivotal Timaean hymn, while expressing them in a new vocabulary. These achieve-

---

[11] As a Protreptikos, see Gruber, pp. 354-355; as a shift to a new ethical and moral form, see Courcelle, *Cons. Phil.,* p. 203. Chadwick (*Boethius,* p. 241) reports Usener's association of the "new beginning" with the phrasing of Cicero's *De Divinatione,* II.xlix.101: "tum ego rursus quasi ab alio principio sum exorsus dicere."

[12] See L. Cooper, *Concordance of Boethius,* p. 163, and Gruber, *Kommentar,* p. 355.

[13] "Omnium generatio rerum cunctusque mutabilium naturarum progressus et quicquid aliquo mouetur modo causas, ordinem, formas ex diuinae mentis stabilitate sortitur" (IV.pr.6.7). Compare III.m.9.1-6: "O qui perpetua mundum ratione gubernas, / terrarum caelique sator, qui tempus ab aeuo / ire iubes stabilisque manens das cuncta moueri, / quem non externae pepulerunt fingere causae / materiae fluitantis opus uerum insita summi / forma boni liuore carens. . . ."

[14] "Sicut enim artifex faciendae rei formam mente praecipiens mouet operis effectum . . ." (IV.pr.6.12). For the sources in Chalcidius, see Gruber, *Kommentar,* p. 356. While the word *artifex* is used nowhere else in the *Consolation* (See Cooper, *Concordance,* p. 33), the phrasing of this passage does echo the vocabulary of craft found in the Timaean hymn: "tu cuncta superno / ducis ab exemplo, pulchrum pulcherrimus ipse / mundum mente gerens similique in imagine formans / perfectasque iubens perfectum absoluere partes" (III.m.9.6-9).

ments assert a new kind of discourse which will characterize the *Consolation*'s final arguments. By expanding the work's basic philosophical vocabulary, and by doing so within a prose rather than a verse context, Boethius explores the possibilities of a discourse suitable for the logical expression of God's works.

The epistemological problems Philosophy confronts once her speech gets underway also assert her mastery of philosophical technique at the expense of the prisoner's inabilities. The very fact that he is bound by the strictures of human language renders any expression of philosophical truth problematic. Her statement on the relationship of fate to providence, for example, reveals a view of man's limited abilities when compared to God's or, indeed, to her own.

> Therefore, the changing course of Fate is to the simple stability of Providence as reasoning is to intellect, as that which is generated is to that which is, as time is to eternity, as a circle is to its center.[15]

This statement implicitly compares the prisoner's rational abilities to Philosophy's intellectual ones, and her word *ratiocinatio* for reasoning brings with it the old Ciceronian meaning of technical, limited skills at argument.[16] The comparison

---

[15] Green, trans., p. 92. "Igitur uti est ad intellectum ratiocinatio, ad id quod est id quod gignitur, ad aeternitatem tempus, ad punctum medium circulus, ita est fati series mobilis ad prouidentiae stabilem simplicitatem" (IV.pr.6.17).

[16] *Ratiocinatio* operates within the realm of probable, rather than certain, arguments, as Cicero states: "Ratiocinatio est oratio ex ipsa re probabile aliquid eliciens quod expositum et per se cognitum sua se vi et ratione confirmet" (*De Inventione*, I.xxxiv.57). Boethius had earlier used the term when the prisoner praised Philosophy's reasoning as being firmly based in *ratiocinatione* (III.pr.10.21). Here, I think, the prisoner is applying his own standards of reasoning to Philosophy's method. Gruber translates the term as "Vernunftschluss," but problems remain. In the *De Inventione* Cicero is contrasting inductive and deductive forms of reasoning (I.xxxi.51), where *ratiocinatio* means the latter. Central to his exposition is that he is characterizing rhetorical, rather than strictly logical forms of argument. Under deduction he describes, not syllogistic reasoning, as he had in *De Finibus*, v.55 (discussing

becomes explicit as, only a few lines later, Philosophy comments on the prisoner's limited grasp of the order of her argument and the order of divinity.

> Therefore, even though things may seem confused and discordant to you, because you cannot discern the order that governs them, nevertheless everything is governed by its own proper order directing all things toward the good.[17]

She reminds the prisoner of what she had earlier demonstrated (". . . ut uberrime demonstratum est . . ." IV.6.22), and she anticipates a series of questions the prisoner might ask. She thus attempts to sustain the dialogic movement herself, asking and answering her own questions. But this kind of dialogue revives itself only to be subsequently dismissed. Her inquiry is inappropriate for public discussion. People's judgments conflict in these matters (IV.pr.6.25), and she passes over problem points by conceding issues and internalizing the dialogue as a process of essentially private meditation. She then selects, "a few things which human reason can comprehend" (Green, p. 93) in an attempt to return the argument to the prisoner's level (IV.pr.6.32). Her emphases here attest that both he and the reader are still creatures of opinion, who need to be convinced and for whom things seem to be rather than simply are. Because we live in a world of becoming rather than being

---

Stoic logic), but rather enthymemes. Comparison with the *ad Herennium* on a similar passage seems only to confuse the issue. There, *ratiocinatio* can mean a figure of thought (IV.xv.23) ("reasoning by question and answer," in Harry Caplan's translation, Loeb edition, p. 285). It can also mean a type of issue (I.xi.19), "reasoning from analogy" (Caplan, p. 35, translating the Greek *syllogismos*). In the context of Philosophy's distinction between *ratiocinatio* and *intellectus* in the *Consolation*, however, I think it remains clear that, whatever the precise meaning of *ratiocinatio*, its connotations all involve rhetorical or probable modes of argument, and that the arena of its operation is the classroom or the law court.

[17] Green, trans., p. 93. "Quo fit ut, tametsi uobis hunc ordinem minime considerare ualentibus confusa omnia perturbataque uideantur, nihilo minus tamen suus modus ad bonum dirigens cuncta disponat" (IV.pr.6.21).

(see IV.pr.6.17), we may not grasp what is apparent and de-
monstrable to God or Philosophy.

> Therefore, when you see something happen here contrary to
> your ideas of what is right, it is your opinion and expectation
> which is confused, while the order of things themselves is
> right.[18]

Philosophy's remarks indicate that the controlling structures of *both* her verbal arguments and God's natural order
can elude the mind. Her advice recalls the prisoner's earlier
confusion over the labyrinth of words she had woven in
III.pr.12; but now she is unconcerned with placating his impatience. The human mind, she implies, is limited in its ability
to perceive order in philosophical argument or in divine creation, for both appear as the developments of two higher
intellects (i.e., Philosophy's and God's). Her demonstration
of intellectual authority, combined with the imagery of her
speech's opening, implicitly link her to God, and she seems
to recognize her own identification with divine control. "But
it is hard for me to recount all this as if I were a god" (Green,
p. 96) and with this Greek quotation Philosophy both apol-
ogizes and reasserts her learning and authority (IV.pr.6.53).
Her Homeric statement augments the collection of *auctores*
Philosophy now begins to use to buttress her arguments.
Earlier in the prosa, she had adduced another Greek line
(whose source is still disputed) as coming from "one who is
better than I" (Green, p. 94; IV.pr.6.38), and her citations of
Lucan's *Pharsalia* comes equipped with the praise of the author
as *familiaris noster Lucanus* (IV.pr.6.33).[19] This battery of *auc-*

[18] Green, trans., p. 94. "Hic igitur quicquid citra spem uideas geri rebus
quidem rectus ordo est, opinioni uero tuae peruersa confusio" (IV.pr.6.34).

[19] For the earlier Greek line, see Gruber, *Kommentar*, p. 361, for possible
sources in Parmenedes and Proclus, and for a review of critical opinion.
Chadwick (*Boethius*, p. 243) argues for its source in the Chaldean Oracles.
For the suggestion that the Greek line and the phrase "me quoque exellentior"
point to an explicitly Christian or Gnostic source, and that they both refer
to the same individual whom Philosophy had spoken of immediately before
("Est alius cunctis uirtutibus absolutus sanctusque ac deo proximus,"

tores contributes to Philosophy's own growing status as an *auctor* and commentator, and her following remarks help define her changing relationships to literary and philosophical discourse.

> It is not fitting for men to understand intellectually or to explain verbally all the dispositions of the divine work.[20]

Philosophy's phrasing, *explicare sermone*, recalls the earlier definitions of her role. At II.pr.8 she announced that what she had to tell the prisoner was too wonderful to put into words (*uerbis explicare*).[21] At the opening of Book Three, she again contrasted the near ineffability of her subject (here, true happiness) with the necessary preliminaries which she had to describe in words (*designare uerbis*).[22] In all three scenes, the techniques of explanation remain limited either to things well known or arguments limited in scope. Philosophy's phrasing highlights the gap between the truths of her philosophy and the tools used to present it. To express the inexpressible becomes one of the central paradoxes of the *Consolation*'s method, and to overcome somewhat the prisoner's and the reader's hesitance, she must assert her authority to make her

---

IV.pr.6.37), see Antony E. Raubitshek, "*Me Quoque Excellentior* (Boethii, *Consolatio* 4.6.27 [*sic*])," in J. J. O'Meara and B. Naumann, eds. *Latin Script and Letters A.D. 400-900* [Bieler Festschrift] (Leiden: E. J. Brill, 1976), p. 62. On the citation of Lucan, Gruber claims that he is "our schoolfellow" because he was a student of the Stoic Cornutus (*Kommentar*, p. 361). On the question of the use of auctores from classical texts, Gruber points to Seneca, *Epistoles*, 88.5, for Homer as an authority (*Kommentar*, p. 363). Courcelle feels that the series of Greek quotations towards the *Consolation*'s close indicates "une culture littéraire issue de l'école d'Ammonius" (*La Cons. Phil.*, p. 299). I am suggesting, rather, that at issue is less the source or analogue for these quotations than the simple fact that they *are* Greek and thus point to Philosophy's use of antique authoritative texts to develop her arguments.

[20] Green, p. 96. "Neque enim fas est homini cunctas diuinae operae machinas uel ingenio comprehendere uel explicare sermone" (IV.pr.6.54).

[21] "mirum est quod dicere gestio, eoque sententiam uerbis explicare uix queo" (II.pr.8.2).

[22] "sed quae tibi causa notior est, eam prius designare uerbis atque informare conabor . . ." (III.pr.1.7).

arguments credible. There are then two fundamental shifts in method as the *Consolation* draws to its close. The first is the change in the text, from a record of dialectical engagement to a document of philosophical reasoning. In tandem with this shift is the change in Philosophy herself, from a teacher drawing out the prisoner's responses, to a lecturer asserting the authority of herself and her sources in order to create the philosophical treatise the prisoner and his audience now read.

The final prosa of Book Four crystallizes these changes. Philosophy distinguishes between the methods of securing belief and assuring proof, arguing that human judgments seldom meet the demands of philosophical demonstration. The gap between her abilities at philosophizing and the prisoner's need for familiar examples, though, seems yet to close. He questions Philosophy from his experience of human opinion. What follows from her arguments on fortune, while truly and soundly reasoned to the prisoner, would appear surprising (*inopinabiles*) to the common run of men: "Because people ordinarily hold that some men suffer bad fortune."[23] Realizing that she must return her argument to the level of probable discourse, Philosophy exclaims: "You mean you want to accommodate our discourse to the common speech so that we will not move too far from ordinary human ways?"[24] Human judgment becomes the criterion for the argument's success here, and Philosophy questions the prisoner, "Do ordinary people judge that [i.e., just punishment] to be bad?" "The people don't think that [i.e., unjust punishment] good, do they?" The prisoner responds that of all conceivable things,

[23] Green, trans., p. 98. The exchange reads: "Nimis quidem, inquam, uera ratio et, si quam paulo ante docuisti prouidentiam fatumue considerem, firmis uiribus nixa sententia. Sed eam, si placet, inter eas quas inopinabiles paulo ante posuisti numeremus. —Qui? inquit. —Quia id hominum sermo communis usurpat, et quidem crebro, quorundam malam esse fortunam" (IV.pr.7.4-6).

[24] Green, trans., p. 98. "Visne igitur, inquit, paulisper uulgi sermonibus accedamus ne nimium uelut ab humanitatis usu recessisse uideamur?" (IV.pr.7.7.)

they judge unjust punishment to be the worst.[25] Their argument concludes with a surprising (*inopinabile*) conclusion, reached by following popular opinion, and to Philosophy's final statement the prisoner responds: "That is true, but no one would dare say so."[26] This exchange, so late in the *Consolation*'s development, may seem out of place and possibly retrograde. Boethius revives both the goals and the form of probable dialectic as outlined in *De topicis differentiis*. The prisoner and Philosophy return to judgment and opinion to secure belief in the arguments on fortune. Moreover, for the last time in the *Consolation*, the disputants revive the rapid exchanges of question and response. Philosophy leads the prisoner back into the old methodology, however, only to reject it once and for all. She lets the prisoner return to the judgments of others, only to have him realize that philosophical reasoning has no need for opinion. In spite of his apparent backsliding, the prisoner *has* progressed. By the end of the exchange, he can separate the method of demonstrating proof from that of securing belief. Through the wordplay on *opinio* and *inopinabile*, Philosophy and the prisoner affirm one of the central definitions of *De topicis differentiis*: that philosophical demonstration may appear suprising or less than credible to most of us. If the force of the discussion is methodological, it is also moral, as the prisoner distinguishes himself from the common run of men. His new self shines against the backdrop of the *vulgi*.

Implicit in this dynamic is a tension between experience

---

[25] Green, p. 98, modified. The exchange reads: "Quid uero iucunda, quae in praemium tribuitur bonis, num uulgus malam esse decernit? —Nequaquam, uerum uti est ita quoque esse optimam censet. —Quid reliqua, quae cum sit aspera iusto supplicio malos cohercet, num bonam populus putat? —Immo omnium, inquam, quae excogitari possunt iudicat esse miserrimam" (IV.pr.7.11-13).

[26] Green, p. 98. The exchange reads: "Vide igitur ne opinionem populi sequentes quiddam ualde inopinabile confecerimus. —Quid? inquam. — . . . Hoc, inquam, uerum est, tametsi nemo audeat confiteri" (IV.pr.7.14,16).

and authority: a tension which motivates much of Book Five's
discussions and which contributes to the prisoner's change
towards the work's close. Book Five opens with the prisoner
dovetailing his own experience with Philosophy's authority,
as if to contrast the two modes of understanding.

> Your exhortation is a worthy one and your authority is great,
> but I know from experience that you are right in saying that
> the question of Providence involves many other problems.[27]

Philosophy's *auctoritas* here has a double focus, referring as it
does to her magisterial intellect as well as to her growing
reliance on, and appearance as, the *auctores*. In Book Five these
developments reach their fullest achievement. Philosophy will
argue throughout the book from classical authors. She refers
to her Aristotle for arguments on causes.[28] She quotes Homer
on cosmology.[29] She addresses Cicero on divination.[30] She
confronts Plato on the perpetuity of the world.[31] She seeks
to ground her arguments in the engagement with a body of
classical texts—texts which comprise the syllabus of literary
and philosophical study. In turn, her statements gain the force
of *sententiae* culled from the authors and their commentators.
If, for example, Philosophy's final arguments owe much to
Ammonius on Aristotle, it may be less an indication of Boe-

---

[27] Green, trans., p. 101. "Recta quidem, inquam, exhortatio tuaque prorsus
auctoritate dignissima, sed quod tu dudum de prouidentia quaestionem plu-
ribus aliis implicitam esse dixisti re experior" (v.pr.1.2).

[28] v.pr.1.12. For the Aristotelian passages at stake, see Courcelle, *Cons.
Phil.*, pp. 218-219, Gruber, *Kommentar*, pp. 380-381.

[29] v.m.2.1-3. For the reconstruction of the Greek and the Homeric texts
in question, see Gruber, *Kommentar*, pp. 385-386.

[30] v.pr.4.1. While the probable reference here is to *De Divinatione*, II.iii.8-
9, Klingner long ago pointed out that, at least in this passage, Boethius gets
his discussion through Augustine's *City of God*, v.9 (see Gruber, *Kommentar*,
p. 396), and Chadwick mentions Augustine's *De Trinitate*, III.iv.9, as another
possible analogue (*Boethius*, p. 242).

[31] v.pr.6, actually challenges Plato's authority and a strict adherence to his
doctrines. See the extended discussions at v.pr.6.9,10,14, and for the sources,
Gruber, *Kommentar*, pp. 409-411.

thius' own training than of his attempt to show Philosophy as a kind of commentator on a par with the Neoplatonist.[32] Her persona takes on the qualities of a schoolmaster grounding his lessons in the *auctores*.

Philosophy lectures. Her partner gradually disappears into a listening and reading pupil. By bringing classical texts so fully into the foreground, Philosophy returns the *Consolation* to its opening scene. The action now fully transpires in that library of the mind where texts articulate the structures of reality, and where the student's goal becomes a life of reading. Philosophy's bibliographic asides direct the prisoner and the reader back to texts. Both figures may spend the rest of the *Consolation* reading and studying such writings. In addition, both may treat the *Consolation* itself as a text to be read, studied, and commented on. In these ways, the status of the work changes, as it explores the various guises in which to engage an audience. At one level, the work has transcribed a dialogue, and it can be approached much like the *Tusculan Disputations* or *De Magistro*. Moreover, the *Consolation* makes its audience readers of poetry; it engages their interpretive skills, and the reader can measure his own as well as the prisoner's progress against Philosophy's metra. Finally, the *Consolation* is a treatise, an authoritative work of prose designed to be studied with the attention paid to an Aristotle or a Cicero. The remainder of Book Five thus explores these various modes of discourse in ways which, once again, rewrite earlier portions of the text to emphasize the development of its characters.

II

The opening exchanges of Book Five hinge on the principles of revision and rewriting articulated throughout the work.

---

[32] For the possible sources in Ammonius, and for Boethius' possible reworkings of the Ammonian idiom in his *Perihermeneias* commentary, see Courcelle, *Cons. Phil.*, pp. 212-224.

They restate the central methodological concerns of the dialogue, while reviving its key metaphors. The prisoner interrupts Philosophy just as she is about to address other problems raised by her review of Fortune and reward posed by the Hercules myth. Philosophy's response returns to the earlier imagery of the *via* and the *patria*. She explicitly reminds the prisoner of her earlier goals, and she recalls for him the by-paths which had previously distracted their arguments.[33] As before, the way is both methodological and moral: her phrasing, "rectum iter," brings to mind the emotional helplessness of the prisoner alone on the road of life in the opening carmen.[34] His own response also takes up the language of philosophical argument, and he praises his teacher, using the same criteria she herself had used to outline the goals of her method. He echoes the promise made by Philosophy at the opening of Book Four: she was committed to explore both sides of an argument to ensure credibility; he commends her for establishing every side of her argument in undoubted belief.

When every part of your argument is convincingly established, none of its implications will cause any doubt.
(v.pr.1)[35]

But, in order to demonstrate this truth fully, I will prove my point in both ways one after another.
(iv.pr.2)[36]

[33] "Festino, inquit, debitum promissionis absoluere uiamque tibi qua patriam reueharis aperire. Haec autem etsi perutilia cognitu tamen a propositi nostri tramite paulisper auersa sunt, uerendumque est ne deuiis fatigatus ad emetiendum rectum iter sufficere non possis" (v.pr.1.4-5). With this passage, compare Philosophy's statements at iii.pr.8.1, which incorporate the image of the way with the notion of promise: "Nihil igitur dubium est quin hae ad beatitudinem uiae deuia quaedam sint nec perducere quemquam eo ualeant ad quod se perducturas esse promittunt."

[34] Compare i.m.1.5-6 (On the Muses): "Has saltem nullus potuit peruincere terror / ne nostrum comites prosequerentur iter," and Philosophy's answer (i.pr.3.5): "Atqui Philosophiae fas non erat incomitatum relinquere iter innocentis."

[35] Green, trans., p. 101. "Simul, cum omne disputationis tuae latus indubitata fide constiterit, nihil de sequentibus ambigatur" (v.pr.1.7).

[36] Green, trans., p. 77. "Sed uti nostrae sententiae fides abundantior sit,

The opening of the Book thus confirms the prisoner's ability to distinguish the truth learned through inquiry from the intuitions of experience, and it demonstrates his grasp of a philosophical vocabulary.

But the prisoner is not yet out of the dark, for after Philosophy's long explanations in prose and verse, he remains still troubled by doubt. While he had denied any ambiguity to Philosophy's arguments in prosa 1, at prosa 3 he states: "En, inquam, difficiliore rursus ambiguitate confundor" (v.pr.3.1). It is at this point that the torments of ambiguity force the prisoner not into passive confusion but into active inquiry. Ambiguity becomes a goad to interpretation, as the prisoner must try to sort out for himself the problems of free will and providence. Prosa 3 represents his one chance to do philosophy: to engage fully in the method of demonstration he had praised in his master.

His argument structures itself along the lines of successive refutations of ill-informed opinion. *Incerta opinio* cannot be attributed to God but rather motivates the arguments of men.[37] The prisoner distinguishes between belief and proof in a way which confirms his command of Philosophy's technique. First, he refuses to agree with the reasoning "by which some people believe they can solve this problem."[38] He recounts their arguments, and then contrasts facts and opinions about observable reality.[39] Necessary arguments, the heart of philosophical reasoning, are central to his point. He then applies the same line of reasoning from temporal experience to

---

alterutro calle procedam nunc hinc nunc inde proposita confirmans" (IV.pr.2.4).

[37] "Nam si aliorsum quam prouisa sunt detorqueri ualent, non iam erit futuri firma praescientia, sed opinio potius incerta; quod de deo credere nefas iudico" (v.pr.3.6).

[38] Green, trans., p. 105. "Neque enim illam probo rationem qua se quidam credunt hunc quaestionis nodum posse dissoluere" (v.pr.3.7).

[39] v.pr.3.10-13.

future events.[40] Human opinion is differentiated from true knowledge.[41] His methodological sophistication extends to the rhetorical structure of his argument. His reasoning proceeds by question and answer. Like Philosophy before him, and like her ancestors in Cicero and Augustine, the speaker attempts to sustain dialogue by preserving the structures of interrogation and response. The pattern of questioning leads him to argument by counter-example. His questions have no right answers: one argument, once accepted, leads to a collapse of human affairs.[42] Another abolishes the possibility of prayer.[43] Together, it follows necessarily that humanity would lose its link to its creator. "So it will necessarily follow, as you sang a little while ago, that mankind would be cut off from its source and dwindle into nothing."[44] The conclusion's phrasing is distinctive for two reasons. First, it shows the prisoner's command of argument by necessity, and his need to preserve something of a rational method. Even though his conclusions are negative, he is in full command of technique. Second, he shows himself to be a good reader. He takes Philosophy's earlier poem, IV.m.6, as a text, a statement of *auctoritas*, which can be used to support a proposition. He re-

[40] v.pr.3.14-17.

[41] v.pr.3.18.

[42] "Quo semel recepto quantus occasus humanarum rerum consequatur liquet" (v.pr.3.29).

[43] "Igitur nec sperandi aliquid nec deprecandi ulla ratio est; quid enim uel speret quisque uel etiam deprecetur quando optanda omnia series indeflexa conectit? Auferetur igitur unicum illud inter homines deumque commercium, sperandi scilicet ac deprecandi . . ." (v.pr.3.33-34). For discussion of this passage in relationship to the final mention of prayer at the end of the *Consolation*, see my arguments at the end of this chapter, and compare Christine Mohrmann, "Some Remarks on the Language of Boethius, *Consolatio Philosophiae*," in *Latin Script and Letters*, pp. 54-61 (arguing that their source lies in the idioms of the liturgy), and C. J. de Vogel, "Boethiana, II," *Vivarium* 10 (1972), 1-40.

[44] I am modifying Green's translation, p. 107, with reference to the Loeb translators, p. 403. "Quare necesse erit humanum genus, uti paulo ante cantabas, dissaeptum atque disiunctum suo fonte fatiscere" (v.pr.3.36).

members and uses a poetry designed to be interpreted; that he does so rightly, and in keeping with Philosophy's own use of *auctores* in Book Five, demonstrates his new-found interpretive skills.

His following poem, v.m.3, also demonstrates a new-found ability. If his remarks in the prose mark him as a good reader, this metrum shows him as a good writer. He incorporates the structures of Platonic epistemology into a reasoned poetic form far different from his last attempt at verse (i.m.5). Taken together, the third prose and verse of Book Five serve as a structural counterweight and a philosophical answer to the desperate sequence in Book One (i.pr.4.-m.5).[45] The two poems are written in the same meter; the two prosae are structured through patterns of questioning. The speech and the poem of Book Five balance the histrionics of Book One's tirade with a calm, philosophical method and tone. At the substantive level, v.pr.3 answers some of the problems of i.pr.4. Broadly speaking, both speeches focus on the problems of reward and punishment; but while i.pr.4 is obsessively autobiographical, v.pr.3 is detached and abstract in focus. In Book Five, no historical examples intrude, while the arguments of i.pr.4 are weighted down with their local resonance. The prisoner had lamented: "Instead of being rewarded for true virtue, I am falsely punished as a criminal."[46] The judges were unmoved by either the whims of fortune or the fallibility of man's mind. In Book Five these specific themes are handled with clearer insight. Fortune is no longer in control, for the prisoner claims that, "it is pointless to assign rewards and punishments to the good and wicked since neither are deserved if the actions of men are not free and voluntary."[47]

---

[45] Parallels between the prisoner's prosimetrical speeches at Books One and Five have been only alluded to, without extensive investigation, by Gruber (*Kommentar*, p. 393), and Scheible (*Die Gedichte*, p. 162).

[46] Green, trans., p. 13. "pro uerae uirtutis praemiis falsi sceleris poenas subimus" (i.pr.4.34).

[47] Green, trans., p. 107. "Frustra enim bonis malisque praemia poenaeue

Again, the issue of judgment hinges on man's mind; but instead of stressing its fallibility or the emotionalism attendant on the court, Boethius focuses on the will's relationship to providence, and on the mind's relationship not to other minds but to God.

The poems also present two sides to the same philosophical issues, and the ways in which they handle their respective source material also mark a radical change in the prisoner's development. While the poem in Book Five has its sources in Plato and the Neoplatonists, I.m.5 lamented the incomprehensibility of the cosmic order in terms taken from Seneca's *Hyppolytus*. The prisoner had become a dramatic figure, and his invocations and interjections gave this poem a self-indulgent theatricality foreign to the spirit of philosophical inquiry. It is worth exploring in some detail the earlier poem's debt to Seneca for two reasons. It illustrates the prisoner's shift in poetic technique from Books One to Five. It also reveals the prisoner's earlier inability to rewrite his Senecan source in the way Lady Philosophy will recast the dramatic choruses into new figures of Orpheus and Hercules. I.m.5 shows the prisoner as an uncritical reader of Senecan tragedy, in contrast to Lady Philosophy and to himself in the *Consolation*'s later portions.

The poem of Book One models itself on the choral address to Nature in *Hyppolytus*, 959-988.[48] Thematically, both speeches contrast the stability of cosmic order with the apparent disorder of human life. Structurally they fall into two parts, praise and lament, while they also share a certain rhetorical pattern of invocation, predication, and supplication.[49]

---

proponuntur, quae nullus meruit liber ac uoluntarius motus animorum" (v.pr.3.30).

[48] See Appendix for complete texts.

[49] Gruber analyses the bipartite structure of I.m.5 and argues that Boethius differs from Seneca in the forcefulness of his prayer and in the shifts in structure which give the metrum a greater "religiös-kultischen Charakter" (*Kommentar*, p. 133). While Scheible does see the centrality of Seneca's chorus

In their first sections, the verses restate the power of nature over earth. The prisoner and the Chorus invoke the Ruler and delineate his or her control over the heavenly bodies. Like Seneca's Chorus, the prisoner attempts to catalogue the myths surrounding diurnal and seasonal change. Astrological signs are named, and the cycle of winter, fall, and summer appears in agricultural imagery. Specifically, both poems see the winter winds stripping the trees.[50] Then, through a sequence of question and complaint, the speakers lament the power of Fortune and man's loss of control in his life. Nature or the *conditor* operate far from human affairs and leave people subject to irrational forces of good and evil. For Boethius, perverts sit on royal thrones; for Seneca, crime sits reigning in the palace.[51] The poems also share metrical strategies for emotional effect. Written in the same anapestic dimeter, they use half-lines to punctuate the argument. Questions interrupt the meter's flow, and there is a certain tension created by the broken metrics of both poems.[52] The prisoner had thus mod-

---

to the metrum she asserts that this example has led readers since Peiper to overrate the influence of Seneca on the poetry as a whole (*Die Gedichte*, pp. 36-39, esp. p. 36, n. 1).

[50] *Cons. Phil.*, I.m.5.14-20:

Tu frondifluae frigore brumae
stringis lucem breviore mora,
tu cum feruida uenerit aestas
agiles nocti diuidis horas.
Tua uis uarium temperat annum,
ut quas Boreae spiritus aufert
reuehat mites Zephyrus frondes.

Hypp., 966-967:

ut nunc canae frigora brumae
nudent silvas, . . .

[51] *Cons. Phil.*, I.m.5.31-2:

at peruersi resident celso
mores solio. . . .

Hypp., 982:

fraus sublimi regnat in aula.

[52] Boethius and Seneca exploit the tendency of the dimeter line to split in half. In complaining of man's limited control over his fortune, both writers culminate an argument with a rhetorical question asked in a half-line.

Cons. Phil., I.m.5.25-29

Omnia certo fine gubernans
hominum solos respuis actus

Hypp., 972-7

sed cur idem qui tanta regis,
sub quo vasti pondera mundi

elled the broad outlines and some of the techniques of his complaint on Seneca's scene. Developing the rhetorical excesses of his forensic display in the previous prosa, the prisoner becomes overtly dramatic in his outburst. He is being theatrical in the worst sense, and he enacts the dictum he will soon hear Fortuna herself utter: "What else does the cry of tragedy bewail but the overthrow of happy realms by the unexpected blow of Fortune?"[53] This is precisely the purpose and tone of his poem, and the clamor of his exhortation, like

merito rector cohibere modo.	librata suos ducunt orbes,
Nam cur tantas lubrica uersat	hominum nimium securus abes,
Fortuna uices?	non sollicitus prodesse bonis,
	nocuisse malis?

Boethius also leaves a half-line uncompleted to emphasize the power of his lament:

> Latet obscuris condita uirtus
> clara tenebris iustusque tulit
> crimen iniqui. (1.m.5.34-6)

Compare Seneca's use of half lines:

> colla leonis Cererem magno
> fervore coquant viresque suas
> temperet annus? (Hypp., 969-971)

> tristis virtus perversa tulit
> praemia recti; castos sequitur
> mala paupertas vitioque potens
> regnat adulter. (Hypp., 985-988)

[53] Green, trans., p. 24. "Quid tragoediarum clamor aliud deflet nisi indiscreto ictu fortunam felicia regna uertentem?" (II.pr.2.12.) It seems that central to Late Antique definitions of tragedy are not the generic or even the moral and thematic content of the work, but rather the sense of *clamor*: the loudness and emotive character of the outburst. Cassiodorus reports the view when he writes: "Tragoedia ex uocis uastitate nominatur, quae concauis repercussionibus roborata talem sonum uidetur efficere, ut paene ab homine non credatur exire" (*Variae*, IV.51, ed. Fridh, CCSL, p. 178). To a certain extent, then, the "tragic" nature of the prisoner at the *Consolation*'s opening may refer as much to his tone of voice as to the details of his fall from power: that is, that Boethius appears tragic because he sounds tragic; because he adopts the voice of the Senecan stage in contrast to Philosophy's calm, philosophical manner.

that of Seneca's chorus, has its place most surely on the stage rather than the library. The prisoner remains subject to those Muses of the theater which turn him to Seneca, not as a foil, but as a source for passion.

In this context, the metrical, structural, and thematic relationships of the poem with v.m.3 are striking. While both use the same anapestic dimeter, the details of myth and agriculture are gone in Book Five. Instead, the concentration on problems of mind and body makes the poem's subject matter more abstract. Gone too are the intrusive O's which mark the emotionalism of his prayer. 1.m.5 had moved from harmony to discord: it began with a praise of creation and creator, but ended with a lament on the instability of Fortune; God ruled in a unity, but man lived in fragments. v.m.3, however, moves from apparent discord to potential harmony. The paradox of providence and free will seems unresolvable. Man seems to wander in blindness, unable to recognize the unity of creation. But the prisoner realizes that from the fragments of remembered knowledge, man can piece together an apprehension of truth. The poem of Book Five now has no use for Seneca, either straight or recast. Central to the prisoner's technique in the poem is the rewriting of Philosophy's own poetry. The blind limbs of the body (v.m.3.8) recall the blindness Philosophy had found earlier in the prisoner. When he asks, "Sed quis nota scire laborat?" (14) he revives the imagery of mental labor which had led up to the Hercules poem and which had looked forward to that hero's higher reward.

Taken together, these two prosimetric speeches bracket the substance of the *Consolation* itself. Within them transpires the dialogue between Philosophy and the prisoner: her initiation of the dialogue comes soon after 1.m.5; its last stages are attained just before v.pr.3. After the prisoner's last poem, the conversation is over, and the *Consolation* presents an unbroken lecture punctuated only by the prisoner's occasional, nearly monosyllabic assents. The principles of rewriting operate at the large structural level, as the speech of Book Five recasts that of Book One. Instead of looking for sources in forensic oratory or Senecan histrionics, the reader finds in Book Five the heritage of Aristotelian method and Platonic myth. In keeping with these patterns of rewriting, Philosophy now answers his poem of Book Five in a way analogous to her response to the poem of Book One. There, immediately after I.m.5, Philosophy had calmly restated the central claims of the prisoner's accusation, and I illustrated earlier how she ordered her response sequentially through a series of distinctive rhetorical markers. After the prisoner's final metrum, she again reasserts her skill with language, only here it is the language of philosophy rather than of dialectic.

She shows herself to be a model of organized thinking and clarity of purpose. She argues that Cicero, Boethius himself, and all mankind have been unable to solve the problem of providence because their reasoning (*ratiocinatio*) cannot grasp divine prescience. Should such reasoning approach divine intelligence, all ambiguities would disappear, and in saying this Philosophy confirms that the human condition will remain one of doubt and approximation.[54] Certainty, for the prisoner, can be approached only through mastery of the arts of inquiry, and philosophy displays her demonstrative skills by presenting a sequence of rhetorical questions, each marked by explicit links.

> Quaero enim . . .
> Num enim . . .
> Si igitur . . .
> Etenim . . .
> Num igitur . . .
> (v.pr.4.4,5,6,7,8).

Her method appears similar to that of I.pr.5; but, instead of putting off the "stronger medicines" for later use, she sets out to demonstrate her philosophical position through rig-

---

[54] "Cuius caliginis causa est quod humanae ratiocinationis motus ad diuinae praescientiae simplicitatem non potest ammoueri; quae si ullo modo cogitari queat, nihil prorsus relinquetur ambigui" (v.pr.4.2).

orous proofs.[55] Her claims for internal arguments and necessary proof read like a textbook definition of philosophical method.

> Moreover, it is clear that firmly based proof does not rest on signs and extrinsic arguments but is deduced from suitable and necessary causes.[56]

Philosophy reminds the prisoner of the key points of her method. Her phrasing returns to the definition of demonstration given in Boethius' *De topicis differentiis*, and it echoes the prisoner's own characterization of her technique in Book Three ("Atque haec nullis extrinsecus sumptis, sed ex altero altero fidem trahente insitis domesticisque probationibus explicabas," III.pr.12.35). By putting her method into action, Philosophy confirms her authority and renders the prisoner's responses minimal. The self-sufficiency of philosophical demonstration needs no outside experiences nor outside interlocutors to develop arguments. Philosophy can ask and answer her own questions, thus internalizing the process of dialogue.

This methodological move complements the *Consolation*'s change in subject. From discussing man's relationship to fortune or the world, Boethius moves to man's relationship to himself and to God. There is a progressive turning inward here, as Book Five explores the workings of mental faculties and the structures of human judgment. The place of action for this topic becomes the mind itself. Philosophy's poem on perception theory (V.m.4) argues for an internalized process of perceiving. Rejecting the Stoic theories of impression, she takes the Platonic psychological vocabulary to show how the mind is no passive tabula rasa but an active seat of power, holding within itself remembered forms.[57] Her repetition of

---

[55] "Quare demonstrandum prius est nihil non ex necessitate contingere . . ." (V.pr.4.12).

[56] Green, trans., p. 109. "Iam uero probationem firma ratione subnixam constat non ex signis neque petitis extrinsecus argumentis sed ex conuenientibus necessariisque causis esse ducendam" (V.pr.4.13).

[57] "cum uel lux oculos ferit / uel uox auribus instrepit. / Tum mentis uigor

phrases for interiority (the words *intus*, *introrsumque*) points the poem to the articulation of interior states, and I would contend that her methodological vocabulary and her philosophical diction dovetail here, as the *Consolation*'s subject and method operate silently within the mind. Metrum 4 thus completes the development of a set of images basic to the work's movement: from external hopes, wealth, fame, and extrinsic arguments, there has been a move to inner reliance, self-sufficient arguments, and rejection of transitory reward. This movement inward informs, too, the central metaphors of seeing expressed in the work's poetry: from the downcast, earth-bound look of Orpheus, the prisoner is meant to move to the upward-looking and heaven-seeking look of Hercules. The goal of this progress is recognition of the soul's true *patria* as well as the awareness of man's own condition under the aegis of a benign God. With this in mind, Philosophy's final poem (v.m.5) reviews the catalogue of beasts familiar from the mythological poetry and juxtaposes a new view of the upright man. She brings out the thematic importance of the man/beast dichotomy which was announced in the Ulysses poem. In Book Five, the animals, for all their physical abilities of flight, power, or endurance, nonetheless possess only *sensus* and no *ratio*. Humankind, however, with their upright bodies, look down upon the earth, and Philosophy's term *despicit* used to describe this process echoes her earlier metrum chronicling the soul's ascent to heaven.[58] Like the final poem of Book Three, the final poem of Book Five also has Orpheus in mind, as the human face and forehead point confidently to the sky, and as the mind itself aspires to heaven.[59]

---

excitus / quas intus species tenet / ad motus similes uocans / notis applicat exteris / introrsumque reconditis / formis miscet imagines" (v.m.4.33-40).

[58] Compare v.m.5.10-11: "unica gens hominum celsum leuat altius cacumen / atque leuis recto stat corpore despicitque terras," with iv.m.1.3-4: "quas sibi cum uelox mens induit / terras perosa despicit."

[59] "Haec, nisi terrenus male desipis, ammonet figura: / Qui recto caelum uultu petis exserisque frontem, / in sublime feras animum quoque, ne grauata pessum / inferior sidat mens corpore celsius leuato." (v.m.5.12-15).

The two last poems of the *Consolation* thus reaffirm through the metaphors for seeing and understanding man's place in the world and in the cosmos. By firmly locating the seat of human reason in relation both to beastly sensation and divine intelligence, Philosophy gives precise meaning to her restatement of the human condition: "homo est animal bipes rationale" (v.pr.4.35). Such a statement had, in the mouth of the prisoner of Book One, appeared simply as a textbook answer, rattled off by a man mired in the limited worlds of rhetoric and dialectic. By Book Five, the definition has a new edge: "rational" now specifically locates man in the schema of mental faculties; "bipedal" can, in the context of Philosophy's final poem, point to the unique human ability to stand erect and fix the gaze to heaven. The definition here both marks man for what he is and for what he can aspire to be. This new interpretation of an old definition reifies whatever changes have occurred in the prisoner; by redefining his species, she redefines him. The prisoner's moral education has culminated through two parallel processes: first, through the active engagement with Philosophy's method of demonstration and the corresponding ability to argue like a philosopher; second, through the explicit teachings of Philosophy herself—teachings which stimulate moral growth through technical instruction.

Philosophy's final arguments take on a didactic tone in v.pr.6, as she proceeds through rigorous demonstration and proof. Her approach summarizes the basic techniques of disputation developed to this point, as her lecture subsumes and reenacts all the previous forms of argument and refutation explored with the prisoner. There is the appeal to human judgment as an initial premise.[60] Then, Philosophy adduces key *auctores*, Aristotle and Plato, only to qualify their beliefs and explain their terminology.[61] Finally, Philosophy takes the

---

[60] "Deum igitur aeternum esse cunctorum ratione degentium commune iudicium est" (v.pr.6.2).

[61] "Quod igitur temporis patitur condicionem, licet illud, sicuti de mundo censuit Aristoteles, nec coeperit umquam esse nec desinat uitaque eius cum

techniques of question and answer to a new level of sophistication by arguing with herself. She anticipates the prisoner's
questions and, in a striking sequence of rhetorical moves,
imitates the dynamic of interrogation and response. She in-
terposes, "if you were to say here . . . ," and quickly offers
her own, "I will respond" (*respondebo*, v.6.25-26). Again, her
imagined version of what the prisoner will ask (her word
inquies, v.6.37) gets another response (her *respondebo*, v.7.38).
Philosophy continues this dialogue with herself, taking the
prisoner's voice right down to the characteristic *minime* which
has become his signature by the end of the work.[62]

In arguing for the distinction between prevision and providence, Philosophy asks a rhetorical question to which the
response is *minime* (i.e., "not at all," v.pr.6.19). Then, at the
prosa's penultimate moment, Philosophy asks, "What will
you say, then?" ("Quid igitur, inquies," v.pr.6.39) to the
query, "Whether God's knowledge is changed by your de-
cisions" (Green, trans., p. 119). Again, the response is *minime*
(v.pr.6.49). Although certain editors have placed the first of
these responses in quotation marks, indicating that the prisoner is, in fact, answering, there is nothing in the manuscripts
to suggest that anyone other than Philosophy is speaking, and
both Bieler and Weinberg print the words as Philosophy's
own.[63] With both responses spoken by Philosophy, prosa 6

---

temporis infinitate tendatur, nondum tamen tale est ut aeternum esse iure
credatur" (v.pr.6.6. On Plato, see v.pr.6.9,10,14).

[62] The prisoner begins his use of *minime* as a form of assent as early as
III.pr.3.9, and uses it twelve more times through the course of the *Consolation*
(see Cooper, *Concordance*, p. 235). On two earlier occasions, Philosophy had
responded to her own rhetorical questions: at III.pr.4.6, she had asked the
prisoner if he thought a wise man unworthy of respect—of course not (*minime*); at II.pr.5.32 she anticipates the prisoner's assent when she asks, "Am I
wrong," and answers herself, "Of course not, you will say" ("minime,
inquis"). Boethius had also used the idiom in the sequence of questions which
closes section III of *De Trinitate*: to those who ask, "Is the Father the same
as the Son," the Catholics answer, *minime* (*De Trin.*, p. 16).

[63] The Loeb editors print the first of the *minime*'s as the prisoner's
(p. 426), and Green, who claims to be following the editions of Bieler and
Weinberg, also translates the first *minime* as the prisoner's (p. 117). Bieler,

becomes an unbroken treatise. She internalizes and sustains a dialogue with a silent—or even absent—partner. Philosophy apes the prisoner's characteristic *minime*, and her question-and-answer technique affirms her role as a Boethian figure of internalized disputation, much like the writer of the tractates: she can anticipate and answer imaginary questions.

Her prose also takes on the status of a written document. Like the meditations of the tractates, her lecture becomes a readable text. The *Consolation* has been moving towards this point since iv.pr.6, both through the gradual disappearance of the prisoner and through Philosophy's own engagement with the written works of Cicero, Aristotle, and Plato. The texture of the *Consolation*'s prose thus becomes a kind of commentary: a self-consciously written document whose authoritative status complements the *auctoritas* of its basic texts. In addition to adopting the idiom of the tractates (especially at iv.pr.6), Boethius has Philosophy return to the voice of the commentaries. In its final and explicit mention of Aristotle and Plato, and in its attempted synthesis of method and theme, the *Consolation* fulfills Boethius' early dream of harmonizing both authors through translation and commentary. If the goals of the project initiated in the *Perihermeneias* commentary were unfulfilled in commentary form, they are completed by the *Consolation*'s close. By bringing together the various facets of the reading and writing persona Boethius had developed throughout his literary career, he affirms the act of reading as the key to intellectual growth and self-awareness.

The tone, structure, and method of the *Consolation*'s conclusion turn the prisoner into a reader who is no longer inside the text but rather outside it. Rather than witnessing him read Philosophy's poems and discuss their meanings within the work's fiction, we are unable to gauge his possible responses to Philosophy's prose disquisitions. This is so, I would suggest, because the prisoner inside the fiction and the reader

---

p. 102, note to l.68, notes "*Minime* Boethio dare solent editores; sed Philosophia ipsa sibi respondere uidetur, cf. infra, 6, 40."

outside it have now merged into one. Throughout the work, the reader has been able to measure his experience against that of the prisoner; Philosophy's exhortations forced him to interpret her poetry and to engage her in discussion. By narrating the prisoner's education, the *Consolation* has been educating the reader, but by the final prosa all that has changed. The prisoner has moved from participant to audience, and his silent accession to Philosophy's authority matches the reader's experience of silently absorbing her doctrine. Philosophy's own form of address confirms the union of prisoner and reader. Her concluding sentences go past the prisoner to the audience, demonstrating an awareness of a public readership for her words. The exhortation which closes the work differs from the injunctions at the conclusions to her mythological metra. Philosophy no longer goads the prisoner to interpret her exempla and to see himself through literary fictions. She now pressures him not to read but to act, and the force of her words suggests one reason for the absence of a final metrum.

> Therefore, stand firm against vice and cultivate virtue. Lift up your soul to worthy hopes, and offer humble prayers to heaven. If you will face it, the necessity of virtuous action imposed upon you is very great, since all your actions are done in the sight of a Judge who sees all things.[64]

Philosophy's final injunction removes the arena of the *Consolation*'s activity from the prison or the library to the world under the sight of God. While her phrasing resembles the concluding lines to the poem on Hercules, there is no *exemplum* of myth or literature from which to learn. By avoiding a concluding metrum, Boethius accomplishes two things. He reinforces the non-dialectical and purely philosophical structure of his concluding argument. The tension between poetry

---

[64] Green, trans., p. 119. "Auersamini igitur uitia, colite uirtutes, ad rectas spes animum subleuate, humiles preces in excelsa porrigite. Magna uobis est, si dissimulare non uultis, necessitas indicta probitatis cum ante oculos agitis iudicis cuncta cernentis" (v.pr.6.47-48).

and reason, and in turn, the prisoner's own problem with wonder and belief, disappear as we are left with a straight-forward piece of demonstrative prose. In addition, there is no final poem because further reading is unnecessary. At the very end of the work, Boethius rejects the very principle of edu-cation and understanding he has developed. Words, and es-pecially poetry, are useless at this point, as Philosophy offers now another, higher form of discourse which is neither vo-calized nor transcribed: prayer.

The mention of prayer at the *Consolation*'s close changes dramatically the tone and purpose of the work.[65] Some have gone so far as to suggest that these final lines are an editorial addition, and that the idiom of prayer is foreign to the *Con-solation*'s non-theological diction.[66] Boethius' conception of prayer, however, makes sense within the structures of dis-course he has developed throughout the work, and within the overall tension between silence and speech whose analogue can be found in the works of Augustine. I had begun this study by suggesting that the prisoner's silence of Book One had as its foil the higher, Augustinian "rhetoric of silence" through which all true reading and understanding transpired. The *De Magistro* outlined the theory of the inner, silent teacher, while at the same time presenting Adeodatus' silence as a model for the student's behavior. As Adeodatus disap-pears from the *De Magistro*'s final sections, his silence reaffirms Augustine's own authority as a teacher, while at the same

---

[65] "Nec frustra sunt in deo positae spes precesque, quae cum rectae sunt inefficaces esse non possunt" (v.pr.6.46), and see quotation from v.pr.6.47. Mohrmann, "Some Remarks," argues that these closing lines echo v.pr.3.33, where Boethius had discussed the possibility of destroying prayer as a form of discourse between man and God. There, the word for prayer was *deprecandi*, which, Mohrmann argues, owes its origins in this context to the Late Latin usage of the Catholic liturgy. She then compares the phrasing *sperandi / deprecandi* in v.3. with the phrasing *spes precesque* at v.6, noting too that *preces* and *in excelsa* "have a certain liturgical flavour" (p. 61).

[66] Gruber summarizes the criticism, *Kommentar*, pp. 414-415. See Mohr-mann, "Some Remarks," and De Vogel, "Boethiana, II," who argues for a pervasive Christian element throughout the *Consolation* drawn primarily from Biblical idioms.

time enacting a form of the silent understanding which Augustine himself is explaining. Save for Adeodatus' final summarizing remarks, his parallel with the *Consolation*'s prisoner is, I think, self-evident. But it is rather with the *Confessions* that the prisoner's, and the reader's, ultimate silence and prayer has its analogue.

Book Ten of the *Confessions* opens with a meditation on the usefulness of writing the book and on the place of its composition in Augustine's spiritual life. As the last book in the larger, autobiographical section of the work, Book Ten summarizes many of the themes of the *Confessions*, and, in particular, it reflects on the processes of reading and writing which, as is well known, structured the key moments of the narrative.[67] "I wish to act in truth," Augustine states, "making my confession both in my heart before you and in this book before the many who will read it."[68] He notes that man's conscience is bared before God's eyes, and for that reason:

> I make my confession not in words and sounds made by the tongue alone, but with the voice of my soul and in my thoughts which cry aloud to you.
>
> . . .
>
> And my confession is made both silently in your sight, my God, and aloud as well, because even though my tongue utters no sound, my heart cries to you.[69]

[67] For the issues of reading and writing in the *Confessions*, from a variety of critical and theoretical perspectives, see Mazzotta, *Dante: Poet of the Desert*, pp. 145-191; Andrew Fichter, *Poets Historicall* (New Haven: Yale University Press, 1982), pp. 40-69; Eugene Vance, "The Grammar of Selfhood in Augustine's *Confessions*," *Genre* 6 (1973), 1-28; Ralph Flores, "Reading and Speech in St. Augustine's *Confessions*," *Augustinian Studies* 6 (1975), 1-13.

[68] Translations from R. Pine-Coffin, trans., *St. Augustine's Confessions* (Harmondsworth: Penguin, 1961), p. 207. "uolo eam facere in corde meo coram te in confessione, in stilo autem meo coram multis testibus" *Conf.*, x.i.1).

[69] Pine-Coffin, p. 207. "neque id ago uerbis carnis et uocibus, sed uerbis animae et clamore cogitationis, quem nouit auris tua" (*Conf.*, x.ii.2). Pine-Coffin, p. 208. "confessio itaque mea, deus meus, in conspectu tuo tibi tacite fit et no tacite. tacet enim strepitu, clamat affectu" (*Conf.*, x.ii.2).

These remarks bear directly on the tone of the *Consolation*'s close. First, there is the awareness of God's ability to see all things, and of his role as judge of man's actions (cf. *Conf.*, x.5, "It is you, O Lord, who judges me").[70] Augustine realizes that even at his most isolated, man is never alone, and Boethius' claim for the eternal presence of God fills the void left by the rejection of worldly goods and human company which the *Consolation* had chronicled. The stark loneliness of the *Consolation*'s opening is thus impossible in a world which admits the presence of God and the continuity of his sight. Second, Augustine distinguishes between the ways of communicating to man and to God. His *Confessions* remain a written text fit for human eyes; that he recounts his life "out loud" signals the fact that his words will speak to the reader. But he also speaks in silence to God, and here Augustine returns to the idiom of silent reading and meditation developed earlier in the *Confessions*. On the one hand, silence is the appropriate medium for reading and learning: witness Ambrose reading in silence or Augustine reading the scriptures silently in the "tolle lege" scene. On the other hand, silence is the ambiance of prayer. Augustine postulates a higher form of discourse for expressing the self to God; the individual articulates itself not through words, but through the voice of the soul.[71]

The prisoner's silence at the *Consolation*'s ending may, in part, be said to enact these Augustinian principles. If he has taken Philosophy's injunction to heart, then his prayers will be unspoken. The written document of his education—*The Consolation of Philosophy* we have finished reading—remains in this schema only half of the prisoner's "confession." It corresponds to that record of the life presented in Augustine's

---

[70] Pine-Coffin, p. 210. "Tu enim, domine, diiudicas me . . ." (*Conf.*, x.v.7).

[71] Compare Boethius' discussion at v.pr.3.34, where the prisoner considers prayer a form of conversation (a *colloquium*) between man and God. Mohrmann's discussion does not focus on this term, but rather on the term *commercium*—man's communication with God as a kind of "commerce," using the idiom of the early Roman liturgy ("Some Remarks," pp. 56-58).

book. In the Saint's words, it remains a confession made "before the many who will read it."

To this point, I have read the *Consolation* as the expression of a life through language: the work of a mind defining and redefining itself through the kinds of discourse it employs. The prisoner's move from lethargic silence, through oratory, rhetoric, dialectic, and philosophy represents the development of a mind traced through different levels of language use. At the top of this hierarchy is prayer. It is essential that Boethius reserve mention of this form of discourse for the *Consolation*'s end, for it is the last stage in the sequence of his education in the arts of expression. Significantly, Boethius does not transcribe whatever his concluding prayer might be, and in this he contrasts sharply with the lush, rhetorically assured Platonic hymn of III.m.9. Philosophy's "prayer" in that poem artfully imitated the controlling power of the Ruler in its own metrical, metaphorical, and rhetorical control. As the centerpiece of the *Consolation*, it symbolically restated the prisoner's moral goal. As a work of poetry, it inspired the prisoner with an almost speechless wonder at the workings of the cosmos. The best and most effective final answer to this prayer would, therefore, not be a transcription of an explicitly Christian act of devotion, but rather no text at all. As a counterpoint to Philosophy's brilliantly executed hymn, there is only silence. To the authority of the Platonic *conditor*, and to the authority of Philosophy herself, Boethius juxtaposes the final authority of God. He replaces the old *auctores* with an authority figure whose ultimate comprehension and engagement demands neither prose nor verse.

There are thus three aspects to the prisoner's silence as the *Consolation* draws to its close. First, there is the silence of the student, listening to the teacher's voice remind him of himself. This is the silence described in the *De Magistro*, where Augustine characterizes the attentive listener and the inner teacher, while Adeodatus enacts the role of quiescent student. Second, there is the silence of the reader. As Philosophy's method changes from dialogue to monologue, her *prosae* become written treatises designed to be read. The prisoner's silent engagement with these new texts is a model for the *Consolation*'s reader, and this stance may owe something to Augustine's formulation of a theory of ideal reading in the *Confessions*. Finally, there is the silence of prayer also characterized in the *Confessions*. Here, Boethius rejects articulated language altogether in favor of a form of communication which cannot be transcribed and which supplants the authority figures of the human judges or of Lady Philosophy with that of God.

With the prisoner's silence, the *Consolation*'s conclusion differs markedly from those earlier texts I had presented as generic and structural backgrounds to the work. Unlike the dialogues of Cicero, Augustine, or Fulgentius, and unlike Boethius' own early *In Isagogen*, there is no final promise of further study with the master, nor is there the explicit commitment to transcribing that study in future literary texts. Biographical arguments would, of course, obviate these problems: the student's commitment at the end of the *In Isagogen* to continue studying *si vita suppetit* ("if life permits") would be pointless in a work written in anticipation of execution. But what I have tried to emphasize throughout this study is the internal coherence of Boethius' literary career, as well as of the *Consolation*'s imagery and method, and for these reasons stress the absence of any need for literal, biographical criticism. The *Consolation*'s close has its meaning within the structure of the text itself; within the tropes and patterns of the reader's life Boethius had created for himself; and within the structures of literary allusions operating through the work. The *Consolation*'s conclusion returns the reader to its beginnings in the texts and contexts out of which it is built, and to the beginning of the work itself. The prisoner's final silence stands in sharp contrast to his opening speechlessness, and his final refusal to transcribe prayer or poetry differentiates him from the creature of lethargy possessed by the difficulty of beginning the text.

APPENDIX

SENECA'S PLAYS IN
The Consolation of Philosophy

Seneca's plays have yet to be given the status demanded for a full understanding of Boethius' poetic technique. Ever since Rudolph Peiper catalogued the echoes and allusions to Senecan drama in his edition of the *Consolation*, scholars have been content to mention the plays as simply one more example of the wide eclecticism of Boethius' reading or the complex syncretism of his method.[1] Joachim Gruber's commentary gives little prominence to Seneca's influence, and Henry Chadwick notes only that Book Four of the *Consolation* "concludes with a poem full of echoes of Seneca's tragedies" (p. 274).[2] Throughout this study, I have taken Seneca's plays as a major influence on the poetry of the *Consolation*. I have

---

[1] R. Peiper, ed., *Boetii De Consolatione Philosophiae* (Leipzig: Teubner, 1871), pp. 228-233. For discussion of Peiper's catalogue, see A. M. Crabbe, "Literary Design," in Gibson, *Boethius*, p. 239 and p. 265, n. 28. In fact, long before Peiper noticed Boethius's use of Seneca, late medieval readers had commented on the similarities of lines in *Hercules Furens* with IV.m.7. On Petrarch's recognition of Seneca in Boethius, see A. C. de la Mare, "Petrarch's Manuscript of the Tragedies of Seneca," *JWCI* 40 (1977), 289, n. 20. Petrarch glossed *HF* 582: "Hinc bo.us in consol." Nicholas Trivet also found echoes. See V. Ussani, Jr., ed., *Nicolai Treveti Expositio Herculis Furentis* (Rome: Edizioni dell'Ateneo, 1959), pp. 82, 169.

[2] Gruber simply reports Peiper's original findings, and Chadwick mentions Seneca only in reference to IV.m.7. Sheible considers Peiper's catalogue to overstate the case, and, as I noted earlier, favors comparison with Greek plays over Senecan dramas for the major mythological poems.

tried to show how Boethius rewrites portions of the plays in order to reinforce the impact of his own arguments. By constantly having the Senecan version as a kind of background or "super-text" to his own verses, he can measure the prisoner against the explicitly Stoic models of Orpheus and Hercules. Moreover, by shifting the speakers of Seneca's lines from such figures as the Juno of *Hercules Furens* or the Argive Chorus from the *Agamemnon*, Boethius replaces one female authority with another, and thus reinforces the dramatic and at times choral power of Lady Philosophy's metrical advice.

Boethius' adaptations of Senecan scenes proceed according to the central principles of the *Consolation*'s argument, and the structure of Senecan allusion chronicles a pattern of Boethius' reading and rewriting which is at the heart of the prisoner's educational experience. Remembering, Lady Philosophy had claimed, is the operation of the learning mind, and through the process of recall the mind reviews its cognitive life both within and before its bodily existence. It is clear from the structures of remembrance in the *Consolation* that the prisoner recalls earlier experiences only to reject them: his profession of an orator and politician; his status as an Academician; his reading of certain texts. The process of growth may be said to parallel Augustine's development in the *Confessions*. Augustine recalls Virgil, Mani, and Cicero only to reject them. Learning not to weep for Dido, to abandon the Manichees, and to turn from the *Hortensius* are all moments which, reenacted in the *Confessions*, reveal a mind reordering itself along the lines of critical reading. Critics of the saint's autobiography have long noticed how the young man's life was shaped, in the text, according to such literary rather than literal experiences.[3] The *Aeneid* is but the most obvious narrative against which Augustine measures his own growth. I tried to draw out the cultural implications of such an attitude towards texts in Chapter I; now, I propose a distinctive literary use of the persona of the reader. We have seen Boethius present himself

---

[3] See the studies of Vance, Fichter, and Flores cited in Chapter V, n. 67.

as a reader and commentator of classical texts, and how he tried to shape his life according to the demands of scholarship. There is another kind of reading in the *Consolation*, perhaps close to Augustine's experience in the *Confessions*, and this is the way Boethius handles Seneca. The reader of the *Consolation* witnesses another reader's progressive engagement with Seneca's plays: from slavish imitation to critical reading, to rejection.

Boethius' use of Senecan material is not without its pattern and logic. The early books draw most heavily on the *Hyppolytus*, while by Book Three the Hercules plays begin to take over.[4] The poem on Orpheus recasts an entire chorus from *Hercules Furens*, and in the final metrum of Book Four Boethius synthesizes material from that play with the chorus of Argive women in the *Agamemnon*, while allusions to the *Medea* and possibly *Hercules Oetaeus* appear at strategic points as well. After the final poem of Book Four, Boethius has no use for the dramatist, and, save for two dubious citations, Book Five is devoid of any allusion to the plays.[5] Boethius' use of Seneca chronicles the growth of a reader's mind, a growth achieved in tandem with his development as a debater and his maturity as a philosopher. His rejection of Seneca as a source coincides with the final turning point of the *Consolation*'s argument, and it follows closely on the "new beginning" offered by Philosophy's prose disquisition (IV.pr.6). Education is a theme and process for the work, and the citations from Seneca inscribe the prisoner's education as a reader.

To put into this sequence the allusions and reworkings of

---

[4] See Peiper's catalogue.

[5] Peiper records one citation from *Octavia* in Book Five: v.m.4.20, "Quae diuisa recolligit." *Oct*, 754, "recollige animum, recipe laetitiam, precor." This parallel is hardly distinctive, and the *Octavia* was probably not part of the Senecan canon as passed down through the earliest MSS Boethius could have seen. The play's authenticity is questioned by virtually all modern scholars (see Tarrant, pp. 23, 157, on the MS's history and the differences in theme and structure of *Octavia* from the rest of the plays). Peiper's other citation in Book Five makes no sense to me: v.m.2.3, "Melliflui canit oris Homerus" compared with *Oedipus*, 194, "quos liberior domus elato."

Seneca which I have presented in this study, I review my basic
arguments. Boethius begins with the *Hyppolytus*. Peiper noticed
echoes as early as Philosophy's first metrum (1.m.2), but it is
with the prisoner's lament at 1.m.5 that the Senecan source has
its full meaning. By following Seneca closely, the prisoner apes
the voice of the tragic chorus. He takes the Senecan scene
directly and without irony; any additions or revisions serve
only to augment the tone of his dramatic source. Both poems
take as their central examples the facts of nature: the changing
seasons or the passage of days. In keeping with the obsessively
earth-bound expressions of the prisoner in Book One, his
poem preserves the imagery of Nature without an awareness
of the benign power which, as Philosophy will later teach
him, disposes all things. After Book One, allusions to Seneca's
plays are scattered throughout the metra, but it is not until
III.m.12 and IV.m.7 that Boethius rewrites in full entire scenes
or speeches. Unlike the prisoner's "straight" adaptation of
dramatic lament in Book One, these poems are in the voice
of Philosophy, and, as I have shown, they recast the Senecan
source material in ways which juxtapose positive and negative
readings of their heroic subjects. Boethius recasts Seneca's
Orpheus into a figure for the prisoner; rather than looking
forward as a warning to Hercules in *Hercules Furens*, the *Consolation*'s Orpheus looks back over the prisoner's life thus far.
Rather than focusing on the legalisms and details of Plutonian
justice (as Seneca's chorus had within the context of the play's
larger structure of judgment and retribution) Boethius' metrum rejects human law in favor of a higher set of commands,
and this rejection participates in the larger dismissal of human
legal systems building from the prisoner's defense at 1.pr.5.
Finally, the poem on Hercules not only summarizes the central
metaphors of the *Consolation*'s text, but also synthesizes a mass
of Senecan material, effectively rewriting a body of female
speeches whose vengeful or angry tones contrast sharply with
the encouraging voice of Lady Philosophy.

  Boethius' experience of the drama may also be said to enact
that rejection which greeted Philosophy's initial appearance:

the banishment of the Muses. While they are, certainly, *poeticas Musas*, they are also *scenicas meritriculas*—whores of the theater—and their aegis would seem to command the dramatic literature so vehemently condemned in early Christian polemic. One might, at first, find it odd if not self-contradictory for Boethius to incorporate so much of Senecan drama into Philosophy's poetry. And yet, this apparent paradox is precisely the point. Rather than rejecting the drama as a source for his diction, Boethius appropriates it, and the place of Seneca's lines in Philosophy's mouth concretizes the actual replacement of her Muses for the whores of the theater.

My reading of Seneca's place in *The Consolation of Philosophy* would make little sense without evidence for the dramatist's survival in Late Antiquity, and in what follows I will attempt a brief chronicle of the plays' fate to the time of Boethius. Our understanding of the place of drama during this period, however, remains inadequate.[6] The early Christian repudiation of the theater survives from Tertullian onward, and for the first six centuries of Christianity attitudes towards Roman drama seem to vacillate between outright condemnation and grudging tolerance.[7] St. Augustine, while associating the theater and the tragic katharsis with the lustful experience of Carthage in the *Confessions* (III.2), nonetheless readily employs theatrical imagery in the *Soliloquia*.[8] In the famous discussion of the theory of representation, Augustine recalls the actor Roscius and the problem of character portrayal.[9] In the *City of God*, moreover, he offers tragedy as a component of a young man's education, and recent studies have suggested the possibility of the Saint's own early participation in dramatic per-

---

[6] For drama in general in Late Antiquity, see H. A. Kelley, "Tragedy and the Performance of Tragedy in Late Roman Antiquity," *Traditio* 35 (1979), 21-44, who summarizes the current scholarly debates and provides much primary source material. See too Mary H. Marshall, "Theater in the Middle Ages: Evidence from Dictionaries and Glosses," *Symposium* 4 (1950), 1-39.

[7] See Heiko Jürgens, *Pompa Diaboli* (Stuttgart: Kohlhammer, 1972).

[8] See the discussion of the *Soliloquia* in Chapter I of this study.

[9] *Soliloquia*, II.x.18.

formance.[10] Records of the reception of Roman drama survive
from other Late Antique writers. Sidonius Apollinaris in the
fifth century records dramatic performances at the Gothic
court, but with a vagueness which makes impossible any lo-
calization of the survival of literary drama here.[11] In the sixth
century, Cassiodorus voices a concern with the need to preserve the architectural heritage of the Roman theaters. His
remarks in the *Variae* indicate a certain familiarity with the
technical terms of drama and dramaturgy, but it is unclear
from his letters whether dramas were still being performed
in those theaters he wished to save, or whether he simply
echoed the tropes of dramatic criticism familiar from his wide
reading.[12]

For all of these historical remarks, and for all the vituper-
ations of the early fathers, it remains unclear how Roman
drama and Seneca's plays in particular were performed and
transmitted. Debate still continues as to whether the plays
were publicly declaimed or acted on the stage. Some have
concluded that the philosophical weight of Seneca's texts
would have precluded their public performance and would
have relegated them to private reading and instruction.[13] In

[10] As cited and quoted in E. K. Chambers, *The Mediaeval Stage* (Oxford:
Clarendon Press, 1903), vol. I, p. 18: "et haec sunt scenicorum tolerabiliora
ludorum, comoediae scilicet et tragoediae; hoc est, fabulae poetarum agendae
in spectaculis, multa rerum turpitudine sed nulla saltem sicut alia multa verborum obscoenitate compositae; quas etiam inter studia quae honesta ac lib-
eralia vocantur pueri legere et discere coguntur a sensibus" (*City of God*, 11.8).
Kelly calls attention to Augustine's remarks in the *Confessions* concerning not
only his enjoyment of the theater, but of his possible participation in tragic
performance (Kelly, "Tragedy," p. 27 and n. 21, citing *Conf.* IV.1,2,3 and
III.6).

[11] See the citations and discussion in Jeff Opland, *Anglo-Saxon Oral Poetry*
(New Haven: Yale University Press, 1980), pp. 53-55.

[12] Cassiodorus, *Variae*, IV.51.

[13] The debate centers on the study of O. Zweierlein, *Die Rezitationsdramen
Senecas* (Meisenheim-am-Glan: Hain, 1966), who argued that the dramas were
recitation pieces, performed not in costume and with stage action, but rather
through public reading. See the discussion and survey of the arguments in
Tarrant, ed., *Agamemnon*, pp. 7-8 and notes.

fact, the major sources for the survival of Senecan drama lie not with historians of the theater but with grammarians. W. Trillitsch's study of the reception of Seneca's *oeuvre* collects a variety of *vestigia* and *testamenta* from the second through the sixth centuries. Grammarians and commentators quoted Seneca's lines often purely as examples of rhetorical schemes and tropes. Pieces of the tragedies survive in Prudentius, Macrobius, Ennodius, and other writers from the fourth and fifth centuries.[14] Yet, we possess no exhaustive commentary on the plays themselves in the manner of Donatus' work on Terence. In spite of Augustine's permission to include tragedy in the curriculum, I have found no explicit mention of Seneca's plays in early writings on education.

The history of Seneca's text also points towards its familiarity in the early Middle Ages.[15] Although no integral manuscript exists prior to the eleventh century, there is extant a fifth century palimpsest (Milan, Ambrosian Library, MS G 82) on which is transcribed over two hundred lines from *Medea* and *Oedipus,* and a ninth century florelegium containing another recension of these texts adds to the evidence for pre-Carolingian interest in the dramas.[16] The researches of modern textual critics posit a fourth-century exemplar for the plays, and Late Antique citations, recorded for virtually all the dramas save *Octavia*, demonstrate either that complete texts were circulating before the earliest separation of the stemma in the

[14] W. Trillitsch, *Seneca im Literarischen Urteil der Antike* (Amsterdam: Hakkert, 1971), pp. 186-206, 384-391. See too his later study, "Seneca Tragicus—Nachleben und Beurteilung im lateinischen Mittelalter von der Spätantike bis zum Renaissanzhumanizmus," *Philologus* 122 (1978), 120-124.

[15] See the discussions in Tarrant, *Agamemnon*, pp. 23-87, and, more recently, in R. H. Rouse, "New Light on the Circulation of the A-text of Seneca's Tragedies," *JWCI* 40 (1977), 283-286. See, too, G. Brugnoli, "La tradizione manoscritta de Seneca tragico alla luce delle testimonianze medioevali," Atti della Accademia Nazionale di Lincei, Classe di Sci. mor., Stor. e fil., s.8, v.8 (Rome: Accademia Nazionale dei Lincei, 1957), pp. 201-285.

[16] Palimpsest edited by G. Studemund, in F. Leo, ed., *L. Annaei Senecae Tragoediae* (Berlin: Weidmann, 1878), pp. xx-xxvii.

eighth century, or that a living tradition of performance or instruction led to their memorization.[17]

St. Jerome offers a convenient example of an early use of Senecan material for a specific literary purpose. In his *Vita Malchi* (c. 390) Jerome rewrites a passage from Seneca's *Troades*, and in so doing he effectively Christianizes the Roman's Stoic outlook, while augmenting the rhetorical force of his own narrative.[18]

Vita Malchi (ch. 9)	*Troades* (510-512)
Si iuvat Dominus miseros,	Fata si miseros iuvant,
habemus salutem;	habes salutem;
si despicit peccatores,	fata si vitam negant,
habemus sepulchrum.	habes sepulchrum.

Scholars have long noticed Jerome's allusion, and the commentary on its effect is extensive.[19] In the *Troades*, the boy Astyanax takes refuge in a literal tomb (Hector's grave); in Jerome's work, Malchus seeks safety in a figurative one (the cave). The sequence of pursuer and pursued resonates with the epic drama at the end of the Trojan war, and Jerome's version of Seneca's lines gives to the life of Malchus a new dramatic significance. Philosophically, too, the death of Astyanax contrasts with the successful escape of Malchus. When the boy leaves his hiding place, he condemns himself to death at Ulysses' hands; Malchus waits, aided by God rather than by fate, and his course succeeds. By juxtaposing Malchus' redemptive escape from the cave against Astyanax' tragic death, Jerome heightens the impact of the Monk's faith and of the resolution of his flight. By rewriting the Senecan scene,

[17] See the review of scholarship in Tarrant, pp. 52-86, with the stemma described on p. 86.

[18] Texts quoted from W. Trillitsch, "Hieronymus und Seneca," *Mittellateinisches Jahrbuch* 2 (1965), 47.

[19] See G. E. Duckworth, "Classical Echoes in St. Jerome's Life of Malchus," *The Classical Bulletin* 24 (1947/1948), 29; H. Hagendahl, *Latin Fathers and the Classics* (Gothenburg: Studia Graeca et Latina Gothoburgensia, 6, 1958), p. 118. For a full commentary, see Trillitsch, "Hieronymus und Seneca," pp. 46-47.

he offers a pagan, tragic background against which a new, Christian scheme of salvation gains in theatrical effect.

The example of Jerome's *Vita Malchi* posits one previous use of Seneca's text rewritten into a new context, and together with references to the plays in intellectual texts, and with what we know of the manuscript traditions of the dramas, may provide the framework in which Boethius came to the playwright. Of course, these historical issues do not explain why Boethius turned to Seneca in the first place. A purely biographical argument might devolve to the availability of certain texts over others, and would claim that the historical circumstances of the *Consolation*'s composition led Boethius to employ Seneca to the exclusion of other authors. While Jerome does posit a Christian use of the drama, we may, I think, safely dismiss the notion of Seneca's supposed links with early Christianity, and in turn, the Early Medieval legend of his correspondence with St. Paul.[20] Instead, we may turn to the presentation of Seneca himself in the *Consolation*, and to the larger structures of imagery through which Boethius fashioned his literary persona. In short, I would suggest that Seneca is an almost natural figure towards whom the figures of the *Consolation*'s fiction may turn.

The figure of Seneca himself enters the *Consolation* twice, first as an example of those philosophers forced to suffer and die for their beliefs, second as a failed courtier too caught up in the power struggles of imperial whim. In 1.pr.3, Philosophy opens the account of herself with a history of her followers: Socrates, Anaxagoras, and Zeno among the Greeks, Canius, Seneca, and Soranus among the Romans, embody the fates of Philosophy's students berated by the mob. Her history of her discipline here, written through capsule biographies of her followers, is clearly modelled on the opening of Cicero's *Tusculan Disputations*, where the Roman traces the history of his subject through a series of men and schools culminating in

[20] See Léon Herrmann, *Sénèque et les premiers Chrétiens* (Brussels: Collection Latomus, 1979).

the Academic heritage he espouses (*Tusc. Disp.* I.i.1-I.v.9; cf.
II.i.1-II.iv.10). Seneca, for Philosophy, stands as one of the
familiar Roman examples of the philosophical life which the
prisoner should know (1.3.9). Such men "were disgraced only
because they had been trained in my studies and therefore
seemed obnoxious to wicked men" (Green, trans., p. 8;
I.pr.3.10). In Book Three, Philosophy argues against the varieties of earthly fame and power which men think bring them
happiness. Association with the noble or the powerful does
not bring one power; if anything, she argues through a variety
of historical examples, the life of the courtier invariably ends
with disappointment or distress (III.pr.5). A man such as Seneca was put to death by the very friend and student whom
he served, and for all his attempts to retire from Nero's court,
he was destroyed by his "very greatness" (Green, trans.,
pp. 51-52; III.pr.5.10-11).

Even these brief appearances in the *Consolation* mark Seneca
as a figure in whom Boethius no doubt saw himself. A mis-
understood intellectual, a failed courtier, Seneca stands as an
historical precedent for the Boethian persona's own struggle
with ignorant readers, aristocratic intrigue, and the vagaries
of Gothic law. The figure of Nero, too, so prominent as an
exemplar of civilization gone mad, foreshadows a Theodoric
who would put his advisor to death. While Seneca is nowhere
mentioned as a playwright, and while none of his specific
philosophical works are mentioned, he nonetheless stands behind much of the emotionalism of the *Consolation*, and from
this perspective it might seem almost natural for Boethius to
turn to his plays for source material. One can construct a
biographical argument which presents Boethius imprisoned
as turning towards his own imagined forefather, and seeking
some inspiration in his dramas of Stoic virtue. But I do not
think there is need for this kind of speculation. Seneca's plays
and Seneca himself figure prominently in the *Consolation*'s
fiction, and, as I have tried to show, those plays participate
in a structure of literary allusion which charts a course of
reading, rewriting, and ultimately rejecting them as source

material for philosophical poetry. We may say instead that the personage of Seneca remains, like those other historical figures which people the *Consolation*'s opening, just one more historical analogue to be brushed away as Philosophy's arguments become more abstract and as the prisoner's abilities rise to the level of philosophical inquiry unhindered by outside examples.

Such then are the possible literary, critical, historical, and textual contexts in which Boethius' use of Senecan drama can be understood. The remainder of the Appendix presents the full texts of Boethius's and Seneca's lines in parallel to illustrate the arguments made in the course of this study.

Cons. Phil., 1.m.5

O stelliferi conditor orbis,
qui perpetuo nixus solio
rapido caelum turbine uersas
legemque pati sidera cogis,
ut nunc pleno lucida cornu
totis fratris obuia flammis
condat stellas luna minores,
nunc obscuro pallida cornu
Phoebo propior lumina perdat
et qui primae tempore noctis
agit algentes Hesperos ortus
solitas iterum mutet habenas
Phoebi pallens Lucifer ortu.
Tu frondifluae frigore brumae
stringis lucem breuiore mora,
tu cum feruida uenerit aestas
agiles nocti diuidis horas.
Tua uis uarium temperat annum,
ut quas Boreae spiritus aufert
reuehat mites Zephyrus frondes,
quaeque Arcturus semina uidit
Sirius altas urat segetes:
nihil antiqua lege solutum
linquit propriae stationis opus.
Omnia certo fine gubernans
hominum solos respuis actus

Seneca, Hyppolytus, 959-988

O magna parens, Natura, deum
tuque igniferi rector Olympi,
qui sparsa cito sidera mundo
cursusque uagos rapis astrorum
celerique polos cardine uersas,
cur tanta tibi cura perennes
agitare uias aetheris alti,
ut nunc canae frigora brumae
nudent siluas, nunc arbustis
redeant umbrae, nunc aestiui
colla leonis Cererem magno
feruore coquant uiresque suas
temperet annus?
sed cur idem qui tanta regis,
sub quo uasti pondera mundi
librata suos ducunt orbes,
hominum nimium securus abes,
non sollicitus prodesse bonis,
nocuisse malis?
Res humanas ordine nullo
Fortuna regit sparsitque manu
munera caeca, peiora fouens;
uincit sanctos dira libido,
fraus sublimi regnat in aula.
tradere turpi fasces populus
gaudet, eosdem colit atque odit.

merito rector cohibere modo.
Nam cur tantas lubrica uersat
Fortuna uices? Premit insontes
debita sceleri noxia poena,
at peruersi resident celso
mores solio sanctaque calcant
iniusta uice colla nocentes.
Latet obscuris condita uirtus
clara tenebris iustusque tulit
crimen iniqui.
Nil periuria, nil nocet ipsis
fraus mendaci compta colore.
Sed cum libuit uiribus uti,
quos innumeri metuunt populi
summos gaudet subdere reges.
O iam miseras respice terras,
quisquis rerum foedera nectis!
Operis tanti pars non uilis
homines quatimur fortunae salo.
Rapidos, rector, comprime fluctus
et quo caelum regis immensum
firma stabiles foedere terras.

tristis virtus perversa tulit
praemia recti; castos sequitur
mala paupertas vitioque potens
regnat adulter.
o vane pudor falsumque decus!

Cons. Phil., III.m.12

Felix, qui potuit boni
fontem uisere lucidum,
felix, qui potuit grauis
terrae soluere uincula.
Quondam funera coniugis
uates Threicius gemens
postquam flebilibus modis
siluas currere mobiles,
amnes stare coegerat
iunxitque intrepidum latus
saeuis cerua leonibus
nec uisum timuit lepus
iam cantu placidum canem,
cum flagrantior intima
feruor pectoris ureret
nec qui cuncta subegerant
mulcerent dominum modi,
immites superos querens
infernas adiit domos.
Illic blanda sonantibus

Seneca, Hercules Furens, 569-91

Immites potuit flectere cantibus
umbrarum dominos et prece supplici
Orpheus, Eurydicen dum repetit suam.
quae silvas et aves saxaque traxerat
ars, quae praebuerat fluminibus moras,
ad cuius sonitum constiterant ferae,
mulcet non solitis vocibus inferos
et surdis resonat clarius in locis.
deflent Eurydicen Threiciae nurus,
deflent et lacrimis difficiles dei,
et qui fronte nimis crimina tetrica
quaerunt ac veteres excutiunt reos
flentes Eurydicen iuridici sedent.
tandem mortis ait 'vincimur' arbiter,
'evade ad superos, lege tamen data—
tu post terga tui perge viri comes,
tu non ante tuam respice coniugem,
quam cum clara deos obtulerit dies
Spartanique aderit ianua Taenari.'
odit verus amor nec patitur moras;

chordis carmina temperans
quicquid praecipuis deae
matris fontibus hauserat
quod luctus dabat impotens,
quod luctum geminans amor
deflet Taenara commouens
et dulci ueniam prece
umbrarum dominos rogat.
Stupet tergeminus nouo
captus carmine ianitor;
quae sontes agitant metu
ultrices scelerum deae
iam maestae lacrimis madent;
non Ixionium caput
uelox praecipitat rota
et longa site perditus
spernit flumina Tantalus;
uultur dum satur est modis
non traxit Tityi iecur.
Tandem 'Vincimur' arbiter
umbrarum miserans ait.
'Donamus comitem uiro
emptam carmine coniugem;
sed lex dona coherceat,
ne dum Tartara liquerit
fas sit lumina flectere.'
Quis legem det amantibus?
Maior lex amor est sibi.
Heu, noctis prope terminos
Orpheus Eurydicen suam
uidit, perdidit, occidit.
Vos haec fabula respicit
quicumque in superum diem
mentem ducere quaeritis;
nam qui Tartareum in specus
uictus lumina flexerit,
quicquid praecipuum trahit
perdit dum uidet inferos.

Cons. Phil., IV.m.7

Bella bis quinis operatus annis
ultor Atrides Phrygiae ruinis
fratris amissos thalamos piauit;
ille dum Graiae dare uela classi
optat et uentos redimit cruore,

munus dum properat cernere, perdidit.
Quae vinci potuit regia carmine,
haec vinci poterit regia viribus.

Seneca, Hercules Furens, 750-9

Rapitur volucri tortus Ixion rota;
cervice saxum grande Sisyphia sedet;
in amne medio faucibus siccis senex
sectatur undas, alluit mentum latex
fidemque cum iam saepe decepto
    dedit,
perit unda in ore; poma destituunt
    famem.
praebet volucri Tityos aeternas dapes
urnasque frustra Danaides plenas
    gerunt;
errant furentes impiae Cadmeides
terretque mensas avida Phineas avis.

Seneca, Agamemnon, 162-173
(Tarrant, ed.)

Pudet pigetque: Tyndaris, caeli
    genus,
lustrale classi Doricae peperit caput!
reuoluit animus uirginis thalamos
    meae

exuit patrem miserumque tristis
foederat natae iugulum sacerdos.
Fleuit amissos Ithacus sodales,
quos ferus uasto recubans in antro
mersit immani Polyphemus aluo;
sed tamen caeco furibundus ore
gaudium maestis lacrimis
    rependit.
Herculem duri celebrant labores:
ille Centauros domuit superbos,
abstulit saeuo spolium leoni,
fixit et certis uolucres sagittis,
poma cernenti rapuit draconi
aureo laeuam grauior metallo,
Cerberum traxit triplici catena,
uictor immitem posuisse fertur
pabulum saeuis dominum
    quadrigis,
Hydra combusto periit ueneno,
fronte turpatus Achelous amnis
ora demersit pudibunda ripis,
strauit Antaeum Libycis harenis,
Cacus Euandri satiauit iras,
quosque pressurus foret altus
    orbis
saetiger spumis umeros notauit;
ultimus caelum labor inreflexo
sustulit collo pretiumque rursus
ultimi caelum meruit laboris.
Ite nunc, fortes, ubi celsa magni
ducit exempli uia. Cur inertes
terga nudatis? Superata tellus
    sidera donat.

quos ille dignos Pelopia fecit domo
cum stetit ad aras ore sacrifico pater
quam nuptiales! horruit Calchas suae
responsa uocis et recedentes focos.
o scelera semper sceleribus uincens
    domus:
cruore uentos emimus, bellum nece!
Sed uela pariter mille fecerunt rates?
non est soluta prospero classis deo,
eiecit Aulis impias portu rates.

Agamemnon, 808-66
(selections, Tarrant, ed.)
tuus ille bis seno meruit labore
adlegi caelo magnus Alcides,
        (812-813)

tibi concitatus substitit mundus,
o puer subiture caelum. (827-828)

Te sensit Nemeaeus arto
pressus lacerto fulmineus leo,
ceruaque Parrhasis,
sensit Arcadii populator agri
gemuitque taurus Dictaea linquens
horrridus arua.
morte fecundum domuit draconem
uetuitque collo pereunte nasci
geminosque fratres
pectore ex uno tria monstra natos
stipite incusso fregit insultans
duxitque ad ortus Hesperium pecus,
Geryonae spolium triformis.
egit Threicium gregem
quem non Strymonii gramine
    fluminis
Hebriue ripis pauit tyrannus:
hospitum dirus stabulis cruorem
praebuit saeuis tinxitque crudos
ultimus rictus sanguis aurigae.
uidit Hippolyte ferox
pectore e medio rapi
spolium et sagittis

nube percussa Stymphalis alto
decidit caelo
arborque pomis fertilis aureis
extimuit manus insueta carpi
fugitque in auras leuiore ramo:
audiuit sonitum crepitante lamna
frigidus custos nescius somni
linqueret cum iam nemus omne
        fuluo
plenus Alcides uacuum metallo.
tractus ad caelum canis inferorum
triplici catena tacuit nec ullo
latrauit ore,
lucis ignotae metuens colorem.
Te duce succidit
mendax Dardanidae domus
et sensit arcus iterum timendos;
te duce concidit totidem diebus
Troia quot annis.   (829-866)

Seneca, Hercules Furens, from Juno's
        speech

quae fera tyranni iura violento queant
nocere iuveni? nempe pro telis gerit
quae timuit et quae fudit; armatus
        venit
leone et hydra. nec satis terrae
        patent;
effregit ecce limen inferni Iovis
et opima victi regis ad superos refert.
vidi ipsa, vidi nocte discussa inferum
et Dite domito spolia iactantem patri
fraterna. cur non vinctum et
        oppressum trahit
ipsum catenis paria sortitum Iovi
Ereboque capto potitur et retegit
        Styga?
parum est reverti; foedus umbrarum
        perit,
patefacta ab imis manibus retro
        via est
et sacra dirae mortis in aperto iacent.
at ille, rupto carcere umbrarum
        ferox,

de me triumphat et superbifica manu
atrum per urbes ducit Argolicas
    canem.
viso labantem Cerbero vidi diem
pavidumque Solem; me quoque
    invasit tremor
et terna monstri colla devicti intuens
timui imperasse.   (*HF*, 43-63)

. . . robore experto tumet,
et posse caelum viribus vinci suis
didicit ferendo; subdidit mundo
    caput
nec flexit umeros molis immensae
    labor
meliusque collo sedit Herculeo polus.
immota cervix sidera et caelum tulit
et me prementem. quaerit ad superos
    viam.   (68-74)

I nunc, superbe, caelitum sedes pete,
humana temne.   (89-90)

Hercules Furens, 524-532 (Chorus)

O Fortuna viris invida fortibus,
quam non aequa bonis praemia
    dividis.
'Eurystheus facili regnet in otio;
Alcmena genitus bella per omnia
monstris exagitet caeliferam manum:
serpentis resecet colla feracia,
deceptis referat mala sororibus,
cum somno dederit pervigiles genas
pomis divitibus praepositus draco.'

Hercules Furens, 566-568 (Chorus)

fatum rumpe manu, tristibus inferis
prospectus pateat lucis et invius
limes det faciles ad superos vias!

Hercules Furens, 1100-1121 (Chorus)

Nunc Herculeis percussa sonent
pectora palmis, mundum solitos

ferre lacertos verbera pulsent
victrice manu; gemitus vastos
audiat aether, audiat atri
regina poli vastisque ferox
qui colla gerit vincta catenis
imo latitans Cerberus antro;
resonet maesto clamore chaos
latique patens unda profundi
et qui medius tua tela tamen
senserat aer;
pectora tantis obsessa malis
non sunt ictu ferienda levi,
uno planctu tria regna sonent.
et tu collo decus ac telum
suspensa diu, fortis harundo,
pharetraeque graves, date saeva fero
verbera tergo; caedant umeros
robora fortes stipesque potens
duris laceret pectora nodis:
plangant tantos arma dolores.

INDEX OF NAMES AND SUBJECTS

structure: structural unity of the
work, 155-160, 164-165, 166-175,
185-186, 193-196, 200-201, 204,
212-213, 216-218, 220-221, 224-
225, 227-228, 236, 239-241; poetry vs. prose, 126-127, 144-145,
152, 167, 175, 201-202, 204-206,
209, 231-232, 235-236; dialogue
vs. monologue, 180, 210, 219,
226, 229-230, 235-236; mythological poetry, 181, 185-202; as a
text to be read, 216, 230, 236;
ending of the work, 230-236;
themes and images in: exile and
alienation, 120-121; loss or absence, 126, 131-132, 164, 193,
234; limits of language, 117-123,
209-212; belief vs. proof, 213-
214, 218; role of the reader, 166-
168, 180, 185, 230-231; tragedy
and theatricality, 221-223; figure
of Seneca, 245-247; discussions of
individual books: Book Two:
forms of argument in, 110-114;
naturalistic poetry in, 114-116,
188-189; Book Three: structure
of, 124-125, 164-165; Platonism
of, 124-125, 138, 140, 141-142,
149-150; critical views of, 124-
125; Book Four: structure and
themes of, 166-202, 204-216;
Book Five: structure and themes
of, 203-204, 215-236; critical
views of, 203-204; see also Timaean hymn (III.m.9), Lady Philosophy, The Prisoner
Cornford, F. M.: 36
Corti, Maria: 12
Courcelle, Pierre: 10, 16n, 18n, 26n,
27, 46, 65n, 86n, 97n, 98n, 102n,
109, 120n, 124n, 138n, 142, 148n,
154n, 182, 203-204, 212n, 215n,
216n
Crabbe, Anna: 11, 33n, 46n, 96n,
237n
Curtius, E. R.: 17n, 57n, 59n, 74n,
89, 187n

Cushman, Robert: 12, 37n
Cynics: 182, 183n

Damon, P. W.: 183n
Dante: 10, 167n
de la Mare, A. C.: 237n
De Rijk, L. M.: 15n, 69n, 70n, 76n
Detienne, M.: 181n
De Vogel, C. J.: 10, 18, 33n, 219n,
232n
disputatio in utramque partem: 33, 35,
42, 43, 175
Donatus, commentator on Terence:
243
Downey, Glanville: 28n
Duckworth, G. E.: 244n
Dwyer, Richard: 154n

Ebbesen, Sten: 19n, 27n
enchainment, imagery of: 194-195,
198
Ennodius, 243
extrinsic vs. intrinsic, imagery of: 8,
112-113, 126, 132-134, 139, 150,
172, 226-227

Fabius, figure of: 70-77, 145
Fichter, Andrew: 233n, 238n
Fish, Stanley: 12, 37n
Flores, Ralph: 49n, 233n, 238n
forms, the Platonic: 9, 37
Fortuna, figure of: 110, 112, 113-
114, 148, 156, 163, 195
fortune: 112-114, 188-189, 213-214,
220, 222-223, 224, 226
Friedman, John Block: 154n
Fulgentius: 5, 10, 12, 19, 32, 56-69,
70-72, 74, 77, 94, 99, 102n, 154n,
183, 193, 236; De Continentia Virgiliana, 5, 10, 19, 31, 56-69, 71,
77, 78; Mitologiae, 65, 102n

Galinsky, G. Carl: 193n
Gegenschatz, E.: 203n
Gigon, O.: 34n

INDEX OF LATIN TERMS

LIBRARY OF CONGRESS CATALOGING IN PUBLICATION DATA

Lerer, Seth, 1955-
Boethius and dialogue.

Bibliography: p.
Includes index.
1. Boethius, d. 524. De consolatione philosophiae.
2. Boethius, d. 524—Technique.   3. Dialogue.
4. Dialogues, Latin—History and criticism.   I. Title.

PA6231.C8L47 1985   100   85-42937
ISBN 0-691-06653-1